THE PLEASURES OF MURDER

Jonathan Goodman, the crime historian, was for some years a theatre director and television producer. As well as being the author of a number of books on criminology, he was general editor of the Celebrated Trials series and has also published four novels and a volume of poetry. He is a member of the British Academy of Forensic Sciences, the Medico-Legal Society and Our Society.

The Pleasures of Murder

Edited by JONATHAN GOODMAN

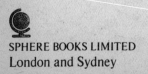

SPHERE BOOKS LIMITED
London and Sydney

First published in Great Britain by
Allison and Busby Limited 1983
Copyright © 1983 by Jonathan Goodman
This collection published by Sphere Books Ltd 1986
30–32 Gray's Inn Road, London WCIX 8JL

Set in 10/11 pt Compugraphic Plantin

Printed and bound in Great Britain by
Collins, Glasgow

Dedicated to the memory of Thomas De Quincey,
who showed how

Contents

Before the Facts

There are any number of ways of categorizing the true-crime literature (which, let the uninitiated realize, is different from – not a segment of – 'criminology', that bubblegum generic that becomes increasingly meaningless as its meanings increase). The best way, though it entails actually reading at least a couple of paragraphs of every item that seems relevant, is to split the literature into that which deserves to be called literature and that which doesn't.

Don't misunderstand me: to divide in this way is much the same as to hang pictures by Rembrandt and lesser artists in one room of a gallery, plans drawn by modern British architects in another – the rooms being contiguous, with an opening, not a door, between. Both rooms should be visited, for an architect who is audacious enough, idiosyncratic if not stylish, may hit upon a design that affords pleasures.

Pleasures. That word in the title of this collection was picked without consideration of others; there was no point in rummaging in Roget. It would have been daring to call the book *The Best of Murder*; something like that. Daring but deceptive. For what on earth would 'best' have meant? I wager that, nine times out of ten, an author's notion of what he has done best does not accord with what his most avid reader thinks. And, of course, there are constraints on 'best' in any anthology. Any? Well, yes, I think so – or rather, I believe there should be. Apart from the constraint of choosing ingredients that don't add up to a tome, there is the aim of offering varied consecution to those invariably dogged readers who, like Carroll's King, begin at the beginning and go on till they come to the end, then stop. Besides, there is the hope, usually forlorn, of steering clear of pieces that have already been anthologized. For instance, I admire – and, more important at the moment, derive pleasure from – the introduction to *Trial of Alma Victoria Rattenbury and George Percy Stoner* in the 'Notable Trials' series; but as it has been republished over and over again, I have chosen something else by F. Tennyson Jesse (*1888–1958*).

Returning, but more pointedly, to categories, let me try to group all but one of the authors of the assembled essays and extracts into types. Arbitrarily, I'm afraid, but there it is.

Fryn Tennyson Jesse (and here, you see, I at once hit a snag: I wonder if I should pair her with my only other woman author, Dorothy Dunbar – but decide that they should be treated as equal writers) ventured into all sorts of genres. As did Rayner Heppenstall, the friend – and, all too often, subsequently the enemy – of more-publicized literary figures of his time (*1911–81*): novelist, poet, translator, critic, diarist, playwright – he moonlighted at each of these occupations while despondently earning a living as a BBC radio producer, and did not exploit his study of the Newgate Calendar and of French crimes and criminals until his retirement.

Edmund Pearson (*1880–1937*), who was a librarian, a researcher into bibliographic oddities, and an editor, is the most consistently pleasurable American crime historian; though his enthusiasm for the Harvard murder case is not contagious to British readers, and though his desire to change the verdict on Lizzie Borden may have caused him to premeditate errors, his delight in the incongruities that crop up in murder cases dovetails, sometimes perfectly, with his ability to lounge without sprawling, which is as adequate a sign of literary elegance as it is of breeding.

I wish I could do without the expression, 'renaissance man', but it applies to – indeed, might have been coined for – Richard Altick, who has used the ample spare time of a professor at an American university to carry out research on a diversity of subjects (including research itself) and to convert his findings into delights.

That leaves us with just one other member of this group. His name is Jacques Barzun, and it is hard to know what to say about him without writing a book. He loves learning and persuading others to learn – not so as to cram the brain with knick-knackery but as the means to the ends of appreciating what is good and making it better. With Wendell Hertig Taylor, he compiled *A Catalogue of Crime* (Harper & Row), which should be owned – and would be treasured – by anyone who uses bookshelves for books.

Then there is a small group, just a trio, of crime historians who, though starting off with the unfair disadvantage of a knowledge of the law, did not let this impede them.

William Roughead (*1870–1952*), who idly enjoyed the prestige of being a Writer to the Signet, the oldest body of law practitioners in Scotland, edited more 'Notable Trials' than anyone else (F. Tennyson Jesse came second); this may have been as much because he lived within strolling distance of the offices of the publishers, William Hodge & Co., in the Old Town of Edinburgh, as because of his literary merits. In the opinion of Henry James, among others, these were considerable. It is a pity, however, that a good many of his essays (which appeared not only as introductions to 'Notable Trials' but also, cannily permutated, in more than a score of omnibuses – or perhaps one should say black marias) sparkle at their beginnings and ends but doze off into unembellished précis in between. Even when writing of forensic battles he had watched from the sideline (and during half a century, he attended many of the piquant murder trials at the High Court of Justiciary, some summers cutting short his holiday on the Isle of Arran rather than miss a cross-examination of Sydney Smith, a speech by Craigie Aitchison, a summation from Lord Guthrie), he only occasionally indicated that he had heard the voices as well as read the words. Excepting the Slater case – in which Roughead, with Conan Doyle, worked to remedy an apparent miscarriage of justice – Roughead garnered virtually all his material from books in his own library or that of the Signet, or from trial transcripts provided by Hodge's, who were the shorthand writers to the Scottish courts.

Whereas Roughead rarely added 'colour' to legal proceedings, Edgar Lustgarten (*1907–78*) was a brilliant court entertainer – though not, one is informed, when he practised as a barrister on the Northern Circuit. The entertainment came later, from his accounts of trials. His one-man radio shows, in which he played all the parts, ranging from crusty judge to harlot witness, gave him a celebrity that entitled him to high fees for series in the Sunday papers. If he had been paid less, he would have written better. Sadly – *like* Roughead now – he rarely ferreted for facts from unpublished sources; and having put together a small repertoire of cases, changed their emphasis to fit different series titles; when he wrote about other cases, the treatment was usually slight – often because, as he admitted to friends, he had little to say. He looked like a weary lizard, and was not much bigger than one. I have several reasons for being grateful to him.

The last of the three procedural experts is Thomas M. McDade, who was for a while an agent of the Federal Bureau of Investigation. At his home, which he calls Scotland Yard, he has an enviable collection of criminous literature; in compiling his bibliography, *The Annals of Murder* (University of Oklahoma Press), he scarcely needed to leave the house in search of titles.

Half a dozen of the authors were journalists at some time or another. Among them is the earliest and only anonymous contributor, the writer of a broadside that predates those discussed by McDade. This unknown ha'penny-a-liner's report of a fatal mugging near St Pancras Church is one of three pieces in the collection in which references to the forbidden fruit of the apple tree prolong the events in the memory.

The two named Englishmen, near opposites in their approach to crime writing, are Kenneth Allsop (*1920–73*), who had a rare knack for untangling skeins of information but was frequently more convinced than convincing when he came to discuss causes and effects of deeds, and Richard Whittington-Egan, one of the last surviving, and most expert

4

exponents of the broderie-Anglaise style of writing, with purple a dominant colour; a tenacious, some might say obsessional, researcher, he delightedly accompanied me as bodyguard and witness when I first accused Richard Gordon Parry of being the killer of Julia Wallace.

As far as the authors here represented are concerned, Whittington-Egan's way with words most closely resembles that of Alexander Woollcott (*1887–1943*), who, when he was not at his Manhattan apartment – nicknamed Wit's End by Dorothy Parker – could often be found at the head, if that is possible, of the 'round table' in the Hotel Algonquin. (Incidentally, Woollcott, a persistent anglophile, was a friend of Fryn Tennyson Jesse and her husband, H.M. Harwood; the Harwoods' correspondence with him and other Americans during the early years of the second world war was published in two books, both from Constable, *London Front* and *While London Burns*.)

I guess that a number of readers will be surprised to find something by James Thurber (*1894–1961*) in a collection like this. (His 'Touché' cartoon and his drawings depicting motives for uxoricide might be apt to a similar but illustrated anthology.) Also, perhaps, some readers will be surprised by the inclusion of newspaper reports by Damon Runyon (*1880–1946*), writing in a more conventional tense than historic present about a murder trial that took place more than somewhat distant from Mindy's.

Dorothy Dunbar (*1923–76*), who edited in several mediums, was stylistically comparable to but less prolific than Edmund Pearson, one of whose favourite cases happens to be the subject of her essay.

Perhaps I am unwise to mention this, considering that a psychiatrist (or, to use Pearson's preferred and preferable term, an alienist) may be present, but I find the Bordens' breakfast menu – itemized by Miss Dunbar – infinitely more macabre than the untidy corpses that caused luncheon to be delayed at the house in Fall River. Similarly, I am less upset by details of the far-flung components of the body in the first Brighton trunk crime (a case – well, yes – in 1831 that

5

receives no other reference in these pages) than by the small revelation that John Holloway was so uncaring as to have sawn off his late wife's legs without first taking off her stockings.

These homicidal asides prompt me to suggest a law of frissonology – *squeamishness increases in inverse relation to the gravity of the cause* – that can be further exemplified by an experience of my own.

During dinner at the Savage Club, my companion, a forensic pathologist, received a message that he was needed at his mortuary to perform an autopsy on the body of a person who, some five weeks before, had been clumsily murdered with a blunt axe. The pathologist suggested that both of us should repair to the mortuary, he to hack, I to admire his deftness, and then, after he had brushed his nails, return to the club to finish the port. I was unenthusiastic, but did not have the courage to demur (a statement that could, but will not, lead me on to a discussion of the equivocal nature of bravery). However, the pathologist, through too hurriedly munching a nutty petit-four, broke a tooth. As luck would have it, a colleague of his, an odontologist, was dining at a nearby table. The pathologist called out to him for help, and the odontologist, an indiscriminate enthusiast, said that, if we could bear waiting a few minutes, he would be delighted to drive us to the mortuary – via his home, where, in the garage, he would remove the stump of tooth. The thought of standing idly by during such an extraction, in such surroundings – and perhaps, my imagination hinted, with the odontologist using inappropriate tools – was harder to stomach than that of observing a month-old corpse being dissected, and I muttered an excuse for leaving and lurched out into St James's.

Taxing my memory now, I recall a party in Liverpool many years ago. It was a sombre affair. None of those invited, nor any of the gatecrashers, seemed to know one another, or to want to, and the host was absent, having accepted a last-minute invitation to a house-warming for a shebeen in Toxteth; no one appeared to have anything in common with anyone else, so none of the introductions developed into conversations, and we just stood and sipped what tasted like a mixture of Merrydown cider and milk stout from glasses the size of Optrex lids. Eventually a small blonde woman complained in an adenoidal voice, 'This isn't a party, whacks – it's a bleeding gathering,' then took off all her clothes revealing that she was not naturally fair, and performed a melancholy dance, humming her own accompaniment, a syncopated version of 'All Things Bright and Beautiful'. When she had quite finished, and had dressed, we all left.

I mention this incident because it seems in a way relevant to the contributors I have not yet referred to: three men who surely never expected their words to be repeated in a criminous anthology. Supposing that one could actually bring them together, they would even *look* ill-assorted. If J. Leslie Hotson, the diligent Canadian-born literary historian, could accommodate the views of the American, Henry David Thoreau (*1817–62*), on essential living (basically, the less work the better – best in a rural setting) and could persuade him to converse rather than be quietly despairing, they might, just might, get on; but Arthur Flegenheimer, also known as Dutch Schultz (*1902–35*), would feel rather left out and might get ominously moody – especially if the two others started chatting about something on which he had practical experience. One can imagine him snarling at the aphoristic Thoreau: 'Sure, some circumstantial evidence *is* very strong – but, Jeez, I can frinstance you a helluva better example than a lousy trout in the milk. Who wants to drink that nil-proof cow's piss anyways?' Mr Flegenheimer, who read little other than the racing form and results in the New York *Morning Telegraph*, and whose writing seems to have been restricted to betting slips (fairly certainly, his orders for illicit booze and the despatch of rivals were oral), intrudes into this anthology by virtue of his last words.

Mine – in terms of this introduction – are fewer: simply that I hope that many of my pleasures of murder will be shared.

Jonathan Goodman
London, 1983

NOTE: Excepting minor deletions, almost invariably of references in extracts to prior or subsequent matter, the contributions are presented as they were originally published. No attempt has been made to correct errors or to add information that has come to light since the contributions first appeared. In some cases, the date of first publication (in a book unless otherwise stated) is shewn beside the author's name.

The Short, Sweet Martyrdom of Jake Lingle

KENNETH ALLSOP

On Monday, 9 June 1930, Alfred J. ('Jake') Lingle, a thirty-eight-year-old crime reporter on the Chicago *Tribune*, was shot to death while walking, smoking a cigar and reading the racing news, in a crowded underpass at Randolph and Michigan during the lunch hour. A noteworthy detail in the plot was that one of Lingle's killers was apparently dressed as a parson.

His death created a furore, the parallel of which it is difficult to imagine in Britain. An American reporter – that is, a reporter on the general news-gathering staff, a position which has a different connotation from the British title, for the American reporter may be merely a leg-man, a fact-gatherer who telephones in his information to a desk re-write man – is not startlingly well paid. Yet he has a place in public regard, a compound of glamour, respect and authority, that has no counterpart in Britain. The murder of Lingle instantly assumed the importance and gravity that had attached to the murder of McSwiggin and other police and Federal officials – and, as in the case of McSwiggin, it was an uprush of moral indignation that plunged in as precipitous a slump of disillusionment.

Lingle's duties on the police beat for the *Tribune* earned him sixty-five dollars a week, a poor sum. He had never had a by-line in the paper; his name was unknown to its readers. Posthumously, when his name was famous (and fast become notorious), he was revealed to have had an income of sixty thousand dollars a year. He owned a chauffeur-driven Lincoln limousine. He had just bought a sixteen-thousand-dollar house at Long Beach, on the Michigan Riviera, where his wife and two children, Buddy (six) and Pansy (five) were to spend the summer months. He had recently taken a suite of rooms at the Stevens, one of Chicago's most stylish hotels. He was an addicted gambler at horse and greyhound tracks. All this was known in a general manner among his colleagues, and the discrepancy between his meagre newspaper salary and his lavish spending was understood to be possible because of a big legacy he had received.

On the day of his death he was on the way to the races. He left his wife packing for her departure to the lake. He himself was that afternoon to go to the meeting at Washington Park, Homewood. Another significant point about that day, 9 June, was that the Sheridan Wave Tournament Club, a society gambling parlour at 621 Waveland Avenue, where the champagne, whisky and food was distributed with the managements's compliments during play, was to reopen that evening, an event of some interest to Lingle.

Retrospectively, it seems certain that Lingle knew he was in trouble. Attorney Louis B. Piquett, former City Prosecutor, later volunteered to tell the police that twenty-four hours before Lingle's death he had met Lingle in the Loop. They stood on Randolph Street talking of the discovery of Red McLaughlin's body from the canal. Lingle was giving Piquett his theory of the killing when 'a blue sedan with two men in it stopped at the kerb alongside us. Lingle stopped in the middle of a sentence, looked up at the two men in a startled way and they looked back at him. He apparently had forgotten what he had been saying for he turned suddenly, walked back the way he had come, hurriedly said "Good-bye", and entered a store as quickly as he could.' And again on the day of his murder, after lunching at the Sherman Hotel he met Sergeant Thomas Alcock, of the Detective Bureau, in the lobby and told him: 'I'm being tailed.'

He was. After buying cigars at the Sherman kiosk, he walked the four blocks to Michigan Avenue to catch the 1.30 p.m. train for the Washington Park race-track, and descended the pedestrian subway to enter the Illinois Central suburban electric railway in Grant Park. At any time of day the subway is as busy a channel as the killers could have chosen, and at lunchtime on this Monday it was swirling with two opposite streams of shoppers and office workers.

A strange aspect of what followed is Lingle's apparent unconcern. He knew he was being followed, and a man of his experience must have known that there was only one purpose in that. Yet, on the evidence of witnesses, he arrived at the entrance to the subway walking between two men. One had blond hair and wore a straw boater and a grey suit. The other was dark in a blue suit. At the entrance Lingle paused and bought a racing edition of an evening paper, and as he did so a roadster swung into the kerb on the south side of Randolph Street and blew its horn to attract Lingle's attention. One of the men in the car called out: 'Play Hy Schneider in the third!' According to Armour Lapansee, a Yellow Cab superintendent who overheard the exchange, Lingle grinned, waved his hand and called back, 'I've got him.'

Lingle walked on into the subway. He was seen by Dr Joseph Springer, a former coroner's physician and a long-standing acquaintance. 'Lingle didn't see me,' Springer stated. 'He was reading the race information. He was holding it before him with both hands and smoking a cigar.'

Lingle had almost reached the end of the subway. He came abreast of the news-stand twenty-five feet short of the east exit, and the dark man who had been walking at his side diverted as if to buy a paper. As he did, the blond man dropped behind Lingle, levelled his left hand which held a snub-barrelled .38 Colt – known, cosily, among police and mobsters as a belly-gun – and fired a single bullet upward into Lingle's neck, which penetrated the brain and left the forehead. He fell forward, cigar still clenched between his teeth, newspaper still in his hands.

Throwing away the gun, the blond killer ran forward into the crowds, then doubled back past Lingle's body and out up the eastern staircase. He jumped a fence, changed his mind again, ran west into Randolph Street, through a passage – where he threw away a left-hand silk glove presumably worn to guard against fingerprints – and, pursued by a policeman, ran into Wabash Avenue, where he escaped into the crowds.

11

Meanwhile in the subway, a Mr Patrick Campbell saw the darkhaired accomplice hurrying towards the west exit. He went to intercept him, but his movement was blocked by a priest who bumped into him. Campbell said: 'What's the matter?' and the priest replied: 'I think someone has been shot. I'm getting out of here.'

Later Lieutenant William Cusick, of the Detective Bureau, commented brusquely: 'He was no priest. A priest would never do that. He would have gone to the side of the stricken person.'

The pattern pieced together. It seemed clear that Lingle had walked into a trap formed by perhaps a dozen men. But what was never put forward as a theory, and which seems the likeliest explanation of his meek and unhesitating advance into the trap, was that, during his progress along the pavement, down the stairs and along the subway between two men, he was being nudged along by a gun hidden in a jacket pocket, under orders to walk naturally and keep reading the paper.

That evening Colonel Robert R. McCormick, proprietor of the Chicago *Tribune*, summoned his news staff together and addressed them on the death of a reporter whom he had never seen and whose name he had never before heard. Fred Pasley, who was there, says he talked for forty-five minutes and pledged himself to solve the crime. Next morning the front page scowled with an eight-column banner headline announcing the sudden end of Lingle. The story read: 'Alfred J. Lingle, better known in his world of newspaper work as Jake Lingle, and for the last eighteen years a reporter on the *Tribune*, was shot to death yesterday in the Illinois Central subway at the east side of Michigan Boulevard, at Randolph Street.

'The *Tribune* offers twenty-five thousand dollars as a reward for information which will lead to the conviction of the slayer or slayers. An additional reward of five thousand dollars was announced by *The Chicago Evening Post*, making a total of thirty thousand dollars.'

Next morning the Hearst Chicago *Herald and Examiner*

also offered a twenty-five-thousand-dollar reward, bringing up the total to fifty-five thousand dollars.

McCormick continued to take Lingle's death as an affront to him personally and a smack at the press which transcended in seriousness all the other hundreds of cases of physical violence and the network of nefariousness. Two days later the *Tribune* carried an editorial headed 'THE CHALLENGE' which read:

'The meaning of this murder is plain. It was committed in reprisal and in attempt at intimidation. Mr Lingle was a police reporter and an exceptionally well-informed one. His personal friendships included the highest police officials and the contacts of his work made him familiar to most of the big and little fellows of gangland. What made him valuable to his newspaper marked him as dangerous to the killers.

'It was very foolish ever to think that assassination would be confined to the gangs who have fought each other for the profits of crime in Chicago. The immunity from punishment after gang murders would be assumed to cover the committing of others. Citizens who interfered with the criminals were no better protected than the gangmen who fought each other for the revenue from liquor selling, coercion of labour and trade, brothel-house keeping and gambling.

'There have been eleven gang murders in ten days. That has become the accepted course of crime in its natural stride, but to the list of Colosimo, O'Banion, the Gennas, Murphy, Weiss, Lombardo, Esposito, the seven who were killed in the St Valentine's Day massacre, the name is added of a man whose business was to expose the work of the killers.

'The *Tribune* accepts this challenge. It is war. There will be casualties, but that is to be expected, it being war. The *Tribune* has the support of all the other Chicago newspapers. . . . The challenge of crime to the community must be accepted. It has been given with bravado. It is accepted and we'll see what the consequences are to be. Justice will make a fight of it or it will abdicate.'

Police Commissioner Russell was galvanized into at least making a statement. It went colourfully: 'I have given orders to the five Deputy Police Commissioners to make this town so quiet that you will be able to hear a consumptive canary cough,' but he added, as a preliminary explanation for any further action: 'Of course, most of the underworld has scuttled off to hiding-places. It will be hard to find them, but we will never rest until the criminals are caught and Chicago is free of them for ever.' An editorial next day remarked bleakly: 'These gangs have run the town for many months and have strewn the streets with the lacerated bodies of their victims. Commissioner Russell and Deputy-Commissioner Stege have had their opportunity to break up these criminal gangs, who make the streets hideous with bleeding corpses. They have failed.' Instantly Russell replied: 'My conscience is clear. All I ask is that the city will sit tight and see what is going to happen.'

All that actually happened was that Russell and Stege, in the words of a newspaper, 'staged a mock heroic battle with crime by arresting every dirty-necked ragamuffin on the street corners, but carefully abstained from taking into custody any of the men who matter'. Meanwhile some of the blanks that until now had remained gaping oddly in the accounts of Lingle's character and circumstances began to be sketched in.

It is fair to infer that up to then the *Tribune* management was genuinely unaware of them. Some of the facts that had so far remained unmentioned were that he had been tagged the 'unofficial Chief of Police'; that he had himself hinted that it was he who had fixed the price of beer in Chicago; that he was an intimate friend of Capone and had stayed with him at his Florida estate; that when he died he was wearing one of Capone's gift diamond-studded belts, which had come to be accepted as the insignia of the Knights of the Round Table of that place and period; that he was improbably maty, for a newspaperman of his lowly status, with millionaire businessmen, judges and county and city officials; that he spent golfing holidays and shared stock market ventures with the Commissioner of Police.

By the time a week had passed certain reservations were beginning to temper the *Tribune*'s anger. It is apparent that more details of Lingle's extramural life were emerging. On 18

June there appeared another leading article, entitled 'THE LINGLE INVESTIGATION GOES ON'. In this the *Tribune* betrayed a flicker of uneasiness about the character of its martyr. 'We do not know why this reporter was killed,' it admitted, 'but we are engaged in finding out and we expect to be successful. It may take time; the quicker the better, but this enlistment is for duration. It may require long, patient efforts, but the *Tribune* is prepared for that, and hopes that some lasting results will be obtained which will stamp justice on the face of the crime.' To endorse its new crusading resolution, two days later the *Tribune* added to its Platform for Chicagoland on the masthead of its centre page, 'END THE REIGN OF GANGDOM'. Appended was an explanatory editorial: 'The killers, the racketeers who exact tribute from businessmen and union labour, the politicians who use and shield the racketeers, the policemen and judges who have been prostituted by politicians, all must go.'

Ten days elapsed, and there had obviously been some concentrated rethinking by McCormick and his editorial executives. The word-of-mouth buzz about Lingle's background and liaisons that was meanwhile racing around Chicago, supported by somewhat less reverent stories in other newspapers, evidently induced the *Tribune* to take a revised, frank, let's-face-it attitude. On 30 June a column-and-a-half editorial was published. Under the heading 'THE LINGLE MURDER', it read: 'When Alfred Lingle was murdered the motive seemed to be apparent. . . . His newspaper saw no other explanation than that his killers either thought he was close to information dangerous to them or intended the murder as notice given the newspapers that crime was ruler in Chicago. It could be both, a murder to prevent a disclosure and to give warning against attempts at others.

'It had been expected that in due time the reprisals which have killed gangster after gangster in the city would be attempted against any other persons or agencies which undertook to interfere with the incredibly profitable criminality. No one had been punished for any of these murders. They have been bizarre beyond belief, and, being undetected, have been assumed, not least by their perpetrators, to be undetectable – at least not to be punishable.

'When, then, Lingle was shot by an assassin the *Tribune* assumed that the criminals had taken the next logical step and were beginning their attack upon newspaper exposure. The *Herald and Examiner* and the *Chicago Evening Post* joined the *Tribune* in offering rewards for evidence which would lead to conviction of the murderers. The newspaper publishers met and made a common cause against the new tactics of gangland. The preliminary investigation has modified some of the first assumptions, although it has not given the situation a different essence.

'Alfred Lingle now takes a different character, one in which he was unknown to the management of the *Tribune* when he was alive. He is dead and cannot defend himself, but many facts now revealed must be accepted as eloquent against him. He was not, and he could not have been, a great reporter. His ability did not contain these possibilities. He did not write stories, but he could get information in police circles. He was not and he could not be influential in the acts of his newspaper, but he could be useful and honest, and that is what the *Tribune* management took him to be. His salary was commensurate with his work. The reasonable appearance against Lingle now is that he was accepted in the world of politics and crime for something undreamed of in his office, and that he used this in his undertakings which made him money and brought him to his death. . . .

'There are weak men on other newspapers and in other professions, in positions of trust and responsibility greater than that of Alfred Lingle. The *Tribune*, although naturally disturbed by the discovery that this reporter was engaged in practices contrary to the code of its honest reporters and abhorred by the policy of the newspaper, does not find that the main objectives of the inquiry have been much altered. The crime and the criminals remain, and they are the concern of the *Tribune* as they are of the decent elements in Chicago. . . .

'If the *Tribune* was concerned when it thought that an

16

attack had been made upon it because it was inimical to crime, it is doubly concerned if it be the fact that crime had made a connexion in its own office. . . . That Alfred Lingle is not a soldier dead in the discharge of duty is unfortunate considering that he is dead. It is of no consequence to an inquiry determined to discover why he was killed, by whom he was killed and with what attendant circumstances. *Tribune* readers may be assured that their newspaper has no intention of concealing the least fact of this murder and its consequences and meanings. The purpose is to catch the murderers. . . .

'The murder of this reporter, even for racketeering reasons, as the evidence indicates it might have been, made a breach in the wall which criminality has so long maintained about its operations here. Some time, somewhere, there will be a hole found or made and the Lingle murder may prove to be it. The *Tribune* will work at its case upon this presumption and with this hope. It has gone into the cause in this fashion and its notice to gangland is that it is in for duration. Kismet.'

Kismet, indeed. For during this revisionary interim, McCormick's investigators and the police had uncovered transactions of a ramification that could not have been anticipated in the affairs of a slum-boy baseball semi-professional who had wormed his way into bottom-grade journalism. Lingle's biography, in fact, accords with the career of any under-privileged opportunist who finds in the gang a reward for endeavour. His first job after leaving a West Jackson Boulevard elementary school was as office boy in a surgical supply house, from where, in 1912, he went as office boy at the *Tribune*. He was at the same time playing semi-professional baseball, and met at the games Bill Russell, a police patrolman, with whom he struck up a friendship, and who, as he progressed through a sergeantcy upward to deputy commissionership, was a valuable aid to Lingle in the police-beat feed work he was now doing for the *Tribune*. Pasley, who worked on the *Tribune* with him during the 'twenties, has described Lingle's relationship with the police and the underworld: 'His right hand would go up to the left breast pocket of his coat for a cigar. There was a cigar for every greeting. They were a two-for-a-nickel brand and Lingle smoked them himself. He knew all the coppers by their first names. He spent his spare time among them. He went to their wakes and funerals; their weddings and christenings. They were his heroes. A lawyer explained him: "As a kid he was cop struck, as another kid might be stage struck." The police station was his prep school and college. He matured, and his point of view developed, in the stodgy, fetid atmosphere of the cell block and the squad-room. Chicago's forty-one police stations are vile places, considered either aesthetically or hygienically. I doubt if a modern farmer would use the majority of them for cow-sheds. Yet the civic patriots put their fledgling blue-coats in them, and expect them to preserve their self-respect and departmental morale.

'In this prep school and college, Lingle learned a great deal the ordinary citizen may, or may not, suspect. He learned that sergeants, lieutenants, and captains know every hand-book, every gambling den, every dive, every beer flat and saloon on their districts, that a word from the captain when the heat is on will close any district tighter than a Scotsman's pocket in five minutes, that they know which joint owners have "a friend in the hall or county", and which haven't. Few haven't. He learned that the Chicago police department is politics-ridden.'

Pasley's view is that Lingle's undoing was gambling – 'he was a gambling fool'. He never bet less than one hundred dollars on a horse, and often a thousand. In 1921, when he was earning only fifty dollars a week, he took a trip to Cuba and came back loaded with gifts for his friends and colleagues, including egret plumes then coveted by women for hat decorations. His big spending and general prodigal way of life began to attract comment, and he gave it to be understood that he had just inherited fifty thousand dollars under his father's will (examination of the probate court records in June 1930 showed that the estate was valued at five hundred dollars). Later he invented a couple of munificent rich uncles. Pasley's deduction is that it was in 1921 that Lingle 'began living a lie, leading a dual life', that the source of his income was not at this time Capone but possibly someone in the Torrio ring – gambling rake-off, slot-machines or police graft. Additional information about his life after office hours was given by John T. Rogers in a St Louis *Post-Dispatch* series. Pointing to the 'mysterious sources of the large sums of money that passed with regularity through his bank accounts', Rogers wrote: 'If Lingle had any legitimate income beyond his sixty-five dollars a week as a reporter it has not been discovered. . . . He lived at one of the best hotels in Chicago, spent nearly all his afternoons at race-tracks and some of his winters at Miami or on the Gulf Coast. . . . At his hotel he was on the "private register". His room was No. 2706 and you could not call it unless your name had been designated by Lingle as a favoured one. . . . All inquiries for Lingle were referred to the house detective. "Sure, he was on the private register," the house officer said. "How could he get any sleep if he wasn't? His telephone would be going all night. He would get in around two or three and wanted rest." "Who would be telephoning him at that hour?" the writer inquired. This question seemed to amaze the house officer. "Why!" he exclaimed, "policemen calling up to have Jake get them transferred or promoted, or politicians wanting the fix put in for somebody. Jake could do it. He had a lot of power. I've known him twenty years. He was up there among the big boys and had a lot of responsibilities. A big man like that needs rest." '

This sketch of Lingle's function seemed to be confirmed by a check made of outgoing telephone calls from his suite. They were mostly to officials in the Federal and city buildings, and in city hall.

That Lingle had operated as liaison officer between the underworld and the political machine was the conclusion of Attorney Donald R. Richberg, who said in a public address: 'The close relationship between Jake Lingle and the police department has been published in the Chicago papers. Out of town newspapers describe Lingle even more bluntly as having been the "the unofficial Chief of Police". But Lingle was also strangely intimate with Al Capone, our most notorious gangster. Surely all Chicago knows that Samuel A. Ettelson,[1] Samuel Insull's political lawyer, who is corporation counsel for Chicago, is also chief operator of the city government. Thompson is only a figurehead. Are we to believe that there existed an unofficial chief of police associating with the most vicious gang in Chicago, without the knowledge of Mr Ettelson – who is neither deaf nor blind but on the contrary has a reputation for knowing everything worth knowing about city hall affairs?'

That he had been on intimate terms with Lingle, that Lingle was 'among the big boys', was readily conceded by Capone himself. He was interviewed on the subject at Palm Island by Henry T. Brundidge of the St Louis *Star*, who on 18 July 1930 published this report of their conversation:

'Was Jake your friend?'

'Yes, up to the very day he died.'

'Did you have a row with him?'

'Absolutely not.'

'If you did not have a row with Lingle, why did you refuse to see him upon your release from the workhouse in Philadelphia?'

'Who said I didn't see him?'

'The Chicago newspapers.'

'Well, if Jake failed to say I saw him – then I didn't see him.'

Asked about the diamond-studded belt Lingle was wearing, Capone explained: 'A Christmas present. Jake was a dear friend of mine.' And he added: 'The Chicago police know who killed him.'

Who in fact had killed Lingle? That aspect of the case seemed to have been temporarily shelved while the fascinating data of his financial state was, bit by bit, exposed for examination. By 30 June 1929, two and a half years of business with the Lake Shore Trust and Savings Bank was on the public record. In that period he had deposited 63,900 dollars.

1. Who wrote the lyrics of Thompson's campaign song 'Big Bill the Builder'.

But, obviously, many of his deals had been in cash, for only one cheque for six thousand dollars related to the purchase of his sixteen-thousand-dollar house. He also carried a large amount of cash on his person – he had had nine thousand dollars in bills in his pocket when he was killed. In March 1930 he paid insurance premiums on jewellery valued at twelve thousand dollars, which was never located. During that two and a half years he drew cheques for the sum of 17,400 dollars for horse-track and dog-track betting.

Another interesting branch of his activities that came to light were his 'loans' from gamblers, politicians and businessmen. He had 'borrowed' two thousand dollars from Jimmy Mondi, once a Mont Tennes handbookman, who had become a Capone gambling operator in Cicero and the Loop – a loan, the report read, which had not been paid back. He had five thousand dollars from Alderman Berthold A. Cronson, nephew of Ettelson, who stated that the loan was 'a pure friendship proposition'; it had not been repaid. He had five thousand dollars from Ettelson himself, who could not be reached but who sent word that he had never loaned Lingle anything at any time, although he 'had a custom of giving Lingle some small remembrance at Christmas time, like a box of cigars'. He had a loan of 2,500 dollars from Major Carlos Ames, president of the Civil Service Commission, and Ames stated that this loan 'was a purely personal affair needed to cover market losses'. He had three hundred dollars from Police Lieutenant Thomas McFarland. 'A purely personal affair,' declared McFarland, as he had been 'a close personal friend of Lingle's for many years'. Additionally it was alleged that Sam Hare, roadhouse and gambling-parlour proprietor, had loaned Lingle twenty thousand dollars. Hare denied it.

Yet further enlightenment thrown by the investigation upon the private operations of Lingle was that he had been in investment partnership with Police Commissioner Russell, one of his five separate accounts for stock-market speculations. This particular one was opened in November 1928 with a twenty-thousand-dollar deposit, and was carried anonymously in the broker's ledger as Number 49 Account. On

September 20, 1929 – preceding the market crash in October 1929 – their joint paper profits were 23,696 dollars; later, a loss of 50,850 dollars was shown. On all his five accounts his paper profits at their peak were eighty-five thousand dollars; with the crash these were converted into a loss of seventy-five thousand dollars. Russell's losses were variously reported as 100 thousand and 250 thousand dollars.

'As to the source of the moneys put up by Lingle in these stock accounts and deposited by him in his bank account,' the report commented with grim formality, 'we have thus far been able to come to no conclusion.'

But the Press and the public had come to conclusions – and they were the drearily obvious ones, the ones that again confirmed that they were the inhabitants of a city that lived by spoliation, that they were governed by dishonourable leaders and venal petty officials. As had happened so monotonously before, the dead hero changed into a monster in this fairy-story in reverse. The newspapers continued to theorize why Lingle had been eliminated, and the public were, flaccidly, interested to know; but the fervour, the righteous wrath, had waned. Both the most likely theories identified Lingle as a favour-seller, and both circumstantially indicted Capone's opposition, the Moran and Aiello merger. One story which had percolated through from the underworld was that Lingle had been given fifty thousand dollars to secure protection for a West Side dog-track, that he had failed – and kept the money. Another implicated him in the reopening of the Sheridan Wave Tournament Club which had been operated by the Weiss-Moran gang, but which, after the St Valentine's Day massacre, and the fragmentation of the gang, had closed. After recouping, Moran had for eighteen months been trying to muster official help for a reopening. It had been in charge of Joe Josephs and Julian Potatoes Kaufman. It was stated that Kaufman, an old friend of Lingle, had approached him and asked him to use his influence to persuade the police to switch on the green light. The Chicago *Daily News* alleged that then, Boss McLaughlin – who on another occasion had threatened Lingle for refusing to inter-

22

cede in obtaining police permission for the operation of another gambling house – was commissioned by Moran to make direct contact with the State's Attorney's Office. Kaufman and Josephs separately approached a police official, who agreed to let the Sheridan Wave Tournament open, if Lingle was cut in.

Following this, according to the report, Lingle called on Josephs and Kaufman and demanded fifty per cent of the profits. Kaufman abusively refused. So the club remained closed.

Another newspaper, the Chicago *Herald and Examiner*, carried a similar story. According to their version Lingle demanded fifteen thousand dollars cash from Josephs and Kaufman, and when this was refused, retorted: 'If this joint is opened up, you'll see more squad cars in front ready to raid it than you ever saw in your life before.'

Three days before Lingle was killed, State's Attorney Swanson's staff of detectives, on the orders of Chief Investigator Pat Roche, raided a gambling house in the Aiello territory, the Biltmore Athletic Club in West Division Street. Within an hour after the raid, Lingle was repeatedly telephoning Roche, who refused to talk to him. Next day Lingle accosted him in person and said: 'You've put me in a terrible jam. I told that outfit they could run, but I didn't know they were going to go with such a bang.'

Meanwhile, Kaufman and Josephs had made up their minds – doubtless after consultation with Moran – to restart the Sheridan Wave Tournament Club in defiance of Lingle. It was widely advertised that it would be opening on the night of 9 June – the day on which Lingle set out for the races for the last time.

An equally plausible theory was that he had got too deeply tangled up in the struggle for money and power in the gambling syndicate. For years there had been bitter war between Mont Tennes's General News Bureau, a racing news wire service which functioned entirely for the purposes of betting, and the independent news services. As an appointed intermediary, in January 1930 Lingle brought the two opposed factions together and a two-year truce was agreed upon. The truce may not have extended to Lingle, whose services perhaps did not satisfy all the parties.

Possibly all are true: it was simply that Lingle, like so many before him, had gone too far out in these barracuda waters of gang-business.

The Man Who Trained
Nude Bicyclists
RICHARD D. ALTICK

While George Chapman briefly operated the Grapes public
house at Bishop's Stortford, Essex, early in 1899, it is conceivable that one of his customers was Samuel Herbert
Dougal. This gentleman, who was about to face the unpleasant necessity of shooting and burying Miss Camille Holland,
might profitably have consulted the landlord, who had
already had initiatory experience in this general line although
for results he relied on the more subtle method of poison and
the incompetence of the attending physicians. Nor did he
object to letting his victims have public burials.

It is appropriate that this, the last of our Victorian cases,
should be especially rich in period charm. The charm, however, is – again appropriately – that of a changing world.
Dougal introduced into Essex one of its first motor cars,
referred to in his diary as the 'loco' or the 'locomobile'. Like
Chapman, he was also, in the best turn-of-the-century fashion, when the invention of the pneumatic tyre had changed
the whole English way of life, a bicycling enthusiast, and he
liked to give lessons in the wholesome art to the girls of the
neighbourhood. In this, however, he had a tendency to con-
fuse his innocent impulses – to share his zest for outdoor
recreation – with others that were less creditable, because
when the girls were on their bikes, they were 'in a state of
nature'. 'What a picture,' comments the editor of his trial,
Miss F. Tennyson Jesse, ' – in that clayey, lumpy field, the
clayey, lumpy girls, naked, astride that unromantic object, a
bicycle, and Dougal, gross and vital, cheering on these
bucolic improprieties . . .!'

Bicycles or not, Dougal was certainly 'gross and vital'.
During his four years at Moat Farm, he seduced ('if,' again

seconding Miss Jesse, 'that term is applicable to those who were, for the most part, such willing victims') a really impressive number of servant girls and others. 'In one case it is known that he had relations with three sisters and with their mother.' In fact, a more suitable name for Dougal's rustic establishment would have been Stud Farm; he hired the girls, put them in the family way, and then discharged them, though continuing to maintain friendly relations with them, as we shall see. None of this side of Dougal's conduct, of course, was brought out in court, because it was irrelevant to the main issue. But his proclivities were notorious in the region. He seems, in fact, to have repopulated a large portion of rural Essex.

With good reason had Sherlock Holmes remarked to Dr Watson, as reported in the *Strand Magazine* for June 1892: 'It is my belief, Watson, founded upon my experience, that the lowest and vilest alleys of London do not present a more dreadful record of sin than does the smiling and beautiful countryside.' Moat Farm, standing neighbourless at the end of a series of country lanes, was the scene of a crime far more sinister than routine fornication. The cold-blooded murder it witnessed amply justified the 'only thought' a criminologist like Holmes had when he beheld these lonely farmsteads – 'a feeling of their isolation and of the impunity with which crime may be committed there'.

Dougal, aged fifty-two when he met his prospective victim in 1898, had been an enlisted man in the Royal Engineers, and upon his retirement after twenty-one years' service he received the golden commendations of his superiors; as a soldier his conduct had been impeccable, irrespective of the number of girls he had seduced off post across the years. After leaving the army, he had launched upon a criminal career which on the whole was more diversified even than Charles Peace's; arson, larceny, and forgery all were in his repertory. His concomitant marital arrangements – there were at least three formal Mrs Dougals as well as informal company of indeterminate number – probably could not stand careful scrutiny. As an adventurer, however, he lacked Peace's picturesqueness; Dougal was nothing if not slick and unprincipled. In 1898 his affairs had come to a crisis. He had lost his army pension long since because of his criminal convictions, his less shady projects for making money had not panned out any better than the others, and now he looked once more to exerting his accustomed powerful influence on a woman, for the sake of the money she possessed. He found her in a lodging house in Bayswater.

Miss Camille Holland, born in India and a lady of comfortable inherited means, was then aged about fifty-six. The landlady with whom she and Dougal stayed at Saffron Walden testified that 'when dressed [she] looked about fifty years of age, but when in bed ten or fifteen years older'. In other words, she was precisely the archetypal lady described by the judge in *Trial by Jury*: she may very well have passed for forty-three, in the dusk with a light behind her. The toilette that knocked a decade or more off her age no doubt consisted of the system of elaborate artifices employed by Mrs Skewton, the berouged and corseted 'fatal Cleopatra' in *Dombey and Son*.[1] She was a perfect mark for a calculating and avaricious man like Dougal – a spinster of blameless life who had managed to make her material circumstances additionally comfortable by being fairly close with the income from her invested money.

In January 1899, some four months after they met, they bought Coldhams Farm, between Saffron Walden and Audley End. She supplied the money and he supplied the new name by which it eventually would achieve notoriety: Moat Farm. One thinks irresistibly of 'Mariana in the Moated Grange'. Miss Jesse, whose great uncle wrote that hauntingly

1. Dickens does not confide the details of what Mrs Skewton wore, but we have the word of the Saffron Walden landlady, who was a dressmaker, as to Miss Holland's customary attire: 'a pair of "natural" woollen combinations, a pair of white linen combinations, a pair of steel-framed corsets, two pink woollen underbodices, black cashmere stockings, a pair of bloomers, and two petticoats' – formidable accoutrement, one thinks, for a spinster lady out to meet the world.

atmospheric poem, describes Moat Farm well in her own prose:

> The house itself is a building that on a sunny day holds something sinister and dreary, a look as of a house in some wild Brontë tale, and that on a wet, grey day might stand for the epitome of everything that is lonely and grim. . . . Surrounded by dark fir trees and gnarled apple trees in a very ecstacy of contortion, it is a small, neat, almost prim house, its deeply sloping roof patterned in diamond shapes with lighter tiles; its famous moat circles it so completely that it is only possible to enter it at one point, where a bridge spans the water. . . . The soil is heavy clay that clings about the feet, and the inhabitants seem to hold in their slouching walk and heaviness of mien some recognition of this fact, as though the perpetual drag of the clay pulled them always downwards, both body and soul.

After staying awhile in lodgings at Saffron Walden, 'Mr and Mrs Dougal', as they now called themselves without warrant, took possession of this depressing retreat, amply furnished with seven rooms' worth of her furniture which was transferred from storage in London.

Two weeks later a maidservant arrived; another week, and Dougal tried to break into her room, allegedly to wind the clock. The girl had hysterics, Miss Holland – as, in the interests of accuracy, we shall continue to call her – intervened, and took the frightened girl into her own bed. Dougal was faced with a heavy decision. His irresistible urge to meddle with toothsome servants obviously did not recommend him to the decorous lady upon whose largesse he was completely dependent. He could not do without either the girls or the money; he could, however, do without Miss Holland, and three days after his attempt upon the servant's virtue, Miss Holland disappeared.

To the girl, whose mother promptly removed her, *virgo intacta*, the next day, Dougal explained that Miss Holland had gone up to London for a day or two. But the days lengthened into weeks, and then into months, and then into years, four of them. Dougal continued to live at Moat Farm, comfortably furnished as it was with Miss Holland's belongings (oddly, she had also left all her clothing behind). He improved his time by giving bicycling lessons in the mire, fathering bucolic brats, and for three of the four years giving shelter to a genuine Mrs Dougal – his third – whom he had invited down to Moat Farm the very day after Miss Holland was last seen. In April 1902, however, this lady eloped with a labourer and the injured husband promptly filed for divorce. She did not contest the suit and he was awarded a decree *nisi* in August.

Meanwhile, by frequent correspondence with Miss Holland's bankers, using her signature, of course, Dougal methodically collected all the cash he needed for a gracious way of life, liquidating an investment or two when current income proved insufficient. This could have continued indefinitely, as long as the money held out, had not one of his seducees, with less forbearance than her several predecessors, sworn out an affiliation order against him. This had the effect of reviving and bringing to official attention the disquieting rumours that had hung in the damp Essex air for several years. The fruits of the police investigation were indications that Dougal had been guilty of extensive and high-handed forgery. The Essex and London police got into communication, and a representative paid him a friendly visit for the sake of obtaining information. The next day, reading the signs aright, Dougal closed out his accounts in two banks and took the outstanding balances in cash. A few days later, appearing at the Bank of England itself, he attempted to cash some ten-pound notes. But the bank had been alerted to watch for those serial numbers, Dougal was arrested, and, after an abortive attempt to escape – he had the ill luck to pick a dead-end street – he was returned, handcuffed, to Saffron Walden.

The question naturally arose, Where was the lady whose bank accounts and broker's portfolio he had been steadily depleting? The Essex constabulary got to work. Failing to find an inch of space inside the house where anything could be concealed, they began to dig up the garden, then the moat. At length someone recalled that shortly after Dougal and Miss Holland had moved in, he had ordered workmen to fill in a drainage ditch leading from the farmyard to a pond. The excavation site therefore was shifted once again. For five weeks the policemen slaved, 'often working up to their waists in slime', slithering in liquid manure, falling into the mess, spraining ankles, finding bones – of animals – , receiving advice from manipulators of divining rods and other specialists in the occult, and eventually, just four years after Miss Holland's arrival at the farm, retrieving what remained of her. It had been the most protracted, and certainly the filthiest, bit of police spade work (in the strictest sense) on record. But it was worth the trouble. The body was identified by its clothing, and the philanderer-forger-cycling instructor was charged with murder, to the applause of a rapt press and public which had watched the marathon digging operations with mounting excitement.

In Chelmsford prison, Dougal passed the time conducting chatty correspondences with acquaintances from the past. Not the least striking of these letters was one he wrote to a girl who had borne one of his more recent by-blows. Always the practical man of affairs, he offered advice on arrangements for a peculiar *ad hoc* journey – the pilgrimage of her numerous peers to bear witness against him:

> I daresay the girls have received their notices, etc., to attend next Monday at Chelmsford, have they not? There will be several from about there, and it would be a good idea to club together and hire a trap and drive all the way. It is a delightful drive through undulating country, and at this time of year it would be a veritable treat for them all.

The notion of a whole sisterhood of young unwed mothers, bound together in common debt to Dougal, chartering a conveyance for a comradely excursion to his trial on a capital charge, is one to occupy the imagination.

What they witnessed, if they all arrived, pink-cheeked after their ride through blossomy Essex, was a trial in which the prosecution held all the cards. The lack of doubt as to the result drained it of drama. But its fundamentally anticlimactic nature was relieved – or perhaps enhanced – by a spot of comedy provided by a flustered witness, the proprietress of the Bayswater boarding house where Dougal met Miss

Holland. She was asked to identify Dougal.

Q.	Do you see him in the Court?
A.	[Looking straight at the jury box] Yes, I see him among those gentlemen over there.
Q.	Will you kindly remove your veil, madam?
A.	Yes. Oh, yes, now I can see him. [Pointing to the same gentleman.]
Q.	Will you kindly listen to me for a moment, madam. Look slowly round the Court again?
A.	Yes, there is the gentleman. [Pointing to the Shire Hall keeper.]
Q.	[By defence counsel] I don't know if I ought to interfere, but I understand this lady has identified a gentleman on the other side of the Court.
Q.	[By the prosecution] Will you do what I ask, madam, and look around the Court slowly, please.
A.	[Pointing to the prisoner in the dock] That is the man sitting there.

The rows of Dougal's erstwhile girlfriends must have got a hearty giggle out of the scene. Dougal's reaction at this point is not on record. His counsel, having called no witnesses, made a gallant but futile address to the jury, which somewhat surprisingly required an hour and a half to come to the foreordained verdict. After sentence was pronounced, the Chief Constable of Essex obtained leave to read a statement bringing to public notice the 'dogged perseverance and unwavering cheerfulness' with which the police of Essex and London, from inspectors to mire-covered constables, had discharged their 'most laborious and unsavoury task'. The practice of ending a murder trial with credit lines was not usual (one rare instance would be the citation of Stokes, in the Wainwright case, for his footwork), but in this instance it was fully justified.

The garland of great Victorian cases begins with the Norfolk police floundering in the muck of James Blomfield Rush's farm: we end it with the constabulary of another eastern county emerging in triumph from the muck of Samuel Dougal's drainage ditch. Even though the latter force, in their deepest and muddiest moments of despair, may not have conceded it, police work, and its appreciative public, had come a long way in half a century. A great novelist[2] had – unfairly, as we now know – derided the Norfolk force for their inability to find what they were looking for; now a Chief Constable gave public praise to his men for persevering to success. To adapt the words of the late Laureate, they strove, they sought, and they found.

2. Dickens.

Murder for Profit and for Science
JACQUES BARZUN

1974

The deeds of the murdering quartette – William Burke, William Hare, and their two women – brought about several important results beyond the death of their victims. Law, medicine, and literature were affected. The story itself is one of the curiosities of capitalist enterprise, and to these interests is also added that of a perfect setting – Edinburgh at the beginning of the nineteenth century, ten years before Queen Victoria.

That the crimes took place in that picturesque but austere city should cause no wonder. Edinburgh was a great medical centre. For nearly a hundred years students had come there from distant places to learn from rival teachers the truth of the systems in vogue – Cullen's and Brown's. Besides the university medical school, still run by a third-generation Monro descended from the founder, there were half a dozen proprietary colleges. Even Dr Benjamin Rush, the self-assured American patriot, went to Edinburgh in the 1760s so that his medical education might be complete.

The teaching was naturally not all 'systems' or 'institutes' (i.e. principles). It included such fundamental sciences as anatomy and physiology, and these entailed dissection, for which a good supply of anatomical subjects was indispensable. It was a merit advertised by each professor that in this regard he 'kept a good table'; it ensured both popularity and fees. The perpetual shortage was due, of course, to the legal requirement of Christian burial and the strength of family feeling. Except for the bodies of felons, which were usually turned over to the schools, physicians had to rely on the recognized but risky trade of grave-robbing.[1] Those engaged

---

1. This familiar phrase is a misnomer. Under the common law there

33

in it earned the imaginative nickname of Resurrection men.

Now the most flourishing course in anatomy and physiology at Edinburgh in 1827 was Dr Robert Knox's. It was consequently the largest market for bodies. His young assistants did all they could to publicize their need, as well as the generous prices that would be paid by the janitor at 10 Surgeons' Square.

In another part of town, outside the West gate, an alley called Tanner's Close was the site of a hostel for vagrants, which offered the comfort of seven beds (three to a bed) for thruppence. It was run by a widow named Log, who cohabited with one of her lodgers, William Hare. He was an Irish navvy, originally a worker on the Union Canal, but now a hawker. As a navvy he had come to know a fellow-countryman, one William Burke, an ex-soldier with a wife in Ireland but living with a woman named Helen MacDougal. He worked as a cobbler and seller of old shoes. All four shared a taste for whisky, a radical improvidence, and a disinclination to hard work.

It was chance that inspired them with the idea for which they became famous. One of the lodgers at Log's died of natural causes, but owing the management £4. Pondering this serious loss, one William or the other recalled what he had heard about bodies and 'selling to the doctors'. The pair emptied the pauper's coffin, put in a load of tanner's bark, and took the corpse to Professor Monro at the university, only to be redirected to Dr Knox. A payment of £7.10s.0d. and the expressed wish of the young students to see the entrepreneurs again seemed an open gateway to affluence. It was clear that deliveries were not met with awkward questions.

But neither were the materials readily procured. Yet in

---

is no property in dead bodies, which makes it impossible to bequeath one's body to a hospital: the executor would lack the power to make delivery. By the same reasoning, body-snatching from cemeteries could only be prosecuted as a trespass. The dangers to the body-snatchers came altogether from the violent anger of the deceased's relatives and friends.

keeping with the new science of political economy, demand *must* create supply. Burke at first tried to find waifs who could be despatched without fear of inquiry. He failed, but the new year 1828 brought fresh resolution and the partners managed not so much to find as to produce sixteen bodies in the next nine months. Prices fluctuated, as in a commodity market, from £8 to £14. Possibly a few more sales went unrecorded.

The first victim, very likely, was Joe the miller, or else it was an old woman from Gilmerton, both ailing. Though Burke always acted under the impetus of liquor, he at first preferred prospects who were ill, or at least feeble. For them too, drink was the preliminary anaesthetic to simple smothering. The system had been created. With a regular income in sight, Log's became a centre of feasting and fighting among the four riders of the Apocalypse.

But like all innovators, they made grave mistakes. The first was to entice to Burke's brother's house Mary Paterson and her friend Janet Brown (both prostitutes) and killing Mary while Janet was in the next room, drunk. Mary was young, beautiful, amiable, well-educated, and widely known throughout Edinburgh. One of Knox's assistants (later surgeon to Queen Victoria) recognized Mary's corpse, for he had known her professionally, as *her* client. But Knox kept mum while Janet continued to search for her friend. He had the body sketched by an artist and kept it unused for three months. Corruption *is* catching.

Other victims followed: a 'cinder woman', who raked through old trash for salables; a sturdy Irishwoman and her deaf-and-dumb grandson; a washerwoman serving the Hares; two more prostitutes, mother and daughter. Even before these achievements, success had become so inspiriting that deliveries to Surgeons' Square were made openly by day, usually in the same capacious tea-chest, which urchins came to recognize and proclaim as the vehicle of a dead body.

In the midst of this prosperity, after a short trip the Burkes took to Ireland, dissension overtook the firm: Hare had indulged in separate trading behind the others' back. And earlier he had annoyed his partner by suggesting that Helen would make a good victim, especially as, being a Scotswoman, she was not to be trusted. A fierce quarrel took place and the Burkes moved to another tenement nearby. Reconciliation came only when a chance arose to kill again. This time it was a young Irish girl, married, and visiting Helen, her relative by marriage. Whether young Ann was invited on purpose or was merely found suitable when she appeared is not known. But we do know that out of delicate feelings for kinship, Burke declined to open the proceedings; he helped Hare only at the end.

Then occurred the second serious mistake: it was to go to work on a retarded youth of eighteen, James Wilson, known as Daft Jamie, whose harmless wanderings through the streets had made him affectionately known to all Edinburgh. Weak in the head, he was strong in body, and Hare later declared in court that 'he fought like a hero'. Into this error of judgement Dr Knox also fell. Public feeling about a second disappearance of notable persons was intense and speculation rife. He quickly had the head and deformed feet removed and denied that the body was Jamie's. For the moment business went on as usual.

Before the next and last victim, a frail beggarwoman who met her end on 31 October 1828, the combine had been planning an expansion of trade, possibly with the help of Dr Knox's janitor Paterson. The idea was to open up branches in Glasgow and Ireland and really make the business pay. Unfortunately, Mrs Docherty, the beggarwoman, had been befriended by a couple named Gray, who were temporarily in close touch with the evil foursome. When the Grays discovered her body on their hosts' premises, they made an outcry, and though penniless themselves, were unmoved by promises of money for their silence.[2] They notified the police, but sounded unconvincing until a discrepancy in the culprits'

---

2. Without the Grays' integrity, the criminals might have escaped. They were ready for flight. They had moreover a kind of hold on the Grays' feelings, for Helen MacDougal had borne two children to

remarks gave everything away. All was over, bar the vast public excitement – and the hanging.

The trial began early on Christmas Eve and lasted uninterrupted through Christmas morning, a full twenty-four hours. It brought into the overcrowded court the town's highest talent in all professions. To prevent general (and mutual) suffocation à la Burke, the windows of the room were opened to the cold blast. Soon everybody's head was muffled up in one of the big coloured handkerchiefs of the time, and the grim scene opened in front of what resembled a carnival.

Only Burke and Helen MacDougal were tried, for the necessary evidence could only come from Hare, who had to be promised immunity. Moreover, of the three murders named in the indictment only the last was prosecuted. This indirectly saved Dr Knox and his assistants from appearing as witnesses, for none of them had seen the last body. Burke was found guilty in fifty minutes' deliberation. MacDougal was let off under the rubric of Not Proven.

Hare, who had joked through his testimony and virtually danced at his partners' downfall, barely escaped the fury of the mob. He was made the object of a technical suit on behalf of Daft Jamie's mother and sister, which resulted in a second trial, on the issue of complicity; but he was not under indictment and he finally went off, to an unknown fate.

Burke was publicly hanged, his skin tanned and sold in strips, and his body dissected by Dr Monro, who lectured upon it for two hours before a huge throng. Those left outside rioted until arrangements were made that allowed some 30,000 to file through the dissecting room and see the remains.

At his next inaugural in Surgeons' Square, Dr Knox proclaimed that he would 'do just as I have done heretofore'. The

---

Mrs Gray's father. A public subscription for Gray, ex-soldier and unemployed, netted less than £10, that is, less than a fresh body at Surgeons' Square.

students cheered, but he was later burnt in effigy and his house was destroyed. He sought and won exoneration by a committee, but the odium persisted. His following gradually dwindled. He moved to another college, then to Glasgow, and finally to London, where he is said to have ended his days as a cheap obstetrician, or again as a demonstrator in a raree show.

Though not an endearing character – and certainly he connived at Burke and Hare's system – Knox was a remarkably gifted man. From early days a traveller and a student, then a surgeon at Waterloo, later a frequent contributor to learned journals, and also the founder of the Museum of Comparative Anatomy (where Burke's skeleton may still be seen), Robert Knox in his late thirties had the energy to lecture three times a day to some five hundred students, larding his instruction with scurrilous attacks on other practitioners. With only one eye, he had more insight into the body's workings than most of his colleagues. To his students, he was 'first and incomparable'.

Clearly Dr Knox was 'all for science'. Burke, while awaiting execution, complained with bitterness of the doctor's failure to pay him £5 still due on the last delivery. That the body had been taken from the surgeon by the police was to him irrelevant. Burke was 'all for business'. And yet, if there are still degrees of turpitude at the lowest level, Burke stands morally well above Hare. After the verdict Burke turned to his 'wife' and said: 'Nelly, you are out of the scrape.' In his confession beforehand, he had absolved her of complicity and Knox and his boys as well: they never 'incoureged me'. At times he had had remorse and bad dreams. But the thin, nervous, insinuating Hare, who may well have been the first begetter of the scheme, showed up in his role of King's evidence as a creature heartless beyond the call of duty. There is no doubt that Hare was 'all for his own skin'.

It remains to say a word about a few of the unlooked-for by-products of the case. One is struck first by the excellence of Dr Christison's medicolegal report on the body of the final victim. Forensic medicine had been and has remained a great speciality of Scottish science. In this case, the differentiation of pre- and post-mortem bruising and lividity was important, as it so often is, and Christison took pains to make 'express trial' to demonstrate effects. He could not prove that murder had been done, but he raised a strong presumption that proved sufficient, and his example encouraged further research.

Nor were men of science done with Burke after the trial. They kept up a fierce polemic over the significance of his cranial configuration. Phrenology was a lively new discipline and criminologists had things to prove, by statistics as well as argument. Fortunately for science, though not for phrenology, Burke's bumps refused to conform to prediction.

The original difficulty of getting subjects for dissection was of course not settled by the murders, either in theory or in practice. Two of Dr Knox's fellow-anatomists had risen to his defence by citing the 'inevitable and necessary' measures used to obtain bodies. They did not mean murder; they meant the deviousness that tempted to it. Here indeed is a prime instance of the way bad laws and confused public sentiment incite to crime. The remedy at law came three years after Burke's trial, in Lord Warburton's Anatomy Act of 1832 (2nd & 3rd William IV, Cap. 75), which authorized the legal custodians of a dead body to allow its delivery to a medical school. These custodians are usually the relatives of the deceased; but failing them, various public officials are named in the Act as having the power. Yet as late as 1921 the state of feeling among officials and laity still denied an adequate supply of subjects for dissection; for the Act of 1832 was only permissive and not mandatory as to the disposal of unclaimed bodies.[3]

In the history of law, the trial about Hare's immunity is important as a review of the law governing the liability of a

3. See the letter to Professor Arthur Robinson in William Roughead, *Burke and Hare*, Edinburgh, 1921, 279–81. The shortage of bodies for medical study continues in the United States today, an indirect result of welfare programmes that defray burial expenses. See the *P & S Quarterly*, Columbia University Medical School, Fall 1973, p. 26, and also *The New York Times* for 7 December 1980.

participant in crime who testifies against his accomplices. Both the Edinburgh trials display in full the scrupulous fair play of British criminal law at its best, to say nothing of the intellectual powers of the lawyers and judges involved.

But perhaps it is literature that has gained most from the emotional upheaval at Edinburgh in 1828. At the time, the journalists and ballad-mongers were fully employed. Even Knox's janitor became a literary man under the name of The Echo of Surgeons' Square, and was bold enough to offer himself as collaborator to Walter Scott. And among the crowd a true genius arose, fired in the forge of public stress, who epitomized the ghastly saga in a definitive quatrain:

Up the Close and doun the stair,
But and ben wi' Burke and Hare:
Burke's the butcher, Hare's the thief
And Knox the boy who buys the beef.[4]

Meantime, Sir Walter Scott had produced a first-rate paragraph of armchair detection to prove that Joe the miller was Burke's first victim, a point on which the witnesses disagreed. More important still, Thomas De Quincey, at the very time Burke and Hare were joining forces, was composing 'Murder Considered as One of the Fine Arts', an epoch-making essay that lifted the tale of crime out of the street-vendor's hands to deposit it in the more manicured but not less feverish ones of the novelist, the psychologist, and the critic.

From the words of De Quincey's twice-revised thesis that murder deserves to be judged and admired by connoisseurs, one gathers that the Edinburgh killings did not fulfil his definition of art. He cheers 'the Burke-and-Hare revolution', no doubt for its attention-getting value which helped to promote his views, but he disapproves the taking advantage of the sick and feeble – they are not really able to stand murder.

---

4. 'But and ben': in and out. The English language was also enriched, at least for a time, with the new verb *to burke*, meaning to murder by strangling or suffocation. According to report, when the crowd caught sight of Hare after his release, the shout went up: 'Burke, the b—!' The word in blank offers two choices to the philologist.

Besides, he wants *one* performer, whose risk is always the greater, surrounded as he is by honest men. Hence our critic prefers the Williams murders of 1812. His sardonic mirth and fanciful points are but a mask for the horror he expresses at the end.

Still, De Quincey's root idea helped create a new literary genre. It begins with Poe and has ended by filling libraries with accounts true and fictional of great crimes and great trials. On Burke and Hare themselves you may read Stevenson's *Body-Snatcher*, you may consult William Roughead in *Classic Crimes*, or you may chance to see James Bridie's *The Anatomist*, where all our characters play out their parts on the stage. The vulgar pruriency which impelled 30,000 to see Burke dissected has been transmuted into an informed intellectual interest which explains, no doubt, the presence of *this* essay, now in the reader's hands.

Far from the Old Folks at Home
DOROTHY DUNBAR

History is not static; it is quivering continuity. There is no such thing as a beginning or end, only illustrative peaks that punctuate the past, emphasize the present, and hint at the future. For example, the frozen body of Burgundy's Charles the Bold on the iceswept battlefield of Nancy is an historical cliché that supposedly marks the end of feudalism and the emergence of Germany and France as national organisms. Actually, Charles's corpse is an illustrative peak in a trend that begins back in the time-shrouded days of Clovis, who divided the Frankist Empire between his four sons, and that can be traced through the shot-up Hapsburg at Sarajevo, into our own atom-ridden times. These illustrative peaks have their heroes, villains, slogans, and symbols – convenient subliminal pegs on which to hang historical hats: white-bearded Moses; Caesar and his to-hell-with-it-all attitude at the Rubicon; the bright flame of Joan of Arc's fire; the blood-stained prints in the snow leading to Valley Forge; Fort Sumter; 'Remember the Maine'; V for Victory.

The history of crime has its own sanguinary thread of continuity, its own bloody peaks and gory symbols. Starting with the truculent Cain, murder has flourished as a national pastime through the ages. David's military tactics with Uriah the Hittite were definitely dirty pool. Nero was most unfilial when he poked holes in his mother's barge. Gilles de Rais (or Retz) had an inordinate amount of young children disappear within the melodramatic precincts of his medieval castle. The Marquise de Brinvilliers favoured arsenic as a solution to family spats, and the examples are numerous in the nineteenth-century Renaissance of murder and in the twentieth-century Restoration period of slaughter. As for symbols, there's Madeleine Smith's tasty cups of cocoa, Dr Palmer's copious beakers of brandy, Neill Cream's 'long pills', the Hauptmann ladder, and the Snyder-Gray sash weight.

For sheer Alpine altitude, however, in the illustrative peaks of crime, the blood-stained palm goes to Miss Lizzie Borden of Fall River, Massachusetts, and her inseparable symbol, the hatchet. Nineteenth-century murder without Lizzie Borden is like Helöise *sans* Abélard, Dr Johnson minus Boswell, or 'Turkey in the Straw' without a fiddle. Lizzie isn't an example of nineteenth-century murder, she *is* nineteenth-century murder – a study in scarlet filtered to a pretty pastel pink by Victoriphobia.

In 1892, Fall River, Massachusetts, was an ugly but productive cotton-mill town of some 75,000 people. There was definitely a right and wrong side of the track, because a foreign-born element had moved in to labour on the business enterprises of the native born. It was one of those towns buttressed with community spirit that might be called nosiness by the uncharitable, and it had its own aristocracy of old Yankee families who defied the contamination of Boston or New York.

One of these families was that of Andrew J. Borden. He was one of Fall River's leading citizens. A home-town boy who made good, he started his business career as an undertaker, and, by a high death rate and caution with the dollar, in 1892 Andrew Borden was worth over a quarter of a million dollars. He was president of a bank, an owner of profitable real-estate holdings. This tall, slightly stooped, white-haired New England magnate was scrupulous and upright in his business dealings, but he was a fatally slow man with the buck. He was not above bringing a basket of eggs from one of his farms to sell in town. Although his one great love affair was with money, he married twice. His first wife obediently produced two daughters and died, and, at forty, Mr Borden took a second wife – a palpitating, grateful spinster named Abby Gray.

For the past twenty years Andrew Borden had lived in a

narrow frame house with the second Mrs Borden and the two daughters of the former marriage. Ninety-two, Second Street was in a neighbourhood that had seen better days, and Andrew Borden's house was situated on a narrow lot, hemmed in by other narrow houses and set almost flush with a busily trafficked street. Downstairs there was a sitting-room, dining-room, parlour and kitchen, while upstairs there was the master bedroom, a dressing-room for Mrs Borden, separate bedrooms for each of the two daughters, and a guest room.

Andrew Borden was seventy with a lean, chipped-away, Grant Wood look. Abby Borden was sixty-four, short, and weighed a regrettable two hundred pounds. Miss Lizzie was thirty-two, a plump, unmarried lady with rimless eyeglasses who liked to try recipes, put bird houses in the garden, and read best sellers like *When Knighthood Was in Flower* and *Alice of Old Vincennes*. She was secretary to the Christian Endeavor Society, belonged to the Fruit and Flower Mission, and was active in the Women's Christian Temperance Union. She also taught a Sunday-school class and had made the grand tour of Europe in 1890. And Lizzie was a young lady with a mind of her own who took a very dim view of some of her father's convictions. She wanted to entertain lavishly, and she wanted a modern bathroom. To Andrew Borden the former was extravagant frivolity; the latter was downright decadent. Emma Borden, although nine years older than Lizzie, was like the negative to Lizzie's positive. She was much less active in church work, her tastes were much simpler, and she was caught up in the apathy of spinsterhood. The fifth resident at 92 Second Street was Bridget Sullivan, the pert, Irish maid-of-all-work.

It was a portrait of New England home life in the nineties. Andrew Borden was one of those I'll-damn-well-have-the-final-word domestic patriarchs. Mrs Borden, although a stepmother, seems to have gone about her household chores and domestic relations in an aura of unquestioning good will and easygoing plumpness. There was nothing of the 'heavy' stepmother about her – except her weight. The two daughters of the house went their rounds of tranquil social life and light domestic duties. If it was a dour household, it was a righteous one, and what the Bordens lacked in humour or gaiety they made up for by relentless virtue and paying their bills on time. But, as in so many cases, this accepted picture of middle-class life had unexpected lights and shadows that blurred the focus, and the home that framed this portrait of domesticity was actually a house divided.

It is unhappy to relate that the two maiden ladies constantly squabbled with their father over property, money, and their standard of living. The girls, particularly Lizzie, wanted luxury – frosting on the cake. Andrew was content with life's necessities. And when Mr Borden showed signs of helping his wife's stepsister financially, a restrained sort of hell broke loose. Lizzie expressed grim displeasure by ceasing to call stepmother 'Mother' and, if forced to speak to her at all, called her 'Mrs Borden'. The two sisters took their meals at pointedly different times than the old couple, and Lizzie even referred to the harmless Abby Borden as a 'mean old thing' on several occasions, a statement that still stands unsupported, as so many of Lizzie's pronouncements do.

The floor plan of the house further strained relations. The upstairs could be split into two separate parts by closing one communicating door, so that the master bedroom and dressing-room could only be reached by the back stairs, the bedrooms of the two daughters and the guest room by the front stairs. The bad feeling seems to have been unanimous. The bolts were drawn on both sides of the crucial communicating door, permanently.

Late in July 1892, Emma Borden went to visit friends in Fairhaven. Lizzie went to New Bedford for a visit but only remained a few days and returned home. On August third, Fall River was in the middle of a suffocating heat wave, but the sweltering monotony was broken by three interesting events. John Vinnicum Morse, a brother of the first Mrs Borden, arrived at 92 Second Street for a short visit. He found Mr and Mrs Borden recovering from a sick spell the night before. They told him Lizzie had also been mildly affected.

45

Miss Lizzie, in spite of the heat, went out on an errand that afternoon. She went to the pharmacy and tried to purchase prussic acid to clean a sealskin cape. The druggist refused to sell her such a potent dry cleaner, but Lizzie was never one to be easily discouraged. Eli Bence and two other drug clerks later identified Lizzie as the would-be purchaser, but she flatly said she wasn't. Then, Lizzie visited a neighbour and family friend, Miss Alice Russell, and carried on like the voice of doom. She told Miss Russell of the daylight robbery that had taken place last year, of the Bordens' illness of the previous evening. She was afraid the milk might be intentionally poisoned.

She feared her father had enemies, the barn had been broken into twice. She was afraid an anonymous *they* 'would burn the house down over us', and her last word on the subject was: 'I feel something hanging over me, and I can't throw it off.' Miss Russell suggested the barn might have been broken into by boys chasing pigeons. As for the other gloomy forebodings, she had no answer. It was probably too hot to cope with such things. Most of this sounds like conversational heat lightening, but one statement was based on fact, not humidity. There had been a daylight burglary at the Borden home in June 1891. Mr Borden's desk had been broken open, and he was relieved of eighty dollars in bank notes, twenty-five to thirty dollars in gold, some streetcar tickets, a watch and chain, and some small trinkets. His thrifty soul outraged, Mr Borden called in the police, who looked helplessly at the ravished desk and nodded sagely when Miss Lizzie said the cellar door was opened and *they* might have come in that way. However, a few days later Andrew Borden told City Marshal Hilliard: 'I am afraid the police will not be able to find the real thief.' Whether it was some inflection of voice, the curious choice of the word 'real', or his uncharacteristic readiness to abandon the inquiry, there was a definite feeling at the local precinct that Mr Borden was not entirely in doubt as to the robber's identity.

At the trial, Lizzie's lawyer blamed the curious conversation with Alice Russell on her monthly female condition. In the neo-Lydia Pinkham era this was a shrewd gambit, and Lizzie, at the inquest, used her condition as a neat bit of insurance just in case any blood was found on her clothes. The assertions about poison were probably wishful thinking about her disappointment at the drug store. The milk and the stomachs of Mr and Mrs Borden all registered negative on poison tests made after the tragedy.

On August fourth, life at 92 Second Street started out in a routine swelter. Mr and Mrs Borden and Mr Morse ate a truly terrifying breakfast at seven, prepared and served by Bridget. There are many elements of horror in the Borden case, but one of the worst was the August fourth breakfast – mutton, sugar cakes, coffee, and mutton broth. Bridget was later ill in the backyard, and if she ate that breakfast she deserved it.

By 9:15, Mr Morse had left the house to visit relatives. Mr Borden set out to make a few business calls, defying the heat in an inferno-like, black broadcloth suit. Miss Lizzie had come downstairs and was in the kitchen, sensibly sipping a frugal cup of coffee, while Bridget washed the breakfast dishes. Mrs Borden asked Bridget to wash the first-floor windows inside and out and said she was going to put fresh pillowcases on the pillows in the guest room. Bridget got her pail, brushes, and cloths and went out through the side door, leaving it unlocked. She talked over the fence to Mrs Kelly's girl for a few minutes and then started sudsing her way methodically round the house. It took an hour, and, as she washed, she looked in each ground-floor room and never saw anyone. Mrs Borden and Lizzie were inside, and it is evident from later medical testimony that Mrs Borden experienced the abomination of foreseeing her own death and knowing her executioner before blood and blackness engulfed her life and her world.

Bridget came in the house, locked the side door, and started washing the windows inside. At about 10:45, Mr Borden pounded on the front door. He had forgotten his key, and that was no light matter if you lived at the Borden house. It was a veritable Bastille. The side and back doors were wooden and locked and they both had screen doors with hooks on them, the front door had three fastenings – a spring latch, a bolt, and a lock which operated by key – and Bridget had to let Mr Borden in. As she fumbled at the three locks, there was a laugh, which has been described in terms running the gamut from 'low and amused' to 'high and maniacal'. Whatever it sounded like, there was no doubt where it came from. Bridget turned around and saw Miss Lizzie standing at the head of the staircase a few feet from the open door of the guest room. Lizzie came down the stairs and told her father: 'Mrs Borden has gone out. She had a note from someone who is sick.' Mr Borden took the key to his bedroom from a shelf, went up the back stairs to his bedroom and a few minutes later came downstairs and went in the sitting-room to rest. He took off his coat and, as further proof that New Englanders are impervious to the weather, put on a cardigan jacket before he stretched out on the couch to rest. He lay on his right side with his congress shoes hanging over the side on the floor. He was in the same position less than an hour later, but he wasn't in such good condition.

In the meantime, Bridget was washing the windows in the dining-room and Lizzie joined her there to start ironing handkerchiefs. Bridget went into the kitchen to wash out her cloths, and Miss Lizzie followed her: 'There's a cheap sale of dress goods on downtown. They are selling some kind of cloth at 8 cents a yard.'

But Bridget was not to be tempted by the vanities of the world. She had been up since six, she had been sick, and the heat was shimmering in a haze off the street. Bridget decided to go up and rest for a few minutes before lunch. Lunch was to be cold mutton and mutton soup, which makes death lose some of its sting.

Bridget lay down in her attic room and heard the clock strike eleven. Fifteen or twenty minutes later Lizzie called up to her, 'Come down quick. Father's dead. Somebody came in and killed him.'

Bridget was sent for the doctor. Dr Bowen, an old friend of the Borden family, found Andrew Borden lying on his side on the couch, his head thoroughly bashed in, blood all over his face. The wounds, it was later proved, were caused by a sharp instrument dealt by a person of ordinary strength and inflicted from behind. But at the moment, the chief fact that struck Dr Bowen was that the face of his old friend was 'hardly to be recognized by one who knew him'.

The neighbours, including Mrs Addie Churchill from next door and Alice Russell, the police, and a curious crowd had gathered with disaster-inspired speed, and Dr Bowen left to send Miss Emma a wire in Fairhaven. By the time Dr Bowen returned to the house, Bridget and Mrs Churchill had found Mrs Borden, adrift in her own blood on the floor of the guest room. And it was written literally in blood that Miss Emma and Miss Lizzie were inheritors of $175,000 each. Coagulation, and lack of it, showed that Abby Borden went to her reward a good ninety minutes before her husband.

In a montage of curiosity, heated discussion, and growing suspicion on the part of the police, the funeral and the inquest took place. Miss Lizzie, so clearheaded and composed during the nerve-racking morning hours of August fourth, a pillar of strength to those who had come to comfort her, at the inquest, under the questioning of District Attorney Hosea Knowlton, became confused and snappish by turn, and she literally just didn't know where she was on the crucial morning. Seven days after the murders, Lizzie Borden was arrested for the murders of her stepmother and father. And the world became 'Lizzie conscious'. Coffee and conversation percolated with equal heat at the nation's breakfast tables, and the question was hotly asked and hotly answered, 'How could a woman do such a thing?' Some people thought it impossible, but some nasty-minded sceptics thought it was not only possible, it was highly probable. But Lizzie had moral support from Lucy Stone and her following of suffragettes. Mrs Susan Fessenden and the W.C.T.U. got behind Lizzie, and she had physical as well as moral support from her pastors, Reverend Buck and Reverend Jubb. She usually made her appearances leaning on the arm of one or the other. 'Unfortunate girl . . . innocent . . . persecuted . . . harshly treated' were adjectives and phrases that were loosely bandied about, until it seemed as if the Commonwealth of Massachusetts should be indicted and tried for their treatment of Lizzie Borden.

Children in the street chanted, 'Mr Borden he is dead, . . . Lizzie hit him on the head.' And one of the barbershop witticisms of the time was: 'What did Lizzie Borden say when someone asked her what time it was? "I don't know, but I'll go axe Father." '

So Lizzie added variety to an already spicy situation by the quantity of answers she gave to the increasingly pertinent question: 'Where were you when it happened, Miss Lizzie?' She always had a ready answer, each one different. She told Dr Bowen she was out in the yard when she heard a groan. Mrs Churchill was informed, 'I went to the barn to get a piece of iron. I heard a distressing noise and came back and found the screen door open.' She told Patrolman Harrington she was in the loft of the barn and heard nothing. The loft was examined and found to contain a pristine layer of dust untouched by human hand or foot. It was so hot in the loft, the patrolman had to leave gasping for air after a few minutes. But 'Asbestos Liz' swore she had been there about twenty minutes. To Miss Russell she again gave the 'looking for a piece of iron to mend a screen door' version. Now, these variations could be excused on the grounds of excitement and confusion, but at the inquest, Miss Lizzie claimed she strolled in from the barn, casually took off her hat, and accidentally discovered her father's body. There's just too much variation between hearing a noise and running in to find your father hacked to bits and hearing nothing and coming upon the disaster accidentally. Also the point was brought up that if Lizzie thought someone had come in and killed her father as she said to Bridget, it was either extremely foolhardy or extremely courageous to stand in the hall, just a few feet from where fresh blood spilled and reeked, and call up to Bridget. Rushing out on the street, away from the carnage, would have seemed more likely. Her account at inquest of her activities during the time between Mr and Mrs Borden's deaths was just as erratic. She gave lie to the axiom that a person can't be in two places at the same time. She was reading an old

Harper's magazine in the kitchen, and she was upstairs in her room sewing a piece of tape on a dress.

Then there was the curious question of Miss Lizzie's elastic wardrobe. At the inquest, she testified that she wore a blue-and-white-stripe dress the morning of the murders but changed to a pink wrapper after somebody told her to. (The case crawls with anonymous collective nouns.) Nobody admitted giving this bit of advice. Both Bridget and Emma Borden said Lizzie was in the habit of wearing a cotton dress of light blue with darker-blue figure in the mornings. At the trial, Dr Bowen confusedly described Lizzie as wearing a drab-coloured calico-type dress. Mrs Churchill said Lizzie was wearing a light-blue cotton with a darker-blue shape. However, when Lizzie was asked by the police to turn over to them the dress she wore on the morning of the murder, she handed them a dark-blue silk dress which she had been wearing during the morning since the murder. Shown the dress at the trial, Dr Bowen had no resort to the indecisive word 'drab'. 'I should call it a dark blue.' Mrs Churchill when confronted with the dark-blue silk reluctantly admitted that: 'I did not see her with that on that morning.'

Then Alice Russell, torn between friendship and conscience, finally told the following story. After a visit Saturday night following the murders from the mayor, who warned Miss Lizzie she was under suspicion, Miss Russell found Lizzie in the kitchen on Sunday morning, burning a light-blue, cotton-cord dress with a dark figure. Emma Borden at the trial said there was paint on it, and she had urged Lizzie to burn the dress. However, police officers who had searched the house said they never saw a dress smeared with paint, and Miss Russell saw no paint on the portion of the dress Lizzie was burning. Lizzie's militant advocates were delighted when the news came out that Lizzie seemed to be the one Borden in the house without blood on her the morning of August fourth. It was proof of her pure innocence. However, the story of the dress could knock the props out of this. Miss Lizzie had some sort of a blue-and-white cotton dress that she was in the habit of wearing in the morning. She was wearing it the morning of the murder, according to witnesses. However, after the murders she changes into a pink wrapper, and for the next few mornings wears a dark-blue silk dress, which she turns over to the police when they request the dress she wore on the morning of the murder. She is found burning a dress that resembles the one she wore on August fourth – after she is told that she is under suspicion. She says she wore the blue-silk dress, which is produced in court. Witnesses say it is not the dress she wore. Emma says the burned dress had paint on it, Lizzie says it had paint on it. Police say there was no paint-stained dress present when they examined the clothes.

The problem of blood could have been easily taken care of after the first murder. There was ample tidying up time, since Bridget was outside washing windows for about an hour. As to the second murder, where time was more tricky, one look at an extant photograph of Mr Borden's body as it was found gives a pretty adequate idea of what could have happened. The couch on which he was lying was directly to the side of the sitting-room door, against the wall. With Mr Borden lying on his side, the back of his head would have been to the door and the murderer could merely have reached an arm and an aiming eye around the door and started banging away. If a few spots of blood were later discovered on the sleeve of the dress, they wouldn't have been obvious to excited eyes, but might have been apparent if tested, so the dress was disposed of just in case. The other theories of Lizzie stripped to the buff or Lizzie in some sort of all-enveloping waterproof garment gave colour to the conjectures of the time, but they don't hold water. Even if Lizzie had betrayed her Puritan upbringing by hacking her father to death without any clothes on, she wouldn't have had time to get dressed again, considering what the ladies of the 1890s considered 'dressed'. Nothing resembling a waterproof garment was ever found.

But whatever theory was believed, there was one certainty in the whole mixed-up matter of Lizzie's dress: Alice Russell was crossed off the Borden Christmas-card list. There was nebulous gossip, too, about Lizzie's lover. The leading candidates were a non-materializing young man she was supposed to have met during her European trip and a shadowy clergyman. But there was never any tangible proof of a romance in Lizzie's life. Like her spiritual ancestress, Elizabeth I of England, she died wearing the righteous if unwelcome crown of virginity, and any tangible lover remained conspicuous by his absence.

There was also the matter of the note Mrs Borden received. Protestors of Lizzie's innocence were faced with the uncomfortable fact that not only did the sick person never come forward, but the messenger also disappeared from the face of the earth. Lizzie's lawyers never made too much of that. The law takes little notice of anything other than the first, second, and third dimensions, and with the eyes of the town, the country, and the world turned on Lizzie, the sick friend and the messenger boy must have indeed been fourth-dimensional characters not to come forth.

On a warm June day in 1893, the thirteen-day wonder, noted in legal documents and court transcripts as the Trial of Lizzie Borden, opened in New Bedford. It was held in a bare, white-walled room with chairs, desks, and settees. The three superior court judges required by law wore regular business suits and fanned themselves with palm-leaf fans. Thirty or forty members of the press, including representatives from the New York *Sun* and the Boston *Globe*, were poised to rush news to a breathless, waiting world, and finally Lizzie Borden made her entrance in the grand manner. Walking sedately, flanked by Reverends Buck and Jubb, she wore a new, stylish black mohair dress with leg-of-mutton sleeves and a black lace hat with rosettes of blue velvet and a blue feather for properly subdued dash.

Mr Hosea Knowlton and Mr William Moody conducted a fair, accurate case for the commonwealth. Under more ordinary, less emotional circumstances they had a case as strong as that which has sent many protesting innocents to their final reckoning with state executioners and the Almighty. The trial revealed little news, although Mrs Hannah Reagan, the matron of the Fall River Police Station, heard the following conversation between Emma and Lizzie Borden: 'Emma,' said Lizzie, 'You have given me away.'

'No, Lizzie, I have not,' was the reply.

But Lizzie insisted: 'You have; and I will let you see I won't give an inch.'

It's cryptic conversation, to put it mildly, and, as it stands so starkly without any context, it is open to all sorts of interpretations. However, Reverend Buck made it seem more important than it actually was, when he visited Mrs Reagan and tried to get her to sign a statement retracting her story of the conversation. It is gratifying to learn that Mrs Reagan refused to sign the retraction, and Reverend Jubb, a vehement and vocal champion of Lizzie's innocence, was told by the Fall River officials in no uncertain terms to mind his own business.

A gruesome touch was added when a plaster cast of Mr Borden's head with appropriate blue marks to indicate the wounds was introduced as part of the medical testimony, and Miss Emma Borden snatched the headlines from Lizzie for one golden moment. Miss Lizzie entrenched herself on her constitutional rights as firmly and eagerly as any object of a twentieth-century Senate investigation, and her sole statement has a familiar ring. 'I am innocent. I leave my counsel to speak for me.'

The only time Lizzie had really run into trouble was during District Attorney Knowlton's merciless barrage of questions at the inquest. She had withdrawn from this encounter bruised and punchy. She wasn't about to get back in the ring for another sparring session with the question-happy District Attorney, and Emma Borden was an ideal substitute. She could testify on everything that happened before and after the murder, but she could not be cross-examined about the morning of August fourth. Emma came out strongly on her sister's side and said it was she who had urged Lizzie to burn the controversial dress.

The commonwealth based its case not only on the fact that Lizzie had the opportunity and motive but the question, 'Was there an opportunity for anyone else?' There was no sign of housebreaking, no struggle, nothing taken. They were hampered by the exclusion of both the pharmacists' testimony on

Lizzie's abortive attempt to obtain prussic acid and Lizzie's suspect inquest testimony. The other weaknesses of the Commonwealth's case were the inability to prove that the axe found in the Borden home was the murder weapon, even though it showed signs of recent washings and scrubbings with ashes and fitted the length of the wounds by an exact three-and-one-half inches; and not being able to come up with conclusive evidence that the blue dress Lizzie wore was the same one that met a fiery end in the Bordens' kitchen stove. Otherwise, the prosecution anticipated Dragnet by fifty years and presented the facts, clearly and damningly. It was an appeal to the intellect.

As for the defence, it was more colourful, if less creditable, and Lizzie had an ideal legal figure in her lawyer. Ex-Governor of Massachusetts, George Robinson was a shrewd Yankee who knew the value of the cracker-barrel approach on a New England jury. Lizzie was her own worst enemy geographically. She was flitting all over the house that morning – upstairs, downstairs, in my lady's chamber – and yet in this narrow house with its communicating doors and thin partitions, the defence maintained, there was a very tangible messenger of death, slaughtering Mrs Borden in her own guest bedroom, waiting in a small closet yet leaving no trace of blood or physical presence for an hour and a half until Andrew Borden decided to come home and lie down and take a nap. This hypothetical killer then struck again, took the hatchet down to the basement and got out of the house without being seen by Bridget or Lizzie, then walked down Second Street invisible to all the neighbours and off into some fiendish limbo.

Lizzie's guilt might have violated every Victorian precept of gently nurtured female, but the story of her defence violated every known limitation of time and space. Ex-Governor Robinson's closing speech for the defence typifies his whole argument: 'To find her guilty, you must believe she is a fiend. Gentlemen, does she look it?'

The jury looked at her, the tasteful clothes, the rimless spectacles, the air of gentility, backed by her pastors and her family, and they brought in a verdict of not guilty.

After the jury congratulated the vindicated darling of the Women's Christian Temperance League, to a man they headed for the nearest hotel bar to celebrate a job well done.

Lizzie may not have been the most beautiful or the sexiest lady ever to flutter a courtroom, but she was the luckiest: She got acquitted. Today a great gulf yawns deep and wide between the jury that acquitted Lizzie Borden and the lawyers, writers, and crime fanciers who study the case today. Faced with the fiction of a church-working spinster who couldn't even have such a thing as murder enter her pure thoughts and the fact that no one else could have done it, the Borden jury bought the whole fiction package. It was dogma in 1892 that a woman couldn't do such a thing, but twentieth-century courts are more sceptical and have been known to hand down verdicts where looks gave way to facts and have indicated that moral turpitude does not guarantee the difference between guilt and innocence on a capital charge.

Anna Marie Hahn looked like a comfortable 'Cincinnati Dutch' housewife, but the mortality rate of old men she loved and left landed her in the electric chair. Mr Chine, the ex-choir singer, appeared like a harmless little man addicted to buttermilk, until he started cremating his wives with undue haste. Major Armstrong was the spit-and-polish image of military propriety, but he bought too much arsenic to take care of his dandelion problems. James P. Watson, alias 'Bluebeard' – and that was no courtesy title with sixteen wives unaccounted for – was a mild-spoken, highly successful businessman who was tenderhearted and easily moved to tears. Louise Peete was the epitome of refinement, but corpses kept turning up with embarrassing regularity wherever she lived. And Dr Alice Wynekoop, well-known doctor, club woman, and social worker, just couldn't account for her daughter-in-law's body in her examining room. None of these ladylike or gentlemanly paragons were acquitted.

There has been no change or developments in the Borden case since the warm June day when the daughter of the house was acquitted to wild cheers and hosannas. There were, indeed, dark hints about a jet-propelled Emma Borden quickly sneaking into her home and then flashing back to Fairhaven. John Vinnicum Morse came in for his share of dark mutterings, but both his alibi and that of Miss Emma were checked and not found wanting. Bridget has been mentioned as a suspect. But she had a good character, was contented with her job, and it was unlikely that she would put such a strain on employer-employee relationships. Also Miss Lizzie was Bridget's alibi, as she could never be Miss Lizzie's. There was, of course, the usual rash of wild-eyed men, maniacs waving hatchets that dripped with blood in broad daylight, and deathbed confessions – all adding up to a big fat zero.

Miss Lizzie and Miss Emma moved to a larger, more spacious home about a mile and a half from Second Street, and it is to be hoped that it had a modern bathroom after all the sisters had been through. In February 1897, Lizzie hit the front pages again. 'Lizzie Borden again. A warrant for her Arrest has been issued. Two Paintings missed from Tilden-Thurber Company's store. Said to have been traced to Miss Borden's Home in Fall River.' No more is heard of this matter except that an 'adjustment was made out of court'. It brings to mind the burglary of 1891.

Lizzie lived on in Fall River in her fine new home. She preferred Washington and Boston, where she was an inveterate theatregoer. She seldom patronized Fall River stores and was not seen on the streets of the town except for brief glimpses of her in her carriage and later her motor car. At any rate, guilty or innocent, it seems that Lizzie, who changed her name to Lizabeth A. Borden, didn't win any popularity polls in her home town. She loved the theatre and seemed to have a school-girl crush on a favourite Boston tragedienne, Nance O'Neil. She shocked Fall River by throwing a big party for Miss O'Neil after a local performance, and there is an even more amazing record that she rented a house at Tyngsboro and entertained Miss O'Neil and her company for an entire week, an almost Roman entertainment for a gentle New England spinster. Evidently, all this was too much for Emma. She left Fall River shortly after this saturnalia and was heard of no more until she and Lizzie got into a legal hassle over the sale of a building from the estate in 1923.

And that's the story of Lizabeth A. Borden, who lived happily until her death in 1927. On 1 June 1927, Lizzie died at her home in Fall River, and on 10 June of the same year, Emma died at Newmarket, New Hampshire. Lizzie left an estate of $266,000 to friends, relatives, and the Animal Rescue League.

Lizzie was not only lucky to get acquitted. She did herself comfortable – to use a local expression – with her home, cars, trips and theatre jaunts, but it all has that 'company look' of dutiful smiles and empty conversation. Did the blood-stained images of Second Street ever gibber idiotically at her memory? Did the wet footprints of the past walk through her mind? There's no way of knowing. Her life after the double murder appeared as placid, although more independent and luxurious, as it had been before the one violent eruption in continuity, and the dark truth lies under a tombstone at the foot of Andrew Borden's grave, marked simply Lizabeth A. Borden.

But she belongs to the world, and it has given her an epitaph in poetry, not in stone:

> Lizzie Borden took an axe,
> Gave her mother forty whacks.
> When she saw what she had done,
> She gave her father forty-one.

Lizzie is a legend. The axe is immortal, and for those interested in the influence of heredity, Lizzie inherited the right to use the Borden coat of arms from her ancestors, Joan and Richard Borden, who pioneered in the locale of Portsmouth, Rhode Island, around 1638. The coat of arms is a 'Lion Rampant, holding a Battle-Axe, proper'.

Something that Shouldn't be Spoken About

ARTHUR FLEGENHEIMER

23 October 1935

Mr Flegenheimer, who was a native of the Bronx, New York City, preferred to be called after Dutch Schultz, the most notorious member of the Frog Hollow gang of ruffians that had caused trouble in the borough towards the end of the nineteenth century.

Taking advantage of Prohibition, Mr Flegenheimer prospered exceedingly as a vintner to the denizens of the Bronx and Manhattan; his bank balances were augmented by other illegal trades. He took a Draconian attitude towards those who rubbed him up the wrong way, and was responsible for the untimely deaths of Jack 'Legs' Diamond ('Just another punk caught with his hands in my pocket' was his post-Legs'-mortem comment), Vincent 'Mad Dog' Coll, Bo Weinberg, et al.

However, in 1935, when he insisted on ridding the city of Thomas E. Dewey, the special prosecutor for organized crime who was actually doing some prosecuting, certain exalted members of the newly-constituted 'national crime syndicate', each no more entrancing than Mr Flegenheimer, felt that the proposed execution would be bad for business, so prevented it by arranging for the biter to be bit while he was dining (to be precise, he was in the lavatory when the shooting occurred) at the Palace Chophouse in Newark, New Jersey. But for the poetry of their names, it would not be worth mentioning that his companions, Lulu Rosencranz, Abe 'Misfit' Landau and Otto 'Abbadabba' Berman, were slain by other bullets from the same gun, wielded by an enthusiastic marksman called Charlie 'The Bug' Workman.

Mr Flegenheimer, being not yet deceased, was trundled to a nearby hospital, where a prodigal amount of perfectly good blood was transfused into him. Here are some of his dying words – which, as Dwight MacDonald has observed, are an

OH OH dog biscuit. And when he is happy he doesn't get snappy. Please please to do this. Then Henry, Henry, Frankie, you didn't meet him. You didn't even meet me. The glove will fit what I say. Oh! Kai-Yi, Kai-Yi. Sure, who cares when you are through? How do you know this? Well, then, oh cocoa know, thinks he is a grandpa again. He is jumping around. No hoboe and phoboe. I think it means the same thing. . . . Oh mamma I can't go on through with it. Please oh! And then he clips me. Come on. Cut that out. We don't owe a nickel. Hold it instead hold it against him. . . . How many good ones and how many bad ones? Please I had nothing with him. He was a cowboy in one of the seven days a week fights. No business no hangout no friends nothing. Just what you pick up and what you need. . . . This is a habit I get. Sometimes I give it up and sometimes I don't. . . . The sidewalk was in trouble and the bears were in trouble and I broke it up. Please put me in that room. Please keep him in control. . . . Please mother don't tear don't rip. That is something that shouldn't be spoken about. Please get me up, my friends, please look out, the shooting is a bit wild and that kind of shooting saved a man's life. . . . Please mother you pick me up now. Do you know me? No, you don't scare me. They are Englishmen and they are a type I don't know who is best they or us. Oh sir get the doll a roofing. You can play jacks and girls do that with a soft ball and play tricks with it. No no and it is no. It is confused and it says no. A boy has never wept nor dashed a thousand kim. And you hear me?. . . . All right look out look out. Oh my memory is all gone. A work relief. Police. Who gets it? I don't know and I don't want to know but look out. It can be traced. He changed for the worst. Please look out. My fortunes have changed and come back and went back since that. . . . They dyed my shoes. Open those shoes. . . . Police mamma Helen mother please take me out. I will settle the indictment. Come on open the soap duckets. The chimney sweeps. Talk to the sword. Shut up you got a big mouth! Please help me get up. Henry

Max come over here. French Canadian bean soup. I want to pay. Let them leave me alone.

Insisting on that final wish, Arthur Flegenheimer, a man who by taking another's name had given all Dutchmen a bad one, said no more before he expired, two hours later, at twenty minutes to nine. A rogue was a rogue was a dead rogue.

Murder by the Scenic Route

JONATHAN GOODMAN

1973

The whole of anything is never told:
you can only take what groups together.
Henry James

Murder for pleasure is almost invariably a solitary vice; indeed, until late in 1965, when the activities of Ian Brady and Myra Hindley were brought to light, one would have needed to pore over very dusty records to find an exception to prove the rule that killing for entertainment's sake is the most unsociable crime of all.

Brady and Hindley were voyeurs, écouteurs, of their own corruption. Enlarging the Freudian pleasure principle, they derived at least as much satisfaction from the shadow of their deeds as from the deeds themselves: from the salacious nostalgia of looking at photographs showing their own intimacy and the obscene contortions of a frightened child; from listening to a tape recording of the child's pleas to be allowed to return to her mother; from hearing another child read a newspaper account of the search for one of their murder victims; and from visiting, and taking others unknowingly to visit, a secret cemetery on a Pennine moor.

Ian Brady, the bastard son of a tea-shop waitress and a man he never knew, was born in a Glasgow maternity hospital on 2 January 1938, and while still a baby was given into the care of foster-parents, a couple with four children of their own who lived in a tenement in the Gorbals slums. His mother visited him frequently, and it seems that she paid for his upkeep, for the foster-parents could not have afforded the neighbours' description of him, when he was five or six, as 'the smartest wee lad in the street'; on Sundays he wore a frilly silk shirt and a kilt, and on weekdays black velvet trousers.

But the little boy's impeccable appearance was deceptive.

Before he was nine, when he moved with his foster-parents to a council house on the Pollok Estate just outside the city, he had gained a reputation for cruelty, not only to animals and insects but also to children weaker than himself. Some twenty years later, people who were at primary school with Brady, their memories perhaps over-coloured by time and newspaper headlines, spoke of his acts of cruelty. One of them was quoted as saying:

> The cats weren't worth bothering with after he'd finished with them. He always carried a flick-knife, and was a great one for a carry-on. He once tied me to a steel washing-post, heaped newspapers round my legs and set fire to them. I can still remember feeling dizzy with the smoke before I was rescued.

In 1949, at the age of eleven, Brady started attending Shawlands Academy in Glasgow. According to a classmate, he was 'a boy who didn't like company, but nae dunderhead'. He was already interested in, if not yet obsessed with, Nazism:

> He read all kinds of books about the nazis and never stopped talking about them. Even when we were playing war games, he made a great point of being a 'German'. . . . When Ian used to shout 'Sieg heil!' and give the nazi salute, people would laugh.

The same classmate also noted that Brady usually had plenty of pocket money, an affluence that may be explained by his appearance at Glasgow Sheriff Court in 1951 on charges of housebreaking and attempted theft, for which he was put on probation for two years. In July of the following year he was admonished on similar charges at Govan Court. Leaving school in 1953, when he was fifteen, he worked for a few months as a butcher's assistant, then as a teaboy in a shipyard. In November 1954 he again appeared at Glasgow Sheriff Court, this time on nine charges of housebreaking and theft, and received two years' probation, a condition of the order being that he returned to his mother, who was now married and living at Moss Side, a grimy suburb of Manchester.

Brady's stepfather found him a job as a porter at the Manchester fruit market, where he himself worked; but the wages were low, the temptations many, and at the city magistrates' court in November 1955 Brady was convicted of stealing lead seals from banana boxes. He was sent to quarter sessions for sentencing, and received a two years' term of Borstal training, which he served at Hull and Hatfield.

On his release, in November 1957, he returned to his mother and stepfather, who were now living at 18 Westmorland Street at Longsight, a Manchester suburb contiguous to, and no less depressing than, Moss Side. (The owner of the house has the dubious, and perhaps unique, distinction of having been landlady to two unconnected murderers; she owns two other houses in the street, and at one of these, No. 10, a tenant was Alfred Bailey, who in 1964 was sentenced to life imprisonment for the murder by strangulation of a six-year-old girl.)

Between April and October 1958, Brady was employed to roll barrels and clean out vats at a brewery close to Strangeways Prison. Before being sent to Borstal, he had been a fairly heavy drinker, so it would be false to assume an occupation syndrome from the fact that during and after the time he worked at the brewery he often drank to excess, receiving a fine in June 1958 for being drunk and disorderly. At the end of the year he went back to work at the fruit market: but for only a few months. During this time – either from a desire to 'better himself' or because, although tall and wiry, he lacked the strength for heavy manual work – he applied for several office jobs, and was eventually taken on as a stock clerk at Millwards Merchandise Ltd, a small chemical distributing firm in Levenshulme Road, Gorton; he started there, at a salary of £12 a week, in February 1959.

He was a good worker, careful and neat, and his employers' only complaints were of his unpunctuality and brief but frequent absences when he slipped out of the office to place bets, always for small amounts and usually each-way, with a local bookmaker. He rarely said more than a few words to the other office workers; during the lunch-break he sat alone in his small office overlooking a yard filled with empty chemical drums and carboys and, after hurrying through a meal usually consisting of cheese and whisked raw eggs, read books on Nazi war crimes and criminals. (His other main literary interest, erotic sadism, was apparently restricted to after-office hours.) He sometimes spent the lunch-break writing orders to record dealers for tapes of German marching songs, speeches by Nazi leaders, and evidence at the Nuremburg war crimes trials; these orders, written in over-large handwriting, often ended with the words 'Thank you, Meine Herren' above the signature.

In January 1961, when Brady had been working at Millwards for nearly two years, a tall, unnaturally blonde girl called Myra Hindley joined the firm as a shorthand-typist.

Like Brady, she had had a disturbed childhood. The daughter of a mixed, Catholic-Protestant, marriage, she was born in Gorton on 23 July 1942. After the birth of her sister Maureen in 1946, she was sent to live with her grandmother in another part of Gorton. Although a reasonably bright child (her IQ rating was 109), she lacked the discipline that a normal home life might have provided. She was allowed to stay out later than other children of her age and often played truant from school. She failed to pass the 11-plus examination, and in her first year at a modern secondary school her report card read;

Progress and conduct	satisfactory
Personality	not very sociable
Attendance	consistently unsatisfactory

The characterism of 'not very sociable' did not apply to her relations with classmates, however: they remember her as 'funny and always singing' and as 'a comedienne, making up ditties and telling jokes'.

In June of 1957, her last year at school, she saw a boy drown in a reservoir. The experience seems to have been traumatic: she organized a collection for a wreath and took a day off from school to attend the funeral; immediately afterwards, encouraged by an aunt and uncle, she embraced the Roman Catholic faith, taking the name 'Veronica' and attending mass regularly.

During the period between leaving school and joining Millwards, she had a succession of office jobs, all with local firms, none lasting more than a few months. Most evenings she spent at cinemas and dance halls. When she was seventeen she became engaged to a childhood friend, but broke it off after a year because, she said, 'he is too childish and we're not saving enough money for marriage'.

It was at this time, if not before, that she became interested in Germany; she began to read books about that country, and early in 1961 obtained an application form for joining the NAAFI so that she could work there. But soon afterwards, still undecided as to whether or not to apply, she was sacked from her job because of absenteeism. The following week, she started work in the stock office at Millwards.

The laws of probability had been defied. It was a millions-to-one chance that brought Brady and Hindley together, to draw from each other, and to exacerbate, a taste for wickedness. Only a slight deviation in the course of either of their young lives would have kept them apart; would have prevented the formation of a synergy, a sum of evil greater than its parts; would have averted several murders and saved a large expenditure of public money in the name of retribution.

From the first moment she saw him, Hindley was attracted to Brady. She made no secret of her fascination, but Brady (who, so far as is known, had never had a girl-friend – a boy-friend either, for that matter) virtually ignored her for almost twelve months, perhaps in the belief that the subtle sadism of disregard gave more satisfaction than would a normal, or even abnormal, sexual relationship.

During her first year at Millwards, Hindley kept a diary. Most of the entries were notes of hairdressing appointments for root toning and pink and blue rinses, or reminders of relatives' birthdays, or sums to show how she had spent her weekly wage of £8.50. But scattered among the mundane words and figures were references to Brady:

> Ian looked at me today. . . . He smiled at me today. . . . The pig – he didn't look at me. . . . He ignored me today. . . . I

wonder if he'll ever take me out. . . . I almost got a smile out of him today. . . . Ian wore a black shirt and looked smashing. . . . He is a loud-mouthed pig. . . . I love him.

At last, just before Christmas 1961, she was able to write:

Eureka! Today we have our first date. We are going to the cinema.

But her joy must have been constrained by the knowledge that the film chosen by Brady for the first date was as important to him as the date itself. The film was *Trial at Nuremburg*, whose subject was Nazi war atrocities.

From now on, however, their relationship quickly ripened, and by the spring of 1962 they were inseparable. Instead of going home for lunch, Hindley brought sandwiches to the office and joined Brady at his desk, where they read aloud to each other from his books on Nazism. Having shown sufficient delight in accounts of the extermination and mass burial of Jews, Hindley was allowed to borrow, for home reading, items from Brady's growing library of books on the history and practice of torture.

There was a marked change in Hindley's appearance and attitude. To coincide with Brady's pet-name for her of 'Myra Hess', and to imply a substance to their conjoined sexual fantasies, she dyed her hair to the extremity of blondeness, exaggerated her small mouth with crimson lipstick and, away from the office, wore sham-suede jackets and leather boots. Before taking up with Brady, she had often spoken of her wish to marry and had shown a love for children in many acts of generosity and in volunteering to baby-sit for neighbours. But now she sneered at marriage, dubbing it 'conventional hypocrisy' and telling a friend: 'I'll never get engaged or marry anybody, because Ian and I have a very good understanding with one another.' Her reaction to a neighbour's pregnancy was the question: 'Why don't you do something to shift it?'

Brady had bought a secondhand motor-cycle, and every night, after having a meal with his mother and stepfather, he drove the couple of miles to the diminutive, dilapidated house in Bannock Street where Hindley lived with her grandmother, a woman in her seventies whose lack of interest, let alone inquisitiveness, in what went on under her own roof was, to say the least of it, unusual. Night after night the grandmother sat in the kitchen, the television turned on, her mind turned off, while upstairs two sane people conditioned themselves to commit insane acts; she ignored even the racket of marching songs and Nazi speeches, just as she ignored the complaints of neighbours at the volume of the recordings – just as later, in a different house, she would ignore a boy's screams and the thump of his falling body.

In 1963 Hindley passed her driving test and, acting on Brady's advice, bought an old mini-van. It seems clear from a letter that Brady wrote to her that they were planning a robbery and had discussed the need for an escape-car: 'Let's capitalize on the situation [of having a car]. I shall grasp this opportunity to view the investment establishment [a bank?] situated in Stockport Road next Friday. I will contact you before then to give other details.' Nothing came of this plan, nor of a similar plan for which Brady tried to enlist the assistance of some ex-Borstal acquaintances.

Brady's driving licence did not cover four-wheeled vehicles, and he never applied for an extension of the licence. Hindley drove him to and from work and did all the driving on their several trips into the surrounding countryside and when they spent a summer holiday in Scotland; also, pandering to his fascination with railway stations, she often drove him to the main-line stations in Manchester and sat in the parked car for sometimes an hour or more while he wandered around. (He said that he went to the railway stations because he 'enjoyed looking at people', but in the light of a subsequent event, a more sinister purpose may be surmised.)

In September 1964, as a result of slum clearance, Hindley's grandmother was given the tenancy of 16 Wardle Brook Avenue, a two-bedroomed council house on the Hattersley overspill estate outside Manchester. Among the modern conveniences of the house was a cigarette machine which was refilled with packets and emptied of coins every Sunday; Hindley, especially, found this useful, since she was a heavy smoker.

Brady moved into the new house, to share Hindley's bedroom, early in 1965. Among the belongings that he brought with him were the paraphernalia of photography, including a developing tank and an enlarger. These last two items were specially necessary, for many of his indoor photographs were not the sort he could have given to a high-street chemist for processing. Some showed Hindley, wholly or partly undressed, in obscene poses; others, taken with the aid of a remote-control gadget, were of her and Brady in the act of coition or entwined in eccentric embraces. There were also a set of photographs of a little girl, naked and gagged, which transcended pornography.

Apart from trades-people, there were few callers at the house in Wardle Brook Avenue. The most frequent visitors were Hindley's sister, Maureen, and her husband, David Smith, who had been married since August 1964, when she was eighteen and he was sixteen. The day after the wedding, Brady and Hindley had taken the couple on a trip to Bowness in the Lake District. Brady already knew Maureen quite well, as she had been working at Millwards for about a year, but it seems that he had met Smith no more than once or twice, and then only briefly. The drive to the Lake District was the first of many such outings, which usually ended back at the Smiths' home, with the sisters sharing a bed while the man and the boy stayed talking and drinking into the small hours, eventually to fall asleep in their chairs.

Brady knew that, between October 1959 and October 1964, Smith had been convicted on three occasions for violent, spur-of-the-moment crimes and once for housebreaking, when three other cases were taken into consideration, and this may explain why, after a few meetings, he began to take the boy into his confidence, first of all showing off his books and extolling the vices of his favourite author and idol as a pioneer of perversions, the Marquis de Sade, and then offering to lend Smith any of the volumes that pricked his fancy.

Later, in the spring of 1965, Brady turned their discussions towards crime – talking generally, testing Smith's reactions, before inviting him to take part in the armed robbery of a bank. He said that he had kept watch on several banks and had compiled detailed notes on their security arrangements. This Smith believed; but he was less convinced by Brady's claim that he had two revolvers, a 0.38 Smith & Wesson and a 0.45 Webley, together with ammunition. To prove that not only did he have the guns (Hindley had bought them from members of a rifle club which she had joined), but also that he was able to fire them with some degree of accuracy, Brady arranged a shooting display on a remote part of Saddleworth Moor, which lies to the north-east of Manchester, close to the Pennine Way. While the two girls sat in the car, he fired some rounds at makeshift targets and allowed Smith to try a few shots, afterwards retrieving the spent shells. As they walked back to the car, Brady asked Smith if he was impressed. Smith said that he was.

Brady and Hindley took the Smiths to the moors on several other occasions, once at eleven o'clock at night. The Smiths enjoyed these outings, but not half as much as did their companions, who obtained a macabre, and almost certainly orgastic, pleasure from the knowledge that they were picnicking within a covert graveyard of their own making.

In July 1965 the Smiths moved into a council flat less than a quarter of a mile from Wardle Brook Avenue. Before, when they were living at Gorton, they had always visited Brady and Hindley by invitation. Now they were made to realize that unexpected calls were not welcomed; within a few weeks of moving to Hattersley, Maureen Smith was twice turned away from her grandmother's house, first by her sister, then by Brady.

Soon after taking possession of the new flat, David Smith went through one of the frequent periods of unemployment which he ascribed to 'regular tonsillitis'. Hearing of this, Brady again spoke of his plan for a robbery, and Smith agreed to 'case' a local bank. (It appears that, all along, his only quibble with the plan was Brady's insistence of the carrying of guns with live ammunition.) He spent a morning watching a bank, and provided Brady with notes of what he observed.

On 25 September, as was by now usual on Saturdays,

Brady and Hindley spent the evening with the Smiths. According to David Smith (in his deposition):

> Myra and Maureen stayed up until about 1.30 a.m. They then went to bed, leaving myself and Brady in the living-room. . . . We discussed the bank job and how the guns would have to be used with live bullets, then he asked me if I was capable of murder. I just gave him a blank look.
>
> He then said: 'I've done it.' He said he had done three or four. He was drunk so I didn't pay much attention. . . . He asked if I believed him. I just looked at him blankly as if I did and I didn't. I wasn't interested.
>
> He then went on to describe how he did it. He said that there were two ways. The first one was to wait in a car in a street chosen beforehand until the right one came along. He would then get out of the car and murder him. He said he didn't like that method very much. He said it took too long just preparing. . . .
>
> The second method was to go out in a car and pick somebody up and take them back to Wardle Brook Avenue, and he did it there. He said he buried the body on the moors. He said he would pick up people between the ages of sixteen and twenty. He chose that age group because they were always listed as missing by the police. He said he had photographs to prove it, but he would not let me see them.
>
> He said that before he killed anyone he used to take a drug. It was Pro-Plus. His books were always removed from the house, and all photographs and tape recordings. I can't remember him saying anything else that night about the killing. I did and I didn't believe him.

The following Saturday, 2 October, there was another late-night session:

> The conversation about murders started up again. Brady said: 'You don't believe I am capable of it, but it will be done.' He said he wasn't due for another one for three months, and this one would not count. . . . We had had a few bottles of wine to drink – about six – and I was more interested in what I was drinking.

Three days later, early in the evening of Tuesday, 5 October, Brady called on Smith and asked him to parcel up the books he had lent him, together with other 'off-beat' items, including Smith's own collection of pornography and an exercise book in which Smith noted his favourite quotations and paraphrased the ostensible philosophies of celebrated perverts. According to Smith, Brady offered no explanation for this request; and again according to Smith, Brady was not asked for one. The same evening, Smith made up the parcel and carried it round to 16 Wardle Brook Avenue. Brady took the parcel upstairs, and came down a few minutes later with two suitcases. As he and Smith helped Hindley to put the cases in the back of her car, he quipped: 'Don't drop them or they'll blow us all up.' Leaving Smith to walk home, Brady and Hindley drove off towards Manchester Central Station.

According to Smith: 'They had not told me what they were going to do with the suitcases, but I had an idea.'

Disposal of the suitcases was part of the preparation for committing a murder. The plan, proved and improved by experience, was impeccable; all that was left to chance was the choice of victim, and this was the least important consideration in the scheme of things. For Brady, the motive on this occasion was more blurred than usual: there was pleasure in killing, of course – a pleasure that would linger in the mind and stimulate the senses; but this time there was, too, the motive of personal aggrandisement. David Smith 'did and didn't' believe that Brady had the ability to kill. He had to be *made* to believe. Evidence was needed.

At ten minutes past six on Thursday morning, 7 October, an emergency call from a telephone box on the Hattersley council estate was received at Hyde Police Station. The caller, David Smith, said that he and his wife were in fear of their lives. A motor patrol officer set off at once, but within a minute of two of his leaving, there was a second call from Smith, who sounded even more frantic than before; terror emphasized his natural slight stammer as he pleaded for protection 'for me and Mo'.

The couple, found cowering in the shadow of the telephone box, were driven to the police station, and David Smith talked to detectives for several hours. As one of the detectives commented afterwards: 'What he said sounded like a nightmare, but it was not the sort of nightmare that anyone in his right mind could possibly dream.'

At 11.30 last night I was at home with my wife. Me and my wife were in bed, but we were awake. . . .

Myra, that's my wife's sister, knocked on our flat and I let her in. She seemed normal at the time. . . . She, Myra that is, was there only about ten minutes at the most, and then she asked me to walk home with her to 16 Wardle Brook Avenue, as she was a bit scared of walking about on the estate in the dark. I'd got dressed after I got out of bed and I left our flat with her about a quarter to twelve midnight, or about that time. . . .

We got almost to Myra's house. I intended to leave her there, then she said: 'Ian has a few miniature wine bottles for you. Come and collect them now.'

As we approached the front door, Myra stopped walking and she said: 'Wait over the road, watch for the landing light to flick twice.' I didn't think this was unusual because I've had to do this before, whilst she, Myra, went in to see if Ian would have me in. He's a very temperamental sort of fellow. I waited across the road as Myra told me to, and then the landing light flicked twice, so I walked up and knocked on the front door. Ian opened the front door and he said in a very loud voice for him, he normally speaks soft: 'Do you want those miniatures?' I nodded my head to show 'yes' and he led me into the kitchen, which is directly opposite the front door, and he gave me three miniature bottles of spirits and said: 'Do you want the rest?'

When I first walked into the house, the door to the living-room – which was on my right, standing at the front door – was closed. After he'd put the three bottles down in the kitchen, Ian went into the living room and I waited in the kitchen. I waited about a minute or two, then suddenly I heard a hell of a scream; it sounded like a woman, really high-pitched. Then the screams carried on, one after another, really loud. Then I heard Myra shout: 'Dave, help him,' very loud. . . .

When I ran in, I just stood inside the living-room, and I saw a young lad, about seventeen years old. He was lying with his head and shoulders on the couch, and his legs were on the floor. He was facing upwards. Ian was standing over him, facing him, with his legs on either side of the young lad's legs. The lad was still screaming. He didn't look injured then, but there was only a

73

small television light on, the big light was off. Ian had a hatchet in his hand, I think it was his right hand, it was his right hand, he was holding it above his head, and then he hit the lad on the left side of the head with the hatchet, I heard the blow, it was a terrible hard blow, it sounded horrible.

The young lad was still screaming, and the lad half fell and half wiggled off the couch, on to the floor, on to his stomach. He was still screaming. Ian went after him and stood over him and kept hacking away at the young lad with the hatchet. I don't know how many times he hit the lad with the hatchet, but it was a lot, about the head, about the neck, you know that region, the shoulders and that. . . .

I felt my stomach turn when I saw what Ian did, and some sick came up and then it went down again. I couldn't move. When he, Ian that is, was hacking at the lad, they got close to me, and one of the blows Ian did at the lad grazed my right leg. I remember, Ian was swinging about with the hatchet, and one blow grazed the top of Myra's head. . . .

After Ian stopped hitting the lad, he was lying on his face, with his feet near the door. I could hear like a gurgling noise in the lad's throat. . . . Ian got a cover off one of the chairs and wrapped it round the lad's head. I was shaking. I was frightened to death of moving, and my stomach was twisting. There was blood all over the place, on the walls, fireplace, everywhere.

Ian never spoke a word all this time, and he got a cord, I think it was electric wire, I don't know where he got it from, and he wrapped it round the lad's neck, one end of the cord in one hand, one end in the other, and he then crossed the cord and pulled and kept pulling until the gurgling stopped in the lad's throat. All the time Ian was doing this, strangling the lad, Ian was swearing; he was saying: 'You dirty bastard.' He kept saying that over and over again.

Myra was still there all the time, just looking. Then Ian looked up at Myra and said something like: 'It's done. It's the messiest yet. It normally only takes one blow.'

Myra just looked at him. She didn't say anything at all. Ian got up then, the little light was still the only one on, and he lit himself a cigarette, after he'd wiped his hands on a piece of some material. Then Ian turned the big light on, and he told Myra to go into the kitchen and get a mop and bucket of warm water and a bowl with soapy water in it and some rags.

Myra did that and Ian turned to me then and said: 'Your stick's

74

a bit wet,' and he grinned at me. The stick he meant was a stick I'd taken with me when I went with Myra from our place. It's like a walking-stick, and the only thing I can think is that when I rushed into the living-room at first I'd dropped it, because it was lying on the floor near the young lad. . . .

Then Myra came in with the bowls of water and that. She didn't appear upset, and she just stepped over the young lad's body and placed the bowls of water and that on the carpet in front of the fireplace.

Then Ian looked at me like, and said: 'Give us a lift with this mess.' I was frightened and I did what he said and I helped to clean the mess up. . . . No one spoke while this was going on, then after we'd cleaned most of it up, Ian – he was speaking to Myra – said: 'Do you think anyone heard the screams?' Myra said: 'Yes, me gran did. I told her I'd dropped something on my toe.' Then Myra left the living-room.

While she was out, Ian offered me a bottle of wine. . . . The young lad was still lying on the floor. Myra came in with a white bed sheet. I think Ian had told her to get one. And a lot of pieces of polythene, fairly big they were, and a large blanket. . . . Ian told me to get hold of the lad's legs, which I did, and Ian got hold of the lad's shoulders and we lifted him into the sheets and blankets. The only reason I did this was out of sheer bloody fear. Then Ian came out with a joke. He said: 'Eddie's a dead weight,' and both Ian and Myra thought it was bloody hilarious. I didn't see anything to laugh about. . . .

On the stick I had, the one I mentioned to you, there is some bound string, and Ian took the stick and unwound the string. He cut it into lengths, about two or three foot in length, and he gave me one end, and he tied the lad's legs up in a funny way, so that the lad's legs were together and bent up into his stomach. Then Ian carried on tying the lad up; it was like a maze of bloody knots. . . .

I had to help him while he folded the corners of the sheet together, with the lad in the middle, and then he tied the corners together. Then he made me do the same with him with the polythene sheets, and last of all came the blanket. He didn't tie that – it was like a kind of cradle. Myra was mopping up all this time. Then Ian told Myra: 'Go upstairs and hold your gran's door to,' and then he said to me: 'Lift your end up,' and between us we carried the young lad upstairs into Myra's bedroom and we put him down near the window.

Then we came downstairs and I saw a wallet lying on the floor. Ian picked it up and pulled out a green sort of card and said: 'That's his name. Do you know him?' I looked at the card and saw the name Edward Evans. I didn't know him. I saw a pair of shoes lying on the living-room floor as well as the wallet, and Ian picked them up, and a couple of letters that were lying there, and put them in a shopping bag. He picked the hatchet up, gave it to me and said something like: 'Feel the weight of that. How did he take it?' I said nothing and gave it him back. I was frightened of him using it on me.

He put the hatchet in with the rest of the things, and he took them upstairs. Myra was still cleaning up, and by this time the house was looking something like normal. . . .

Then Ian went on to describe how he'd done it. How, he said, he'd stood behind the settee looking for some miniatures for me, and the lad Eddie was sat on the settee. He said: 'I held the axe with my two hands and brought it down on his head.' Myra said: 'His eyes registered astonishment when you hit him.' Those are the exact words she said.

Ian was complaining because he'd hurt his ankle and they'd have to keep the lad's body upstairs all night, and he wouldn't be able to carry the lad down to the car because of his ankle. Myra suggested that they use my wife's and my baby trolley to carry the lad's body into their car. Well, it's Myra's car. I agreed straight away. I'd have agreed to anything they said. We arranged to meet where Myra works in Manchester tonight, that's Thursday, at five o'clock. . . .

After we had cleaned up Evans's blood, Myra made a cup of tea, and she and Brady sat talking. She said: 'Do you remember that time we were burying a body on the moors and a policeman came up?' Then she drew me into the conversation and said: 'I was in the mini with a body in the back. It was partitioned off with a plastic sheet. Ian was digging a hole when a policeman came and asked me what the trouble was. I told him I was drying my sparking plugs and he drove off. I was praying that Ian wouldn't come back over the hill whilst he was there.'

. . . I said I'd better be off, I wanted to go and they let me go, and I ran all the way home. They were both unconcerned. I let myself into the flat right away, woke Maureen up and had a wash. I didn't tell her what had happened and I got in bed. It was about three to half past in the morning then. I couldn't get to sleep. I kept thinking about the lad, about the screams and the gurgling he was making. I got up after a bit, put the light on, woke Maureen up and told her all about it. Then she got up, she was crying and upset, and we sat down and tried to decide what to do. . . . It got to about six o'clock. We decided it was the best time to go out, there were milkmen and that knocking about, so I armed myself with a carving knife and a screwdriver, in case I meet Ian and Myra. Maureen came with me and we walked to the telephone kiosk in Hattersley Road West and telephoned the police. That's it. . . .

David Smith also told the police, among other things, about Brady's firearms, so at 8.15 a.m., before knocking at the back door of 16 Wardle Brook Avenue, Superintendent Robert Talbot, the head of the police division in which Hattersley is situated, took the precaution of borrowing a bread-roundsman's white overall to hide his uniform jacket.

Hindley came to the door, and Superintendent Talbot asked her if her husband was at home. She said she was not married. Revealing his uniform, Talbot asked if there was a man in the house. 'There is no man here,' she said. Talbot then pushed past her into the kitchen, and Hindley at once said: 'He is in the other room in bed.' Followed by Detective Sergeant Alexander Carr, the superintendent walked into the living-room.

Brady, wearing only a vest, was lying on a divan bed. He was writing a letter to a director of Millwards, saying that he had injured his ankle and was unable to come to work. He continued to write, glancing up only when Talbot asked him his name.

The superintendent said that he was investigating a report that an act of violence had taken place in the house.

'There was nothing wrong here,' Hindley claimed

Leaving Detective Sergeant Carr in the living-room with Brady, the superintendent went upstairs, accompanied by Hindley. He found the grandmother in bed in the front room. The other bedroom door was locked, and when he asked Hindley for the key, she told him that she had left it at work and that it was inconvenient for her to go for it.

They returned to the living-room. Talbot said that he was

not leaving until he had searched the bedroom, and eventually Hindley said to Brady: 'Well, you'd better tell him.'

'There was a row last night,' said Brady. 'It's in the back bedroom.' He told Hindley to hand over the key, and she took it from her handbag and gave it to the superintendent.

By now, other policemen had arrived. Talbot and Carr went upstairs and unlocked the bedroom door. Beneath the window of the sparsely furnished room was a body wrapped in a blanket. Some books had been thrown on top of the bundle, and beside it on the floor were a carrier bag and a stick, both saturated with blood.

The victim was soon identified as Edward Evans, a seventeen-year-old apprentice machinist who had lived at Ardwick, Manchester. It appears that he was homosexual. He had left home early on the Wednesday evening, telling his mother that he was going to a football match at Old Trafford. He was last seen at seven o'clock in a public house in the centre of Manchester, close to a railway station where he could have caught a train to the football stadium.

Brady and Hindley were driven to Hyde Police Station and interviewed separately. Brady stated that he had met Evans in Manchester and taken him back to the house. 'We had an argument and we came to blows. After the first few blows the situation was out of control. . . . Eddie kicked me at the beginning on my ankle. There was a hatchet on the floor and I hit Eddie with it.' He said that Smith was at the front door when the argument started; Hindley had called Smith into the living-room and he had joined in the fracas, hitting Evans with a stick and kicking him. Brady made no mention of having strangled Evans: 'When Dave and I began cleaning up the floor, the gurgling stopped.'

Hindley refused to say very much, but most of what she did say conflicted with Brady's statement. Whereas Brady admitted being in Manchester the night before, she claimed that they had bought some wine at a nearby off-licence: 'Then we went up to Glossop and sat talking for ages. It was just a normal evening out before all this happened. It was the same as hundreds of other evenings out.' She repeatedly said: 'Ian didn't do it. I didn't do it. David Smith is a liar.' At subsequent interviews she added little to this story, refusing to answer questions unless she were allowed to see Brady.

At midday Detective Chief Superintendent Arthur Benfield, who had been appointed head of Cheshire CID only six days before, went with the Home Office pathologist, Dr Charles St. Hill, to the house in Wardle Brook Avenue. Dr St. Hill made a preliminary examination of the body, which was then taken to the mortuary, where a post-mortem revealed that Evans had died from a fractured skull, his death being accelerated by strangulation. There were fourteen lacerations of the scalp, which could have been caused by the hatchet found in the carrier bag in the back bedroom. Dr St. Hill also observed widespread bruising on the back of the head and across the shoulders, and several 'defence wounds' on the arms and hands. There were indications (trouser fly buttons undone; fibres in the region of the anus which bore similiarities to fibres found in the living-room) that some form of sexual activity had taken place.

The police began to search the house. Among the articles they took away were the two loaded revolvers and a quantity of ammunition; numerous photographs and negatives; books about Germany and Nazi atrocities during World War II; and a notebook containing doodles, sketches and a jumbled list of names in Brady's handwriting.

On the parcel shelf in Hindley's car, which was parked outside the house, the police found a wallet containing sheets of paper divided into columns of words and abbreviations. Brady admitted to Chief Superintendent Benfield that the wallet was his; the notes, he said, were 'the plan for the disposal of Eddie'. He insisted that this 'disposal plan' was prepared after Evans was killed, but careful analysis of the entries convinced the police that the plan referred to a premeditated murder. Most of Brady's explanations for the words and abbreviations were probably true – 'ALI' meant alibi, 'POLY' stood for polythene sheets, 'PRO-P' for Pro-Plus tablets and 'HAT' for hatchet – but his assertion that 'P/B' stood for Penistone Burn, a place on the moors, was soon shown to be false.

Forensic examination of the living-room carpet revealed no trace of blood, and this negative finding seemed to provide a further indication that the murder of Evans was planned: the only way the carpets could have escaped being stained was if they had been taken up before the boy was brought to the house and replaced after the living-room was cleaned. David Smith insisted, however, that, according to his recollection, the carpets were on the floor the whole time. This conflict between expert forensic opinion and the word of an eye-witness remains one of the minor mysteries of the case.

Smith had told the police about the early-morning conversations during which Brady boasted that he had committed three or four murders and buried the bodies on the moors. While a squad of uniformed policemen and detectives ransacked the house, scraping plaster from the walls, removing the floorboards, and digging up the garden, the investigation spread out: house-to-house inquiries were made on the Hattersley estate and in Gorton, all known associates of Brady and Hindley were interviewed, and information was sought at places where they had lived or worked. At the height of the investigation, the police team consisted of officers from Cheshire, Lancashire, the West Riding of Yorkshire, Derbyshire, Manchester City, and the newly formed No. 1 Regional Crime Squad.

As a result of the house-to-house inquiries, the police interviewed a twelve-year-old girl who lived next door but one to 16 Wardle Brook Avenue. With her mother's consent, she had spent several evenings with Brady and Hindley, who had given her wine and spirits to drink; she had been on trips to the moors with them, one of the last occasions being on Christmas Eve, 1964, when they had stayed there until past midnight. Some time in January 1965 (probably New Year's Day), Brady had recorded a conversation between Hindley and the child, part of which referred to a report in a local newspaper of the search for Lesley Ann Downey, aged ten, who had disappeared from a fairground near her home in Ancoats, Manchester, on Boxing Day.

The police drove the neighbour's child to Saddleworth

Moor, and she pointed out the area where Brady and Hindley had taken her; it was around Hollin Brown Knoll, on the A635 road between the villages of Greenfield and Holmfirth. Police officers immediately began to search the area, continuing through the night with the aid of arc lamps. At three o'clock in the afternoon of the following day, Saturday, 16 October, the remains of Lesley Ann Downey were found buried in the peat about 90 yards from the road. The body, which was naked, was lying on its right side with the legs doubled up towards the abdomen. The child's clothes and a string of beads were in the grave. A post-mortem examination was conducted by Dr David Gee, lecturer in forensic medicine at Leeds University, but the body, having lain in the damp peat probably for nine months, was too decomposed for the cause of death to be established.

On 20 October, Detective Chief Inspector John Tyrrell made an important discovery while searching through some of Hindley's possessions. Hidden in the spine of a white prayer book called *The Garden of the Soul*, a souvenir of her first communion, were two left-luggage tickets for articles deposited at Manchester Central Station. The abbreviation 'P/B' in the disposal plan was now explained: the letters stood, not for Penistone Burn, as Brady had pretended, but for prayer book.

The tickets were for the two suitcases taken from the house on the night before the Evans murder. As well as books belonging to Brady and Smith, the suitcases contained coshes, wigs, masks, notes on the security arrangements of banks and company offices, a large collection of photographs and negatives, and two tape recordings. Among the photographs were nine that showed Lesley Ann Downey, naked and with a scarf tied over her mouth, posed obscenely.

One of the tape recordings bore the voice of Hindley and the neighbour's child talking about the newspaper report. The other recording, the ultimate horror in Brady and Hindley's contract of depravity, was of Lesley Ann Downey pleading with them not to undress her but to allow her to go home: 'I have got to get home before eight o'clock. . . . I will get killed if I don't. . . .' Several times during the recording, both Brady and Hindley could be heard ordering the child to put something – a gag, perhaps – in her mouth. The recording ended as if it were a radio programme, with Christmas music faded in and growing in volume. This music helped the police to fix the time of recording as round about Christmas 1964, when the child had disappeared.

During a long interrogation, Brady said that he knew of the tape recording; he also admitted taking the photographs of Lesley Ann Downey in the back bedroom at Wardle Brook Avenue. His story was that two men had brought the child to the house for the purpose of taking the photographs: 'One [of the men] stayed outside. I don't know him. The other man I do know. . . . She left the house with the man who brought her. . . . I'm not saying who it is. I know his name. I've met him in Manchester, and he goes into Liston's Bar.'

Hindley was more specific. She asserted that Lesley Ann Downey had been brought to the house by David Smith and taken away by him after the photographic session. (At the trial both Brady and Hindley tried to put the blame for the murder on Smith, and a half-hearted and quite unsuccessful attempt was made to implicate a schoolfriend of Smith's as the 'other man'.)

Twenty-two of the photographs found in the suitcases were of moorland scenes, some showing Brady or Hindley, others the scenery alone. It struck the detectives as odd that Brady had considered it necessary to remove such seemingly innocent pictures from the house before the Evans murder. Bearing in mind Smith's statement that Brady had told him he had 'photographic proof' of earlier murders, the police enlisted the aid of farmers, shepherds and members of rambling and rock climbing clubs to identify the scenes, and within days each photograph had a twin photograph taken by the police.

One of Brady's photographs showed Hindley holding a puppy under her coat; she was crouching on one knee and looking down. The identical scene was located by the police on Thursday, 21 October, 373 yards from the grave of Lesley Ann Downey and on the opposite side of the A635. When

Inspector John Chaddock removed a stick that he had plunged into the ground to indicate the spot, there was a strong smell of decomposition. The police carefully scraped away the soil to reveal a body lying in a twisted position, the lower limbs facing downwards while the upper part of the trunk and the head were turned to the left. The body was fully clothed, but the trousers and underpants were rolled down to the thighs, indicating sexual interference. As in the case of Lesley Ann Downey, the post-mortem examination (conducted by Professor Cyril Polson, professor of forensic medicine at Leeds University) failed to reveal the cause of death. The face was unrecognizable, but the body was identified from the clothing as that of John Kilbride, a twelve-year-old boy who had disappeared from a market near his home at Ashton-under-Lyne almost two years before, on 23 November 1963.

The discovery of the body of John Kilbride shocked the police but did not surprise them, for they had come across the boy's name in Brady's notebook. Asked to explain its presence on a page that contained sketches and other names, Brady had lied that it was the name of someone he had known in Borstal.

A significant piece of evidence came to light when the police checked the records of vehicles used by Hindley. She had not owned a car in November 1963, but on the day when John Kilbride disappeared she had hired a Ford Anglia. The foreman at the garage remembered that when the car returned the following morning, 'It looked as if it had been through a ploughed field.' He had thought to himself: 'Who's going to touch for the job of washing that?'

To establish the approximate date of the photograph of Hindley crouching over the grave, the dog (a mongrel called Puppet, which also appeared in several of the indoor photographs, contributing to their obscenity) was taken to a veterinary surgeon so that its present age could be estimated. The dog had to be anaesthetized while its teeth were x-rayed, and it died during the examination. When Chief Superintendent Benfield broke the news to Hindley, she lost control and screamed: 'You fucking murderer!' But this was her last show of emotion; during her many interviews she admitted virtually nothing, and the police came to realize, both from her refusal to answer questions and from her general demeanour, that she was the tougher member of the 'evil partnership'.

The detectives engaged on the case suspected that at least two other bodies were buried on the moors. In July 1963 a sixteen-year-old Gorton girl had disappeared on her way to a dance; her home was two doors from where David Smith then lived, and she was known to Hindley. At the time of her disappearance, trenches to take gas pipes were being dug on the moors; the pipes were laid by the beginning of September, two months later. One of the photographs of Hindley on the moors bore a striking similarity, in dress, stance and facial expression, to the photograph of her beside the grave of John Kilbride. In the former photograph her gaze was directed at a spot covered by the gas pipe, and the detectives found it hard to resist the conclusion that if they had received permission to have this stretch of pipe deflected, another body might have been found.

In July 1964, almost exactly a year after the girl's disappearance, an eleven-year-old boy had left his home near the University of Manchester to stay the night with his grandmother. His mother, who was going to a bingo hall, had walked a short distance with him. If he took the normal route to the grandmother's house, he must have passed the corner of Westmorland Street where Brady then lived and where, at that time of the evening, Hindley might easily have been waiting to drive him to Gorton. The boy never arrived at his grandmother's, and is still missing.

Before the passing of Sydney Silverman's *Murder (Abolition of Death Penalty) Act*, which came into operation on 9 November 1965, the police held a trump card in murder cases in which other killings were suspected; playing on the theory of 'the more the madder', the accused might be induced to reveal other crimes to support a plea of insanity, which, if accepted, would substitute life in a mental institution for death on the gallows. The Moors case was the first case of mass murder under the new Act ('Silverman's Folly', as some policemen, the polite ones, refer to it). In Chief Superintendent Benfield's words: 'There was no question of capital punishment in the Moors case. Brady and Hindley were not fools, so why should they admit any more? If they did, there might be no possibility of release in the future.'

As a result of the publicity attached to the case, the police were almost inundated with telephone calls and letters, many of them referring to suspicious incidents witnessed on the moors during the past two or three years. People were asked to report to mobile police posts on roads over the moors, one each in Cheshire, Yorkshire and Derbyshire, where particulars were taken of the incident; they were then asked to lead the police to the spot, which was ringed with a yellow dye and later searched. Before long, the moors looked like a plantation of giant marigolds; but, although 400 reports were investigated, nothing of significance to the murder case was found.

An RAF photo-reconnaissance unit took a series of aerial photographs of the area, which showed clearly where the ground had been disturbed. Again, each place was located, marked and searched. The only bodies found were those of animals.

The days, the weeks, passed, and the search became a race against time. Winter comes early to Saddleworth, which is 1,600 feet above sea level, and winter is the season to stay away from the moors, a time of foul weather in a place where earlier winters have precluded shelter; the ground is often covered with snow, and is almost always threaded with ice, making it rock-hard.

The search was called off in November. Already the bright yellow circles, symbols of the investigators' thoroughness and perseverance, were flecked with snow and being brushed away by the wind.

The municipal borough of Hyde – which has been described, amusing but unjustly, as 'an S-bend with chip shops' – is tacked to the eastern suburbs of Manchester as if as an afterthought. It was here, in the magistrates' court, a place of dark panelled walls surmounted by a white domed ceiling, that the committal proceedings were held in the case of The Queen against Ian Brady and Myra Hindley.

The chairman of the Bench was a woman who served on several local committees for the public good, and thus had earned herself an MBE. The popular press decided that she was newsworthy, not because of her personality, intelligence or standing in the community, but because of the excessive collection of almost identical toque hats which she wore, a different toque each day, during the proceedings. There were two other lay magistrates, one a retired confectioner, the other a retired trade union official.

The task of the magistrates to decide whether or not there was a *prima facie* case for Brady and Hindley to answer was really no task at all. On 21 December 1965, at the end of an eleven-day hearing of evidence which the prosecution witnesses had already given to the police and which most of them would have to give again at Chester Assizes, the two accused were formally committed for trial – an object which, in Scotland, would have been achieved as efficiently, far less expensively, and without squandering many people's time, by the Lord Advocate's weighing-up of evidence contained in statements (precognitions) taken in private by a procurator fiscal.

The magistrates had been faced with a far more difficult decision on the first day, when David Lloyd-Jones and Philip Curtis, representing Brady and Hindley respectively, had pleaded for the committal proceedings to be held *in camera*. In Curtis's words:

> Magistrates have always been entitled as examining justices to sit in private if they wish. What are the advantages of sitting in open court and having the whole of the evidence produced in such a way that it will make it impossible for any juryman ever to come to this case without preconceived notions of what the case against the accused is?

It would be incorrect to suggest that, in ruling against the defence submission, the magistrates were swayed by their egos – by even an unconscious wish to elevate their names from the limbo of local press reports into the lurid limelight of the front pages of national newspapers. All one may say is that there was a serious defect in a system which allowed lay magistrates to decide whether publicity for committal proceedings was right or wrong, and which presented the temptation to some magistrates to make a choice between what seemed right in their own interests and what was right in the interests of justice.

(The defect was cured by the *Criminal Justice Act 1967*, ss. 1–4, which, in addition to reducing the time and effort spent on committal proceedings, limited the scope of press and broadcasting coverage to the barest outline, and allowed full publicity only when a defendant requested it or was not set for trial. As in 1958, when the Tucker Committee had recommended rather less stringent restrictions, a number of journalists supported their arguments in favour of publicity by quoting Lord Hewart's dictum on visible justice; but one thing is certain, and that is that Lord Hewart did not mean that justice should manifestly and undoubtedly be seen to be done in order to boost newspaper sales, which was the sole reason why the prosecution evidence in sensational cases was reported twice over – once pre-trial, once again at trial.)

As much, perhaps more, publicity was given to the proceedings at Hyde as to the trial, and there can be no doubt that this was prejudicial to the accused. To say that Brady and Hindley would have been convicted anyway, pre-trial publicity or not, is to say that there should be one law for the obviously guilty and one law for those whose guilt requires some effort to prove. The prejudice was aggravated by the way in which certain newspapers censored the non-salacious testimony and by the way in which the reports were presented, with headlines, sub-headings and bold or italic type emphasizing specially ghoulish or sexy aspects. For these newspapers, probably the highlight of the proceedings was when Lesley Ann Downey's mother shouted at Hindley from the witness box: 'You beast! You killed my little girl and you sit there staring at me. . . . You tramp!'

The extravagant nationwide coverage ruled out a defence

request for a change of venue for the trial, and made it difficult, perhaps impossible, to find twelve people unaware of, and unaffected by, the publicity, who were yet worthy of serving on the jury.

Every decade has at least one 'crime of the century', and in the sixties this label was attached to the Moors case. If ticket touts had turned some of their profiteering energies from the sporting and theatrical to the legal, then the trial, which opened in the spruced-up No. 2 Court at Chester Castle on 19 April 1966, would have provided very rich pickings indeed. Only sixty seats were available to the public, and for these a queue formed in the early hours of each of the fourteen days of the trial. The public was outnumbered by a motley, many-tongued corps of reporters, augmented by a pack of authors, each of whom was hoping, as someone commented, to turn the 'crime of the century' into a Book of the Month. Security precautions reduced the usual number of public seats: the gallery was speckled with policemen on the look-out for signs of disturbance and for known troublemakers who might have evaded the screening process in the courtyard; the front row of seats, directly behind the dock, was kept empty. There were other precautions, the most spectacular of which was a shield of reinforced glass at the sides and back of the dock: a 'draught excluder', the police called it.

The case was tried before Mr Justice Fenton Atkinson – the son of a judge, Sir Cyril Atkinson – who had been appointed to the Queen's Bench in 1960.

Sir Frederick Elwyn Jones, QC, MP, the Attorney-General, led the prosecution, the first time that the senior law officer had taken part in a murder trial since the case of Dr John Bodkin Adams at the Old Bailey in 1957. Elwyn Jones (whose knowledge of Nazi war crimes and criminals was probably more extensive even than Brady's, since he had served on the British prosecution team at Nuremburg) had to be in London on several days during the trial, once for the opening of Parliament, at other times for cabinet discussions on the Rhodesia crisis, and his role was then assumed by

William Mars-Jones, QC (now a High Court Judge), an efficient and perseverant silk who had prosecuted in the Lime fraud case, Carmarthen, 1962, a trial which lasted fifty-five days, at that time the longest criminal trial this century. Junior Crown counsel was R.G. Waterhouse.

Brady was defended by Emlyn Hooson, Liberal MP for Montgomeryshire, who had taken silk six years before, when, at the age of thirty-five, he was the youngest QC since David Maxwell-Fyfe in 1934. Hooson led David Lloyd-Jones, who had represented Brady at the Hyde committal proceedings.

By a poignant coincidence, on the first day of the trial, Hindley's counsel, Godfrey Heilpern, QC, learned that his sister-in-law, the manageress of a Salford dress shop, had been murdered. Consequently, he had to be absent from court on the day of David Smith's cross-examination, which was conducted by his junior, Philip Curtis, who had been Hindley's counsel at Hyde.

Four women were called to serve on the jury, but Mr Hooson and Mr Heilpern each made two peremptory challenges of them so as to form an all-male jury.

Brady was charged with the murders of Edward Evans, Lesley Ann Downey and John Kilbride. At the committal proceedings, Hindley had been charged with two murder counts – Evans and Downey – plus a third count of harbouring Brady while knowing that he had murdered Kilbride; but before trial, she was also charged with a fourth count – the murder of Kilbride. Like Brady, she pleaded not guilty to all the charges.

While the evidence of David Smith furnished the Crown with the corner-stone of its case, there also existed a wealth of circumstantial evidence which alone, by its cumulative power, was capable of sending both the accused to prison for life. It must be borne in mind, however, that prison for life often means far less than the words seem to threaten. The legal definition of 'life', its meaning in terms of years, is inexact, affected as it is by many factors – for example, the circumstances and number of crimes of which the prisoner is found guilty; his behaviour before the crime, after arrest, and while serving sentence; the shifting whims and beliefs of politicians, penologists, and people whose names inspire respect or, at least, ensure the publication of their letters to *The Times*.

In the cases of Brady and Hindley, the defence could not possibly hope for acquittals; prison terms were inevitable. But there was a faint hope that reasonable doubt could be implanted in the minds of the jury as to whether the accused were guilty on all counts. If the jury were to find them guilty of some, not all, of the charges, their chances would be improved of serving only a fraction of the lifetime penalties which the Crown clearly sought to have imposed.

Defence counsel concentrated their main attack on David Smith, the Crown's strongest yet most vulnerable witness, treating him as an accomplice in the murder of Edward Evans, and suggesting that it was he who had killed Lesley Ann Downey and John Kilbride. It was a simple matter to discredit Smith as a person, but as a witness he was virtually incontrovertible; allied with the natural arrogance of semi-education was the knowledge that he was 'in the clear', for he gave evidence on the understanding that no proceedings would be taken against him in respect of any statements he had made to the police. He not only answered most of the defence questions with swaggering ease but often answered back. (Mr Hooson's sarcastic 'And you're a man in the habit of holding a stick in your hand all the time?' was met with the cutting irony of: 'But I'm not in the habit of witnessing murder, sir.')

The defence was handed what the judge called 'a stick with which to beat Smith' by the revelation that since November 1965 he had received an average of £15 a week from the *News of the World*, and that this newspaper (slogan: 'All human life is here') had promised him a lump sum of at least £1,000 for the use of his name on a series of articles that would appear only if Brady and Hindley were convicted. Clearly, 'this quite extraordinary arrangement' (the judge's words again) might have caused him to fabricate evidence against the accused.

As it happened, Smith's first statement to the police, made

before the *News of the World* approached him, was rather more prejudicial to the accused – Hindley especially – than the evidence Smith gave at the trial. The contagious effect of his interviews with the newspaper's representatives was to supplant simple words and phrases in the statement with gaudy-coloured imagery (the plain 'Ian' of the statement became a 'butcher' from the witness box, and Evans's body became a 'rag doll'), but it seems that there was also a sub-editing influence on his memory. The Attorney-General was able to cut short the defence attack by applying for the statement (which the jury had not heard) to be compared with Smith's evidence; this, of course, was the last thing the defence wanted, and, on the tacit understanding that there would be no further reference to the possible effects of the newspaper's compact with Smith, the judge refused the application.

It is surprising that no action was taken against the *News of the World*. The fact that Smith's evidence was, in some respects, diluted in comparison with his statement does not mean that the newspaper's influence was negative, or even benign to the defence. Who can be sure that if there had been no implied financial incentive to ensure conviction, Smith would not have examined the statement, and his conscience, more closely so as to be sure that any errors that might have crept into the statement were not repeated as evidence? The inglorious history of 'cheque-book journalism' is almost as old as the press itself, and there are several instances of newspapers being fined for contempt of court. (The best-remembered example, perhaps, relates to the second 'Crumbles case' [Patrick Mahon], 1924, when three newspapers were charged, and one of them, the *Evening Standard*, was fined £1,000 for hiding a witness and then allowing her story to appear while the case was *sub judice*. Passing sentence, Lord Hewart wondered if, 'with unlimited enterprise and wealth, we may reach a time when witnesses on both sides will be bound by contract and lodged by this or that newspaper'.)

The *News of the World*'s interference in the Moors case was condemned by the Press Council; but any hope that the Council's words were in any way a deterrent to chequebook journalism must be tempered by the knowledge that in 1963 the Council condemned the *News of the World* for publishing the life story of Miss Christine Keeler, the star witness in the Stephen Ward case, and that five or six years later the same newspaper published a revised version of Miss Keeler's memoirs.

For much of the time that Brady and Hindley were in the dock – he in a chain-store suit of unassuming grey, she usually wearing a black and white jacket and skirt, her hair silver-lilac at the start of the trial, melon-yellow at the end – their behaviour seemed to imitate the way they must have spent the days at Millwards. There was an air of casual efficiency about them. The copious notes they made were flicked from the pads, passed across the rail of the dock, forgotten; it was the practised motion of an invoice being handed over for checking. Occasionally, and especially at the approach of an adjournment (in their terms, lunch-break or knocking-off time), they nudged one another, to offer a mint-sweet from a tube, or to share a smile when a witness's remark jogged a memory of some out-of-office-hours experience.

Brady went into the witness box three times: twice during legal arguments in the jury's absence, and notably once to give evidence in his own defence, on which occasion he was examined for eight and a half hours. The relentless cross-examination by the Attorney-General caused Brady to tell lie after lie – lies at times so blatant and reckless as to seem like a burlesque of untruthfulness. He admitted that if the blows from the hatchet caused Edward Evans's death, then it was he who had killed him, but he denied premeditation; he maintained stoically that he had played no part in the other two murders. There were periods of the cross-examination when Brady gave quite detailed answers, and when he argued with the Attorney-General over trivial points that to him, lacking the perspective of morality, were more relevant than the fact of murder itself; then, realizing the hopelessness of his case, the uselessness of lengthy denials ('My train of thought now is that I will be convicted anyway'), he answered in as few words as possible. He slipped up just once, and that was not during cross-examination, but in examination-in-chief: while describing Lesley Ann Downey's visit to the house – a visit which, he said, was arranged by Smith and was for the sole purpose of photographing the child – he told Mr Hooson: 'After completion, *we all got dressed* and went downstairs.'

Hindley was in the witness box for nearly six hours. Only in minor respects did her evidence conflict with Brady's. She said that she was 'horrified' at the killing of Evans, and that her treatment of Lesley Ann Downey, recorded on the tape, was 'indefensible', 'cruel' – mere words to her, perhaps, ingredients of what the Attorney-General called 'counterfeit shame', yet in a case that extended the dimensions of evil, even a semblance of regret was welcome.

Closing speeches and the judge's summing-up occupied most of the last three days of the trial. The summing-up, precise yet colloquial, deliberately low-keyed (as was Mr Justice Fenton Atkinson's whole handling of the trial), was spoken directly to the jury, and so quietly that people in the well of the court had to lean forward to catch all that was said. The two accused made no effort to hear, and at one point Brady appeared to be asleep.

The jury retired at twenty minutes to three on Friday, 6 May. At five o'clock they returned to pronounce Brady guilty of all three murders, and Hindley guilty of the murders of Edward Evans and Lesley Ann Downey; she was found not guilty of the murder of John Kilbride, but guilty of harbouring Brady, knowing that he had committed the crime.

Asked if he had anything to say before sentence was passed, Brady again revealed his obsessional regard for detail. In anyone else, it might have seemed pathetic. 'No,' he said; then, referring to a question which the jury had interrupted their deliberations to ask: 'Except the revolvers were bought in July 1964.' Hindley had nothing to say.

Mr Justice Fenton Atkinson, as quietly as ever, passed concurrent life sentences ('the only sentences which the law now allows') for each of the murder charges, and a sentence of seven years, also concurrent, for the charge against Hindley of being an accessory after the fact.

* * *

Brady did not appeal. On 17 October the Criminal Division of the Court of Appeal dismissed Hindley's appeal, which had been argued on the ground that she should have been tried separately. Giving judgement, Lord Chief Justice Parker said that the Court was satisfied that there was no miscarriage of justice:

> There was, no doubt, in this case a danger of grave prejudice from the fact that that man was a really terrible murderer and that she had throughout admitted a very close association with him, taking part in all his activities and, indeed, being in the house, if not in the room, on the occasion of two of the murders. . . . [But] that was a prejudice which was inevitable, and was there just as much, if not to a greater extent, if she were tried separately. . . . The evidence against her was overwhelming.

Brady, at his own request, is serving his sentence under rule 43 of the Prison Regulations, which restricts contact with other prisoners. Until 1971, when he was moved to Parkhurst on the Isle of Wight, he was kept in the maximum security 'E' wing of Durham Prison. At one time virtually the sole occupants of this wing were child murderers. Keeping company with Brady was John Straffen, the shambling lunatic who is in prison only because no mental institution is secure enough to guarantee his confinement; also Raymond Morris, the murderer of Christine Darby at Cannock Chase in 1967, who developed so intense a hatred of Brady that he several times tried to wound or scald him. Three child murderers: one of them, Brady, a sadist with homosexual tendencies, the second hopelessly insane, and the third a libidinist. It would require some ingenuity to devise a more sinister trio than this – or, for the two sane prisoners, an existence more comparable to hell; here was the near-reality of Sartre's *Huis Clos*.

Brady has petitioned the Home Office to allow him to see Hindley, who he claims is his common-law wife. He has emphasized later applications by fasting, and in the spring of 1971 went for more than two months without taking solid food.

Hindley, too, it is reported, claims a common-law alliance.

Her pleasures are circumscribed in Holloway, but she appears to accept the bounds. She reads a lot, chiefly books that assist her endeavours to pass O-level examinations, and has acquired a delicate skill, almost akin to art, at embroidery and crocheting. Within the last year or so she has returned to the Roman Catholic faith, confessing her sins and patching a wall of her cell with pictures of favourite saints.

When Lord Stonham was under-secretary at the Home office, he visited Hindley and was much impressed by her quiet manner and intelligence. Afterwards, he was quoted as saying that he was worried that a person like her could be in prison – a sentiment that was reversed by William Mars-Jones, who spoke for the majority by saying that he would be worried if she were not.

The Half-Hanging of Ambrose Gwinnett

RAYNER HEPPENSTALL

The broadsheet in which the story of Ambrose Gwinnett first appeared did not find its way into any of the Newgate Calendars. It might well have done, and it is certainly the most interesting of the stories of the period in which a person (in this case, a young man) survived hanging. Its peculiar interest lies equally in the circumstantial evidence which led to the hanging and in the many surprising consequences of survival. It begins in the reign of Queen Anne, a few years after half-hanged Smith's already remarkable series of escapes. It continues into the reign of the third George.

Ambrose Gwinnett was the young son of a man who kept shop for seamen's slops (ready-made clothes and bedding) in Canterbury, at the sign of the Blue Anchor. Being a well-schooled youth, he had been articled for some years to an attorney in the town. At Michaelmas, in 1709, he had received permission from his master to visit his sister, a Mrs Sawyer, who kept an inn near Deal, between ten and twenty miles away. He set out on foot.

The road was full of men and horses coming from the Michaelmas fairs at Sandwich and Eastry, and he was not accustomed to long walking. Besides, he had a colic. He got to Deal and felt he could go no further. The inns were full with officers and sailors from ships in the Downs. At the New Inn, however, the landlady knew his sister. The two had done each other many a favour. She said Ambrose could sleep on a chair in her parlour and go on his way in the morning.

On the chair where he was to sleep sat a man in nightgown and cap, by a dying fire, counting money. This was the landlady's uncle by marriage, Richard Collins. He was boatswain of an East Indiaman then at anchor in the Downs. It would be better if he shared his double bed with the newcomer. This he reluctantly agreed to do.

He put his money in a money belt, strapped this about him and took up a candle. The two men went up to bed.

They had not been long abed when Ambrose Gwinnett's colic began to trouble him. He awoke his bedfellow and asked the way to the privy. This was, of course, in the garden. The string which lifted the sneck was broken, said Collins, and you needed a knife to lift it. If the young man felt in the right-hand pocket of Collins's trousers, he would find a pen-knife which he could use.

Gwinnett found the knife and, making as little noise as possible, set out in the dark for the garden and the privy. When he opened the penknife, a coin dropped out of the handle. This he put in his pocket and without difficulty raised the sneck and opened the privy door. His bowels were very troublesome, and he stayed quite a long time on the privy seat.

When he returned to the room in which he had been sharing a bed with Richard Collins, he felt around for the trousers, but they had gone. So had Collins. Gwinnett got back into his side of the bed and dozed uneasily until first light, the sun being up at about seven o'clock. Then he arose, dressed and went downstairs. The landlady got up, half-dressed. He paid his reckoning and was instructed on the road to take to his sister's, a distance of three miles, along the coast, we shall suppose, to Kingsdown, possibly to what is now the Rising Sun. It seems likely that he said nothing to Mrs Collins about the disappearance of her uncle and that he did not give her the penknife and the coin, feeling perhaps very poorly and thinking of nothing but how to get to his sister's.

Sawyer himself had been a seafaring man, latterly serving aboard a privateer in the late French war, so that it was with prize money he had bought the inn and married the daughter of a trader in seamen's slops in Canterbury. He would have known whether the level of a spring tide had in the night joined with a fair wind to hasten the sailing of an East Indiaman and so accounted for the abrupt departure of her boatswain, Richard Collins, from the New Inn.

Breakfast was interrupted by the arrival of constables from Deal, who constituted Ambrose Gwinnett the Queen's prisoner on charges of theft and murder. Made to turn out his pockets, he revealed a penknife and a William & Mary guinea, both scratched with the initials 'R.C.'. Of the money belt there appeared to be no trace, nor had Gwinnett an excess of money on him. For the fact that no such excess had been entrusted to his keeping Sawyer's word would be accepted, for he was respected locally. Apart from her uncle's disappearance, the murder charge was based on the fact that Mrs Collins had found the sheets of her double bed stained with blood and the discovery that a trail of blood led downstairs and out of the house all the way to last night's high water mark of the sea.

Ambrose Gwinnett was tried at Maidstone assizes, and a jury convicted him of both theft and murder, despite the absence of a sufficient *corpus delicti* on either count. Sentence was passed that he was to be taken to Deal and hanged near the scene of his crime, to be afterwards hung in chains outside the town.

From Maidstone to Deal, the distance is forty miles. If Gwinnett was trundled the whole way by cart (the halter tied round his arms, so that he could not move these), he cannot, that Wednesday, leaving Maidstone at six o'clock in the morning, have been in Deal until fairly late in the afternoon.

It was a stormy day, the wind and rain so violent that the sheriff and his officers, soaked to the skin, could barely sit their horses. The hangman, we may imagine, did his job hastily and left the body hanging less than the customary half hour (it was sometimes an hour), then cut it down and dumped it at the New Inn to be prepared for gibbeting. This meant wrapping it in tarred calico and fastening the parcel up with iron bands. Then it was taken some way south of the town to the gibbet erected on common land and hoisted up to a swivel, carelessly no doubt.

Officers from a privateer were staying at the Sawyers' inn. Perhaps they expressed sympathy with a landlady known to be under a strain. A boy had been sent out to bring cows home for milking from the northernmost of Sawyer's meadows. He, no doubt, had gone a little further towards Deal, to look at the newly hanged man.

He heard the man groan. Moreover, the calico had come loose from the face, and the eyes were open otherwise than in a lifeless stare. Hurrying back to the inn, he announced that the hanged man was still alive.

We may imagine Sawyer out of the house with all speed, followed by inn servants and privateer officers, calling to neighbours to bring an axe, a saw, a ladder, while a man from the privateer rowed out to the ship to fetch the ship's surgeon. They hacked and sawed the gibbet down, took the body to the inn, stripped it of its iron bands and calico and put it into a warm bed. The surgeon bled it.

Ambrose Gwinnett had to be got away before the destruction of the gibbet became known to the authorities. The captain of the privateer offered to take him aboard. A literate young man would be useful in keeping the steward's accounts.

The ship sailed for the West Indies. A Spanish ship engaged and defeated it. The surviving crew were taken prisoners to Cuba. There were forty of them. They included Ambrose Gwinnett.

Three years later, Spain and Britain being momentarily at peace, the captives were to be put on board transports and shipped to Pennsylvania. It would not have suited Gwinnett to return to English jurisdiction, despite his having been once hanged. He solicited the head gaoler to allow him to remain, and the governor of the island was persuaded that an employee who knew both English and Spanish and was a lawyer's clerk into the bargain would be very useful in dealing with British and American pirates.

Two years later still, a Spanish man-of-war engaged a British pirate ship and reduced its crew to nine hands. These were brought to the gaol in Havana that morning. Among them was Richard Collins. He was slow to recognize the man at the table, with writing materials before him. Gwinnett looked at the name he had written down.

'Were you ever in Deal?' he asked.

'I was pressed there,' said Collins.

'Then,' said Gwinnett, 'I was hanged and gibbeted on your account.'

And he explained. Collins in turn told his story.

The day Ambrose Gwinnett had come to the New Inn, he had been blooded. While Gwinnett was out attending to his colic, the wound had opened. He had left his bed and gone out to knock up the surgeon. In the street, he had been seized by a press gang, dragged (the surgeon's cut still bleeding) to a boat at the sea's edge and conveyed aboard a privateer in the Downs, which presently sailed. His wound attended to by the ship's surgeon, he had been compelled to serve on board the privateer, which in truth was no better than a pirate ship, whether it had always been such or had turned pirate on the conclusion of peace with Spain. In the end, it had been engaged in desperate conflict by a Spanish man-of-war off Yucatan and what remained of it brought into the harbour of Havana.

As far as English law was concerned, the two men could now very well go home together, and Gwinnett would be pardoned. The governor of Cuba would no doubt be sorry to see him go, but he was no longer a prisoner. The governor was a fair-minded man and would probably, for Gwinnett's sake, accept Collins's plea that only *force majeure* had impelled him into courses of piracy.

But the chain of coincidence was not yet broken. It is to be supposed that Richard Collins boarded the right ship, but this time, walking along the Cuban shore at night in the wrong direction, it was Ambrose Gwinnett who fell in with pirates, and was impressed into their service.

Their captain was Brian Walsh, an Irishman. He befriended Gwinnett and made him purser, in charge of enormous riches stowed on the pirates' centre of operations, Swallow island, twelve leagues inside the gulf of Mexico. Gwinnett was later to describe Walsh as a most execrable and bloody villain. This was ungrateful. After capturing a Jamaican ship loaded with a cargo of sugar and rum, Walsh drank himself to death, leaving a will which made Gwinnett sole heir to a fortune of forty thousand pounds sterling, which would make him almost a millionaire today. As he now owned the ship as well, Gwinnett appointed the first mate captain and ordered him to make for Port Royal, it being his intention that on Jamaica his crew should abandon their piratical ways and settle down.

On the voyage from Swallow island, however, their ship went down, with all its treasure. Those who remained afloat in the ship's boats included Ambrose Gwinnett, but the others threw him overboard, perhaps understandably. Once again he was lucky, in that a Spanish ship picked him up, but unlucky in that the Spaniards decided that he was a pirate. They were right, of course, unless he had meant, on arrival in Jamaica, to disgorge all Brian Walsh's ill-gotten gains, which he was never to claim that he had intended to do. As to the men in the boats, they had probably suspected all along that there was something fishy about Brian Walsh's will, as there probably was. We can hardly suppose that, after so many years, Ambrose would remain quite the spotless child of misfortune we first met.

The Spaniards sentenced him to serve in their Mediterranean galleys, which he did for two years. Then, in an engagement with an Algerian chebec, he suffered a real misfortune. He lost a leg. He was to say that, in consequence of this loss, he escaped from the Spaniards, but that seems unlikely. The fact of the matter is that a galley-slave with one leg is not of much use. Perhaps he was encouraged to escape. At any rate, he arrived back in England to find all his relations dead. Richard Collins had not reached home.

The date is said to have been 1730. The years accounted for since 1709 are a long way short of twenty-one. The likeliest guess is that twelve or so had been spent with Brian Walsh.

It may be assumed that he landed either in Deal or at Kingsdown, for all ships into or out of London lay up, however briefly, in the Downs, waiting for a change of wind to take them either round the South Foreland or into the Thames estuary, so that sometimes there were as many as four hundred sail there at a time. Ambrose Gwinnett would either take a ship's boat or engage a local hoveller to convey him to shore.

Finding new people at what had been his sister's, he would next call at the New Inn in Deal, where he would want to know if Richard Collins had appeared. He had not. Gwinnett might try to convince Mrs Collins that he had met her uncle in the West Indies and seen him off back to England, but, as Collins had never returned, she would not believe him. Much as she might pity him for his leglessness, he would still be to her her uncle's murderer, and she might threaten him with the authorities, so that he would have to leave Deal quickly.

He ended up a roadsweeper, who from 1734 onwards swept the way between Mews Gate and Spring Gardens, Charing Cross. There is a broadsheet which contains his purported autobiography. The copy in the British Library is a second edition of 1770. On it, somebody has written: 'Dr Percy told me that he had heard that this pamphlet was a mere fiction written by Mr Bickerstaffe the Dramatic Poet.' Dr Percy we may presume to have been the vicar of Easton Maudit, North-amptonshire, and rector of Wilby in the same county, later bishop of Dromore, whose *Reliques of Ancient English Poetry* had become famous in 1765 and have justly remained so. Isaac Bickerstaffe, one of the first of our Irish dramatists, was a successful playwright in London between 1760 and 1771, when he fled on account of charges of sodomy, then a capital offence, for which he had earlier been deprived of a commission in the Marines.

That the story of Ambrose Gwinnett was a mere fiction is hardly to be believed. Had he invented so remarkable a plot, Bickerstaffe would have made a play of it, not a mere broad-sheet. If Gwinnett had lived until 1770, he would have been eighty-one. Well, it is possible. We may have to imagine a roadsweeper of that age talking to a young Irish playwright, who was certainly not well acquainted with Deal. Men of literary note had before then compiled the autobiographies of disreputable persons from their conversation. Six years before Ambrose Gwinnett returned to Deal, Daniel Defoe had done it for Jack Sheppard. Of course, Gwinnett might have done it for himself.

Tracking Down a Murderer

J. LESLIE HOTSON

Ancient murderers arouse in some of us a deep detecting interest. To ferret them out and to turn the world's eye upon them gives a peculiar pleasure. The modern criminal, on the other hand, leaves us comparatively cold. We abandon him, with his large fortune and temporary mental aberration, to the sordid pillory of the headlines. Our preferred murderers are those far figures who, having drawn a cloak of centuries over their crime, are trying to slip unnoticed down the dark highway of history. Such we like to tap on the shoulder.

But 'First catch your hare,' says the oracle of the kitchen. And the greatest initial obstacle to the exposure of lost murderers is of course the catching them. Clues are clues only to those who have their eyes open. As a specimen of ancient hidden murder, I take the case of Nicholas Colfox. This man, we have just discovered, was a murderer denounced, under a cloak of poetry, by Geoffrey Chaucer. An obscure corner of history shows Colfox as the chief accomplice of Thomas Mowbray in the abduction and secret murder of Thomas, Duke of Gloucester, in 1397. This discovery has now for the first time opened our eyes to the damning finger which Chaucer points in his 'Tale of the Cock and the Fox':

> A Colfox, ful of sly iniquitee . . .
> Wayting his tyme on Chauntecleer to falle,
> As gladly doon thise homicydes alle,
> That in awayt liggen to mordre men.
> O false mordrer, lurking in thy den!

But the story we have to tell here is not the Hunting of the Colfox. We shall come down two centuries, and relate the chase of the man who killed the dramatist Christopher

103

Marlowe. And the beginning of the story lies in Bloomsbury.

You must know, first, that the houses in Bloomsbury are all alike – on the outside. Idiosyncrasy may find a place within door, but it is drab uniformity which orders the antique right-dress and the jaded eyes-front of the smoky exteriors. In a garret of one of these indistinguishable houses, one raw November night, we were huddled over the gas stove. Mary was trying to toast bread and, Jupiter-like, I was pouring a well-aimed shower of coins into the lap of that Danaän stove, to coax from it a complaisant warmth. No one who has not experienced it can know the joy of an English fireside. When the ponderous penny has dropped, and the eager gas has launched its cheerful roar – then is the moment for scorched shins, shivering backs, and little abortive attempts to mitigate the monotony of the English cuisine.

To us enters our literary friend, partly for hot buttered toast, and partly for companionship. Our literary friend is an authority on Christopher Marlowe and his writings. Being on tour, he has paid a visit to Marlowe's college at Cambridge, he has walked from the Bankside to Shoreditch, and is projecting a pilgrimage to the poet's birthplace, Canterbury. Before taking his leave, our literary friend learns that we are spending our days in Chancery Lane, grubbing among the musty parchments and papers of the Public Record Office, finding here a new fact about John Harvard, and there a lawsuit concerning some property of John Milton's. Thinking at once of the unknown man who destroyed the greatest early genius of the English drama, he shakes his head. Not much chance of finding a trace of that criminal in the Public Record Office. Scholars have ransacked the place in search of him. But Deptford, now – where Marlowe was killed? Why not try Deptford? No telling what you might find there, in some obscure corner.

After our literary friend had gone, I endeavoured to think why I ought not to try Deptford. One very good reason that came to me was, I remember, that Peter the Great, Tsar of Muscovy, had tried it: and tsars were notorious for their bad taste – whether it were shown in accidentally beating their children to death, or in fostering revolution with the knout. The story goes that Peter went to Deptford ostensibly to learn shipbuilding as a common workman. But King Charles lodged him and his retinue in Sayes Court, the handsome Deptford mansion of John Evelyn. When the Muscovites came to move out, Evelyn made a bitter complaint to Parliament of the horror wrought within the house by the nasty nobility, and of the destruction of his cherished hedges by Peter. The potentate, it seems, as shipbuilding palled, would seat himself in quest of excitement in a wheelbarrow, and get a powerful gardener to rush him full tilt through a hedge. Evelyn naturally could not be expected to understand what an intoxicated thrill of Tsarility it gave one to smash through those hedges.

Then, too, I reflected that though Deptford, even as late as Peter's time, may have been in a condition to be visited, it now was unquestionably a city slum. On picking up the *Evening Standard* I read that health officers were urging the establishment of public baths in Deptford, since it had been estimated that there was one bathroom for every one hundred houses. Finally, where in Deptford should I find an archive – a commodity no doubt scarcer even than bathrooms?

No; the prospect of Deptford was lacking in charm. Instead, I went to the British Museum to find out exactly what was already known of Marlowe's murderer.

It took but a very short time to find that nothing was exactly known. Turning to the *Dictionary of National Biography*, I found this:

> In the register of the parish church of St. Nicholas, Deptford, appears the entry, which is ordinarily transcribed thus: 'Christopher Marlow, slain by ffrancis Archer, 1 June 1593.' Mr Halliwell-Phillipps read the surname of the assailant as 'Frezer', *i.e.* Fraser.

Here at once was mystery full-fledged. The authorities did not agree even on the murderer's name. Some read 'Archer', and others 'Frezer'. Plainly the first step would be to settle the question to my own satisfaction by studying the original writing. But the burial register that contained it was still kept in the church at Deptford where Marlowe was buried. For some moments a bus pilgrimage to Dismal Deptford loomed up unavoidable – but I was spared. From the dim stack a book on Marlowe was produced, whose author had thoughtfully enriched his work with a photographic facsimile of the disputed entry. One careful glance proved beyond a doubt that the 'Frezer' reading was right and the 'Archer' reading impossible. The scholars and parsons had mistaken the *ff* of *ffrezer* (which was the old way of writing capital F) for a capital A, owing to the two uprights and the crossbar; and to take *ez* for *ch* in an Elizabethan hand is not so stupid as one might suppose. But 'Francis Frezer' was unquestionably the name written by the parish clerk.

So much for the name. What other dim light was there on Marlowe's death? Well, there were two ancient brimstone accounts of the violent and well-merited end of Marlowe, the reputed atheist, which have survived. The first, written by Thomas Beard four years after Marlowe's death, in his *Theatre of Gods Iudgements* (a collection of terrific obituaries), runs as follows:

> Not inferiour to any of the former in Atheisme & impiety, and equall to all in maner of punishment was one of our own nation, of fresh and late memory, called *Marlin* [marginal note: *Marlow*], by profession a scholler, brought vp from his youth in the Vniuersitie of Cambridge, but by practise a playmaker, and a Poet of scurrilitie, who by giuing too large a swinge to his owne wit, and suffering his lust to haue the full raines, fell (not without iust desert) to that outrage and extremitie, that hee denied God and his sonne Christ, and not only in word blasphemed the trinitie, but also (as it is credibly reported) wrote books against it, affirming our Sauiour to be but a deceiuer, and *Moses* to be but a coniurer and seducer of the people, and the holy Bible to be but vaine and idle stories, and all religion but a deuice of pollicie. But see what a hooke the Lord put in the mosthrils of this barking dogge: It so fell out, that in London streets as he purposed to stab one whome hee ought a grudge vnto with his dagger, the other party perceiuing so auoided the stroke, that withall catching hold of his wrest, he stabbed his owne dagger into his owne head, in

such sort, that notwithstanding all the meanes of surgerie that could be wrought, hee shortly after died thereof. The manner of his death being so terrible (for hee euen cursed and blasphemed to his last gaspe, and togither with his breath an oth flew out of his mouth) that it was not only a manifest signe of Gods iudgement, but also an horrible and fearefull terrour to all that beheld him. But herein did the iustice of God most notably appeare, in that hee compelled his owne hand which had written those blasphemies to be the instrument to punish him, and that in his braine, which had deuised the same.

It was to this story that Francis Meres, writing a year later, added the famous embroidery of scandal: '*Christopher Marlow* was stabd to death by a bawdy Seruing man, a riuall of his in his lewde loue.' Historians of literature, novelists, and playwrights have seized on this last unsavoury morsel of gossip and have served it up under such an ingenious variety of forms that those who have heard nothing else about Marlowe have heard that.

William Vaughan, the author of the second long account, tells a more circumstantial and less expansive tale in his *Golden Grove* (1600):

Not inferior to these was one Christopher Marlow by profession a playmaker, who, as it is reported, about 7. yeeres a-goe wrote a booke against the Trinite: but see the effects of Gods justice; it so hapned, that at Detford, a little village about three miles distant from London, as he meant to stab with his ponyard one named Ingram, that had inuited him thither to a feast, and was then playing at tables, he quickly perceyuing it, so auoyded the thrust, that withall drawing out his dagger for his defence, hee stabd this Marlow into the eye, in such sort, that his braines comming out at the daggers point, hee shortlie after dyed. Thus did God, the true executioner of diuine iustice, worke the ende of impious Atheists.

It is to be noticed here that Vaughan gives the assailant's name as one 'Ingram', while the burial register, we remember, reported it as 'Francis Frezer'. Which was correct? Someone had blundered over this name, but from this distance no one could tell where the age-old mistake lay.

Out of this tangle I took small encouragement. How could I hope to discover anything about so shadowy a criminal? In the first place, he was reputed to have been a serving man; and men of that class do not figure largely in the public records. Secondly, his very name was a matter of doubt. So hopeless it seemed that I gave up all thought of tracking him down, and returned to my other research.

Months passed, and took me far from Chancery Lane. But the magnetic power of the archives, that subtle and incalculable force, drew me back; and somewhere in the unconscious part of memory the names 'Ingram' and 'Francis Frezer' were still lurking. One day the gods of chance were propitious. I was going through the pages of one of the old index-books to the Close Rolls of the Chancery, searching it for Walter Raleighs, Francis Drakes, and the like. As my eye travelled through the entries for the year 1596, it was suddenly caught and held by the name 'Ingram Frizer'. In a flash came revelation. Something shouted in my brain that I had my finger on Marlowe's murderer, whose trail I had so long abandoned. The mystery of the name was solved: Vaughan had mentioned the murderer as 'Ingram', apparently taking this as his surname, while the parish clerk, though writing 'Frezer' correctly, had mistakenly substituted 'Francis' as his Christian name.

The date here was 1596, three years after the crime, and Frizer had not been hanged by the neck; on the contrary, here he was, indexed in the Close Rolls of the Chancery. What was he doing there? Referring to the enrolled document, I found it to be merely a deed of bargain and sale, by which Ingram Frizer of London purchased two houses and some land in Buckinghamshire; and in this, of course, there was no clue to the crime. But we had crossed a hot trail. A hazy contradiction of names had leaped into life as Ingram Frizer, a London man of business, living, moving, and having his being three years after killing Marlowe. He challenged me to a chase.

How was I to recover a trace of his crime of 1593? I could

not believe that he had not come to some kind of trial for killing Marlowe, even though he had been acquitted. There must have been a record, somewhere. Casting about, I thought first of the great series of ancient Criminal Inquests – those investigations by coroners' courts into questionable deaths – included in the Chancery records. Unfortunately this collection upon examination proved to contain nothing later than the reign of Henry VI.

Baffled here, I had to lead off in a new direction. It occurred to me that although Marlowe was killed at Deptford in Kent, perhaps the case was not tried in Kent. Perhaps Frizer had been indicted for Marlowe's death in the great Court of the Queen's Bench, Westminster, the highest criminal court in the realm. I therefore got out the Queen's Bench Controlment Roll for 35 Elizabeth (1593) – a thick bundle of dark-brown parchments sewn together at the top. For two days I strained my eyes searching in the dim and difficult script for an indictment of Ingram Frizer, and I finished by finding nothing.

Once more I paused and considered. The possibilities of Kent were not yet exhausted. Marlowe's murderer might have been tried by the Justice of Assize, on circuit there. Hope rode high when the bundle of ancient rolls of the South-Eastern Circuit for 1593 was brought out for me. Black with thick dust they were, and appeared not to have been opened for centuries. I thought surely to make a discovery here. But as they slowly passed in dim and fragmentary procession under my eyes hope seemed to pass with them. In the long files of criminals I found no Ingram Frizer.

This was a dark moment. I could see nothing in any direction. While waiting for light, I read over the two old narratives of Marlowe's death once more. Was there a possible clue still hidden there? What was Vaughan's view of the circumstances of the fight? According to him Marlowe, dagger in fist, had attacked Ingram, who drew his own poniard and killed the poet in self-defence. If this were true, could Ingram properly be called a murderer? To freshen up my imagination I made an effort to put myself in his place. Here lay Kit Marlowe, whom I had stabbed to save my life. Was I to look forward quietly to a trial for murder, and then the gallows? But I killed him in self-defence! I thought that I could prove as much to the coroner's jury. And after proving it, what then? Why, then I could appeal to the Queen for a pardon.

A pardon. A clue! A clue which – presto! – turned me back into my natural shape of a researcher. Where would the royal pardons be entered? Of a sudden I recalled having seen them mentioned in a description of the Patent Rolls of the Chancery. This series is made up of copies of the *Litterae Patentes* or open letters from the sovereign to the subject (the originals are so called from being written upon open sheets of parchment with the Great Seal pendent at the bottom). Among many other kinds of documents, pardons of all sorts were issued through the Chancery as Letters Patent.

Now the index books to the Patent Rolls stand most conveniently on the shelves of the Legal Search Room, just a step down the gloomy corridor from the Round Room where I was working. In a moment I was there, taking down the volume containing 35 Elizabeth (1593), and running my excited finger down the time-faded names noted in the margins.

A dozen rapid leaves, a score or so of names, and treasure-trove! – 'Frisar' lay before me like a jewel on the page. I could not believe my good fortune. There beside it was the laconic description of the pardon, clearly written in the customary abbreviated Latin:

> R[egina] xxviij° die Junij con[cessit] Ingramo ffrisar p[er]don[am] de se defend[endo]

This may be put into English roughly as:

> The Queen 28th day of June granted pardon to Ingram ffrisar [for homicide] in self-defence.

In a kind of whirling daze I realized that Marlowe's name was not there. Still, the date was right: four weeks after Marlowe's burial was sufficient time for issuing a pardon. This *must* be the pardon I was after. But before I could rest I must see the document to which this entry was the index. In an unsteady hand I made out the call ticket for Patent Roll

1401, to which the index referred me, only to find that the hands of the Record Office clock pointed to 4:15 – too late to see the roll that afternoon! That was another dark moment.

Conquering an absurd fear that the attendants must have guessed my secret from my face, I found my way out from the dark musty halls of the archives to the green quiet of the Rolls Yard, past the reflective eye of the guardian bobby under the massive gateway, and into the narrow rapid roar of Chancery Lane. Law clerks passed like so many hasty puppets. Nothing stood in my mind's eye but the shining hope of finding the first authentic account for the death of Christopher Marlowe. That hope would be dashed or realized precisely at ten o'clock on the morrow, when the fatal roll would be waiting on my table. There would be a pardon, I knew; but suppose it should turn out to be only a bare statement, with no thrilling details? As I faced this staggering doubt in Holborn, I was very nearly juggernauted by a Charing Cross bus.

This would not do. I had no right to risk a violent death, when such a secret would die with me. I must live at least until 10 a.m., and that right rapidly. But my desire to speed the parting minutes fell beneath the inexorability of routine. I had to make my usual way by tube to Paddington with other 'season ticket-holders' (an Englishman never *commutes*) and take my seat in the customary Beaconsfield train. We were staying then at Jordans Hostel, which lies halfway between Chalfont St Giles, where Milton wrote, and Beaconsfield, where Chesterton might still be seen from afar off, similarly occupied. On this night of nights the Great Western Railway dropped me in the most ordinary fashion at my little station, and the engine puffed off, remarking, 'What*ever* you *may* or *may* not dis*cover*, the *world must go on, world-must-go-on, worldmustgoon*.' I walked up past the old Friends' Meeting House, through the orchard to the Hostel, and divulged the tremendous secret to Mary. Then followed an attempt to kill the long evening hours by means of a furious game of badminton with a small boy in the Mayflower Barn (a three-centuries-old affair, affirmed by tradition and at least one eminent scholar to be built from the timbers of the Pilgrim ship). The

111

night which succeeded was long, unusually long for the season. But morning came at length, and with it the London train.

III

Life goes by contraries. When I approached the Record Office as the bells of St Clement's were striking ten, I ought, no doubt, to have quickened my steps. Contrariwise, I fell into a kind of fatalistic saunter. If I should find it, well; if not, why, no need to have hurried. . . .

I reached my table. There was the brown roll waiting, as it had waited these three hundred years. Almost calmly I began to unroll the heavy involute of parchment, ten inches wide. But as I noted the length of the average entry my excitement waxed. Faster I rolled – faster, faster – until Frizer's immortal name flashed into view, at the head of a pardon *more than a foot long*.

Surely an angel – perhaps the recording angel – had preserved me for this, or this for me. For me? I cast a furtive glance, half expecting the sharp-eyed double circle of searchers to rise in a body and pounce on my roll – but they were deep in affairs, mostly genealogical, of their own. My eye raced over the pardon – it was written in Latin – and I saw that it quoted in full the details of the inquest held by the Queen's Coroner, William Danby, on 'the body of Christopher Morley, lying dead and slain' at Deptford. *Christopher Morley*. Was this Christopher Marlowe the dramatist? My heart skipped a beat. It must be. The same name in a different spelling. Scholars had seen Marlowe's name written 'Marlin' and 'Marley'; but 'Christopher Morley' was a new and modern-sounding form. In passing I realized that the author of *Shandygaff* had here found a great namesake across three centuries.

No matter for the spelling – here was the previous story, the only authoritative and complete story of Kit Marlowe's mysterious death. How did he die? What was the quarrel?

112

Was there a woman in the case? I found the answers to these questions in the findings of sixteen men under oath – the Coroner's jury. Stripped of a little verbiage, here follows a direct translation from the Latin:

. . . When a certain Ingram Frysar, late of London, gentleman, and the aforesaid Christopher Morley and one Nicholas Skeres, late of London, gentleman, and Robert Poley of London aforesaid, gentleman, on the thirtieth day of May in the thirty-fifth year above mentioned, at Detford Strand aforesaid . . . about the tenth hour before noon of the same day, met together in a room in the house of a certain Eleanor Bull, widow; & there passed the time together & dined & after dinner were in quiet sort together there & walked in the garden belonging to the said house until the sixth hour after noon of the same day & then returned from the said garden to the room aforesaid & there together and in company supped; & after supper the said Ingram & Christopher Morley were in speech & uttered one to the other divers malicious words for the reason that they could not be at one nor agree about the payment of the sum of money, that is, *le Reckoninge*; & the said Christopher Morley then lying upon a bed in the room where they supped, & moved with anger against the said Ingram Frysar upon the words as aforesaid spoken between them, and the said Ingram then & there sitting in the room aforesaid with his back towards the bed where the said Christopher Morley was then lying, sitting near the bed . . . & with the front part of his body towards the table, & the aforesaid Nicholas Skeres & Robert Poley sitting on either side of the said Ingram in such a manner that the same Ingram Frysar in no wise could take flight: it so befell that the said Christopher Morley on a sudden & of his malice towards the said Ingram aforethought, then & there maliciously drew the dagger of the said Ingram which was at his back, and with the same dagger the said Christopher Morley then & there maliciously gave the aforesaid Ingram two wounds on his head of the length of two inches & of the depth of a quarter of an inch; whereupon the said Ingram, in fear of being slain, & sitting in the manner aforesaid between the said Nicholas Skeres & Robert Poley so that he could not in any wise get away, in his own defence & for his saving of his life then & there struggled with the said Christopher Morley to get back from him his dagger aforesaid; in which affray the same Ingram could not get away from the said Christopher Morley; and so it befell in that affray that the said Ingram, in defence of his life, with the dagger aforesaid of the value of twelve pence, gave the said Christopher then & there a mortal wound over his right eye of the depth of two inches & of the width of one inch; of which mortal wound the aforesaid Christopher Morley then & there instantly died; And since that the said Ingram killed & slew the said Christopher Morley aforesaid at Detford Strand aforesaid . . . in the manner & form aforesaid in the defence and saving of his own life, against our peace our crown & dignity, as more fully appears by the tenor of the Record of the Inquest aforesaid which we caused to come before us in our Chancery by virtue of our writ; We therefore moved by piety have pardoned the same Ingram Frisar the breach of our peace which pertains to us against the said Ingram for the death above mentioned & grant to him our firm peace. . . . Witness the Queen at Kew on the 28th day of June.

It will be noticed that this pardon, near the end, refers to the record of the inquest as though it were in the Court of Chancery; and yet I had searched the whole collection of Chancery Inquests with no result. I felt that to complete my documentary record I must find that inquest. But where could it be? I took up the printed description of the Chancery documents and thrashed through every item. At length, in an obscure corner of the Miscellany of the Chancery, a title met my eye: 'Writs and Returns, Henry III to Charles II'. This looked hopeful, for, as I had just seen, the inquest had been returned upon a writ into Chancery; and I got out the Index and Calendar to the Chancery Miscellany. Though the documents well merited the title of 'miscellaneous', they had been roughly grouped together by counties. By going through all the items listed under Kent, I found at last what I wanted – the indented Coroner's inquest (so called because two copies were cut apart on a wavy or indented line for purposes of tallying – whence *indentures*), and the Queen's writ which summoned the case into Chancery. A comparison showed that this inquest had been copied word for word into the pardon, except for the jurors' statement that 'the said Ingram after the slaying aforesaid, perpetrated and done by him in the manner aforesaid, neither fled nor withdrew himself. But what goods or chattels, lands or tenements the said

Ingram had at the time of the slaying . . . the said jurors are totally ignorant'.

With all the documents before me, every step in the proceedings was clear. Ingram Frizer killed Christopher Marlowe on the evening of Wednesday, 30 May 1593. The inquest was held on Friday, 1 June; and on the same day they buried Marlowe's body. Coroner Danby sent the record of the inquest into Chancery in obedience to a writ dated 15 June. And Frizer's pardon was granted at Kew on Thursday, 28 June.

So much for the new dates. Returning to the scene of the inquest, we notice that there were two eyewitnesses to the killing, doubtless friends of Marlowe and Frizer, since they had been feasting with them. Coroner Danby opens his inquiry. The jury examines Marlowe's body, the dagger used in the scuffle, the scalp wounds on Frizer's head, and hears the oral testimony of the two eyewitnesses, Poley and Skeres. Upon deliberation, the jury brings in its finding of homicide in self-defence.

Two courses are open to us: (a) to believe as true the story of Marlowe's attack on Frizer from behind, corroborated in so far as it is by the wounds on Frizer's head, which wounds must have been inflicted *before* Marlowe received his death-blow; or (b) to suppose that Frizer, Poley, and Skeres after the slaying, and in order to save Frizer's life on a plea of self-defence, concocted a lying account of Marlowe's behaviour, to which they swore at the inquest, and with which they deceived the jury.

The latter seems to me a possible but rather unlikely view of the case. In all probability the men had been drinking deep – the party had lasted from ten in the morning until night! – and the bitter debate over the score had roused Marlowe's intoxicated feelings to such a pitch that, leaping from the bed, he took the nearest way to stop Frizer's mouth.

We learn that the quarrel which brought on the fight was a dispute over the reckoning. Money is cause sufficient for a fight; there is no need to drag a woman into the case. The imaginary object of Marlowe's so-called 'lewde loue', about whom so much has been written, is noticeably absent from the picture, both as a cause and as a witness of the fray. In spite of the wishes of Francis Meres and his followers, she must now be returned with thanks to the fertile brain from which she sprang.

IV

Such is the true story of the death of Christopher Marlowe, as I found it in the records, stripped of scandal, and told by sixteen good men and true. But was this to be the end? Who could rest content without finding out more about Ingram Frizer than his mere name? What manner of man was he? What's Christopher to him, or he to Christopher? Questionings of this kind urged me along still farther on his trail; and before many days I had run down such a quantity of facts about his position and personal character that through them the killer of Christopher Marlowe will stand out as a living figure.

And as for Marlowe himself, the spelling of his name as 'Morley' afforded a pregnant suggestion. It led me to an official letter of the highest importance bearing on the dramatist's early life; but that, as Kipling says, is another story.

Halliwell-Phillipps, great biographer of Shakespeare and a mighty man with the records, spoke once and for all for the Nimrods of the archives: 'Which sport is it that elicits the keenest and most genuine enthusiasm – fox-hunting or record-hunting? Undoubtedly the latter.

'For what devotee to field amusements, after galloping day after day for three months in search of a possible fox that does not turn up, would commence another session of the same description with undiminished alacrity? Where is the determined sportsman to be found who would continue to traverse downs and morass if he only winged a miserable sparrow once in a month? Would he persevere for a year or two on the chance of eventually bringing down a woodcock?

'Not a bit of it! The record-hunter is your only true sportsman. Undeterred by hundreds of obstacles – carrying any height of fence – disheartened by no number of failures – merrily henting the stile-a – and, above all, when he once does catch a sight of his bird, never missing it!'

Foxes? Sparrows? Woodcocks? If such small deer stir his blood, picture the high adventure of a chase through a noble forest of parchment three hundred years old – and, at the end of the day, big game.

Dr Hubert
EDGAR LUSTGARTEN

On holiday by the sea you may dispense with the conventions
that normally govern the acquirement of new friends. What is
strictly taboo for the respectable citizens of London or
Birmingham when they are at home is perfectly good form for
those same respectable citizens when they are at Brighton or
Weston-super-Mare.

Especially does this operate among the younger folk. The
retrieval of a beach ball, adjacent deckchairs on the pier, an
involuntary smile at a third encounter on the front – these
will sometimes fulfil the same purpose as the most formal
introductions do elsewhere.

So nobody need be shocked because Miss Doreen Marshall – a charming girl of good family and irreproachable
background – struck up chance acquaintance with a smooth-
mannered young man while staying at Bournemouth in the
July of 1946. Nobody need be shocked because she – who
had served in the WRNS during the war – accepted from
him – who plausibly styled himself an RAF Group Captain
– a proposal that they should dine at his hotel. Nobody need
be shocked even though he escorted her when, at midnight,
she departed.

Not shocked at all; just perhaps surprised. Unless – like
me – you have ceased to be surprised at women's woeful,
often catastrophic, lack of judgement in reading the pointers
to a character from a face.

Neville Heath – for such in reality was the man known to
Doreen Marshall as Group Captain Brooke – has been
described by some as 'handsome' or 'good looking'. Perhaps I
do not correctly understand these terms. His low forehead,
his gelatinous eyes, the ugly and sinister curtailment of the

skull, his anomalous dimpled chin, his anomalous cupid's bow, above all the parted mouth with its hint of uncontained saliva – these would always suggest to me, without profit of hindsight, some form of depravity or perversion.

In that respect, however, through age and sex and – unsought – experience, I should have had what is called the edge on Doreen Marshall.

She did not guess that her new friend was a cheap crook and show-off, with a criminal record overshadowing all his adult life. Still less did she guess that, at the very moment they were exchanging dinner-table banter, he was wanted – urgently wanted – by the Yard.

Still less did she guess the reason why: that they suspected him (and rightly) of murdering a woman two weeks ago in London – a murder accompanied by mutilations so sadistic and obscene that it is agony to read the pathologist's report.

Doreen Marshall guessed nothing. She was as naïve as she was pretty. Untroubled, she walked with him through the pine-scented Bournemouth night.

Five days later her corpse was found in Branksome Chine – torn and outraged even more than that of her London predecessor. . . .

Heath met police questioning with a complete denial. He had left Doreen Marshall at the pier, he said; while still in his view she had crossed the road and gone into the gardens; what happened to her after that was not within his knowledge. (He gave this lie some colour by adding that he had been half expecting her to phone.)

Thus Heath bluffed it out in the station-house at Bournemouth. But it was – literally – a different story at his trial.

Though Heath had also been *charged* with murdering Doreen Marshall, that trial concerned his earlier victim, Margery Gardner. And under the rules that protect a prisoner in our British courts, during that trial the prosecution were debarred from making any reference to his second crime. It was the *defence* that deliberately introduced it, admitting – or rather, insisting on – Heath's guilt, in an attempt to buttress their plea of insanity without which there would have been no defence at all.

The two murders in succession – so ran the argument – indicated 'progressive mania'; especially as the injuries in the second murder achieved the grisly feat of being worse than in the first. J.D. Casswell, Heath's highly skilled defender, made great play with this in opening his case. This progressive mania, he said, formed the foundation for the evidence to be given by Dr Hubert – the latter being the psychiatrist on whom rested the success or otherwise of Heath's insanity plea.

'In having Doctor Hubert as a witness,' Casswell told the jury, 'you are extremely fortunate.' Considered in perspective, these words have an ironic ring. Certainly Doctor Hubert boasted a long and resounding list of psychiatric qualifications. But the jury's good fortune – if it were such – in having him as a witness resided less in these than in his enlightening if unwilling demonstration of the arrant rubbish that may be talked upon occasion by a highly qualified person in the box.

The keen mind that enforced and controlled this demonstration was that of Anthony Hawke, leading counsel for the Crown.

His cross-examination vied in its economy with its effectiveness.

'Doctor Hubert, may I take it from your evidence that at the time Heath murdered Margery Gardner he knew that he was doing something that was wrong?'

'No,' said the psychiatric expert flatly.

'May I take it that he knew what he was doing?'

'Yes,' conceded the psychiatric expert.

'So he knew when he inflicted seventeen lashes on her with a thong that he was inflicting seventeen lashes on her with a thong?'

'Yes.'

'But he did not know that that was wrong?'

'No.'

Hawke neatly inverted his previous question.

'Then at the time he was inflicting those injuries he thought that it was right?'

'Yes,' said Doctor Hubert, after a short pause.

'Because he is a sadist?'

'Yes,' said Doctor Hubert.

'A person who acquires satisfaction by inflicting cruelty?'

'Yes,' said Doctor Hubert.

'Because he could only obtain satisfaction by inflicting cruelty, you say that he thought he was *right* to inflict it, do you?'

'Yes,' said Doctor Hubert.

Hawke, with infinite restraint, never raised his voice.

'Are you saying that a person in that frame of mind is free from criminal responsibility if what he does causes bodily harm or death?'

Doctor Hubert – rather late – began to feel the skids beneath him. He answered affirmatively, but without enthusiasm.

Hawke played his ace.

'Would it be your view that a person who finds it convenient to forge a cheque in order to free himself from financial responsibility is entitled to say that he thought it was right?'

Doctor Hubert temporized and argued; but in the end there was no escape.

'Would such a man be entitled to claim exemption from responsibility on the grounds of insanity?'

'Yes,' Doctor Hubert ludicrously said.

More followed, but the Crown was already home. Heath's insanity defence rightly met rejection and his conviction for the murder of Margery Gardner brought upon him the appropriate penalty.

So it has never been formally and officially proved that he murdered Doreen Marshall. That would have been superfluous. It is impossible to hang even a monster twice.

A Pennyworth of Murder
THOMAS M. McDADE

No collector should try to explain what prompts him to collect the things he does; it would only be a rationalization of impulses not clearly understood. There is even less reason, in my own case, to account for a passion for collecting the literature of crime in the form of books, pamphlets, newspapers or reward notices. It is better, perhaps, that I am ignorant of the inner conflicts which compel this morbid and sanguinary interest.

Whatever the unconscious reasons may be, I know I will read through a stout volume of some forgotten trial to discover one incident which makes the scalp tingle and brings that sensation which the French describe as 'frisson'. Such an episode was that described in the trial of Maria Manning, who murdered Patrick O'Connor. Having buried her friend under the floor of her kitchen, for some days thereafter that young woman went calmly about the business of preparing meals, with no thought of Mr O'Connor in his cramped quarters underfoot.

It is claiming too much, perhaps, to count the reporting of these events as literature, and I shall be the last to defend my taste on that ground. On the other hand, certain publications devoted to this gory subject can claim at least honourable mention in the history of the graphic arts.

During the eighteenth and nineteenth centuries, there was sold on the streets of England's principal cities a kind of literature devoted to the bloody details of the latest murder or a thrilling account of the most recent public execution. 'Written expressly for the amusement of the lower orders', as one commentator notes, these penny or halfpenny sheets were hawked by street vendors who shouted the headlines, startling the populace with 'Dreadful Murder', 'Pool of Blood', 'Female Body', 'Eaten by Rats', 'Missing Head'.

These broadsides were known in their day, at least by the men who sold them, as 'Dying Confessions', or 'Dying Speeches'. In a sense they were not unlike the extra of our newspapers of the pre-radio era, except that each issue was generally devoted to a single crime, a paper with a single story. In addition, the vocabulary of the editors was so rich in sanguinary adjectives and visceral details as to make twentieth-century journalism appear anaemic by comparison.

That this appetite for gore is not confined to the 'lower orders' has been remarked by De Quincey. 'The world, in general, gentlemen, are very bloody-minded; and all they want in a murder is a copious effusion of blood; gaudy display in this point is enough for them.' If we, today, can be said to be less attracted to the purely crimson aspects of crime, it is for reasons more closely related to our subconscious desires than our conscious ones. As one observer has noted, the preoccupation of the Victorians with murderous melodrama was closely related to an extreme sexual prudery in literature. Whatever the reason, no writing of today matches these vignettes of the horrendous.

The shops in which these papers were produced did a regular business of job printing, pouring out a wide selection of chap books, children's spellers, story books, lampoons, political satires, squibs, ballads, valentines, almanacs, hymns, and poetry. In London most of them clustered about the Seven Dials, which Dickens, as Boz, sketched in 'Meditations on Monmouth Street'.

'Seven Dials! the region of song and poetry – first effusions, and last dying speeches.'

Many of the facts which made up the 'news' story were lifted from the regular newspapers which the poorer classes rarely saw. While the type was being set, a woodcut to illustrate it was either made up or, more frequently, selected from a stock on hand. The supply of such woodcuts included standard scenes; such as a hanging, with one, two or three victims; a scene of a man killing a woman; a woman killing a man; or courtroom views. The illustration was not always exactly appropriate to the text, for the crime may have taken place in the street where a woman shot a man, while the woodcut shows the victim being stabbed in a boudoir.

In the selection of type for the headlines, the greatest variety and imagination were shown. The result is eye-catching, though some of the more quaint examples suggest a self-conscious naïveté which looks like an imitation of itself. The whole composition of the page was often enhanced by running part of the caption up the left-hand side of the sheet and down the right, framing the page in bold-faced type. As a further touch, ornaments and borders of printer's flowers were often added, sometimes ending in a tailpiece. Some printers would engage in a little self-advertising at the bottom when space permitted, for example:

London; printed by G. Smeeton, 74, Tooley Street, Southwark; where are constantly on Sale a great Variety of SLIP SONGS, BALLADS &c. carefully printed on yellow wove paper – 'PATTERS', detailing AUTHENTIC Narratives of Remarkable ACCIDENTS, SHIPWRECKS, MURDERS, EXECUTIONS, &c. &c. Shopkeepers supplied on liberal terms. Country and Foreign Orders particularly attended to.

No piece of gallows literature would be complete without the appropriate 'Lamentable Verses'. These most frequently purported to have been written by the murderer but were actually the product of a small fraternity of hacks. Publishers tried to hold on to a good verse writer, but these gentlemen often sold the same script to two different printers. They could get away with this occasionally, as each printer accused the other of plagiarizing from his paper.

In his *Curiosities of Street Literature*, Hindley quotes one of the writers, 'I get one shilling for the verses *written by the wretched culprit*, the night previous to his execution.'

All such verses have a stylized beginning, of which this is a typical example:

You feeling Christians give attention,
Young and old of each degree.

A tale of sorrow I will mention,
Join and sympathize with me.

After this appropriate invocation, there follows a recital of
the facts of the crime. While, in most cases, these verses were
of the crudest, with scant attention to rhyme and metre, on
occasion one rises above the mass and achieves wider fame.
Due in part, no doubt, to the recognition of Thackeray, Scott,
and other British writers, one verse of a ballad on the murder
of William Weare by John Thurtell has earned 'its place
among the gems of British national poesy'. Like that American classic of *poetica criminis* which tells of Lizzie Borden and
her axe, it draws a vivid picture in four short lines:

His throat they cut from ear to ear,
His brains they punched in;
His name was Mr William Weare,
Wot lived in Lyon's Inn.

The verse invariably concluded with a fine show of pen-
ance and resignation, acknowledging the justice of the fate the
criminal was about to receive and admonishing others to
avoid the path of evil.

Oh, pray, young man, by me take warning
Remember me and what I done,
Ponder yes, oh! and consider,
Let passion you not overcome.
I did the deed in the height of passion
I had no animosity
Little thought my tender parents,
I should die upon a gallows tree.

Of that poet one may say, as was said of Probert, one of
Thurtell's accomplices, that his grammar was almost as bad as
his heart.

When there was no crime in real life to report to the masses,
the publishers were not above inventing a faked crime or
'dreadful calamity'. Such false reports were known as 'cocks'
or 'catch-pennies'. Hotten's Slang Dictionary defines 'cocks'
as 'fictitious narratives, in verse or prose, of murders, fires

and terrible accidents, sold on the streets as true accounts'. The word 'cock' may possibly be a corruption of cook, a cooked statement.

Nor did the event need to be entirely fictitious. Hindley quotes one vendor of papers in his *History of the Catnach Press*:

> I remember well the falling of the Brunswick Theatre, out White Chapel way. It was a rare good thing for all running and standing patterers in and about ten miles of London. Every day we all killed more and more people – in our 'Latest Particulars'. One day there was twenty persons killed, the next day thirty or forty, until it got at last to be worked up to about a hundred and all killed. Then we killed all sorts of people, the Duke of Wellington, and all the Dukes and Duchesses, Bishops, swell nobs and snobs we could think of at the moment.

The cock is distinguished from the genuine report by its lack of particularity as to dates, names and places. There is a general vagueness on these matters which permits its use on any occasion.

The vendors of these papers were a breed apart, many of them having spent forty to fifty years in selling them. Mayhew in his *London Labour and the London Poor* gives a good description of these men. There were known as patterers, the running patterer moving freely about the city, usually in groups of three or four, and descending upon a neighbourhood, creating an air of tremendous excitement and urgency by their terrible cries. The standing patterer, like the kiosk news vendor of today, had a permanent stand from which he shouted his wares.

When there were no 'dying confessions' or 'cocks' to sell, the patterer fell back on a staple known in the trade as 'ballads on a subject'. This was a set of verses on a subject of popular interest, such as the royal family or a local anecdote or story. These were sung by the patterer to a popular tune and, given a good tune and the right neighbourhood, the patterer could sell them steadily. The right neighbourhood was important: 'Ratcliff Highway – that's a splendid quarter for working – there's plenty of feeling – but, bless you, some places you go to you can't move no how, they've hearts like paving stones. They wouldn't have the "papers" if you'd give them to 'em – especially when they knows you.'

The crime of James Greenacre in December 1836 was of such notoriety as to be comparable to the Snyder-Gray case. On January 6, 1837, a bargeman pulled out of the Regent's Canal a human head which had been caught in the lock gate. It was fitted to a human trunk found some distance away, and the legs were found later in an osier bed in Camberwell. The remains could only be identified as an unknown female, and the head was preserved in spirits of wine in the hopes it would be recognized.

In March it was identified as that of Hannah Brown, a widow who had been missing since Christmas. James Greenacre, an intended husband of the deceased, was arrested, as was his paramour, Sarah Gale. In his confession Greenacre claimed that he had quarrelled with Mrs Brown and knocked her down in a moment of anger. Thinking he had killed her, he decided to dispose of the body. While she was senseless, but still alive, he cut off her head and then dismembered the body.

The most ghastly part of his measures to dispose of the body deal with his getting rid of the head. This, wrapped up in a silk handkerchief, he carried under his coat flaps through the streets. Boarding a crowded London omnibus, he nearly passed out with fright when, on asking the conductor the fare, he received the stunning reply: 'Six pence a *head*.'

Because of the cold-blooded brutality of the crime, the case aroused the greatest interest. It was estimated by Hindley that over 1,650,000 broadsides were issued describing the crime, trial, confession, and execution. Despite this great volume, one of the street vendors reported: 'Greenacre didn't sell so well as might have been expected for such a diabolical out and out crime as he committed; but you see he came close after Pegsworth, and that took the beauty off him. Two murderers is no good to nobody.'

Another broadside, reporting the arrest of Thomas Ainslie and James Martin on suspicion of the murder of Henry Shepherd, is rare, in that the illustration depicts the actual crime and is not a standard cut. The description of the crime is in the best tradition of the horripilant school of reporting:

> The unfortunate man was found inhumanly murdered in his counting house, his head had been smashed to atoms, the brains were strued & a piece of the scull from the back part of the head lying about 2 ft. from the body; at a distance from the deceased a Poker with which no doubt the bloody deed was committed was found cover'd with blood, the brains was covered with hair, and found spattered on the ceiling of the room, and on the door of the Iron Safe about 7 ft. high.

This broadside may be unique in having a flowered border containing the rose, thistle, and shamrock, emblematic of England, Scotland and Ireland. I have been unable to discover whether Ainslie and Martin were ever tried for this crime, which occurred in December 1832, or whether they were victims of a police round-up of known criminals.

Another broadside in my collection reporting a famous case concerns the murder of Carlo Ferrari. This lad was the victim of the London 'Burkers', in 1831, and the crime revived a public horror which had swept England three years before. In December 1828, the people were fascinated and terrified in turn by the revelations of the deeds of Burke and Hare, the body-snatchers of Edinburgh. Too lazy or timid to steal the bodies of the newly interred from the churchyard burying grounds, these two culprits had dispatched sixteen persons and sold the bodies to the anatomical schools which sought cadavers for instruction. Burke had been hanged for one of these crimes and himself dissected by Dr Alexander Monro, in what was probably the premier autopsy in history, some thirty thousand persons parading through the doctor's rooms to view the body and hear the lecture on it. Thereafter Burke's name became synonymous with murder for profit.

On November 5, 1831, James May, who had regularly made his living supplying the hospitals and anatomical schools of London with dead bodies, and a companion, John Bishop, asked Hill, the porter of King's College, if he 'wanted anything', the euphemism for offering a body. When asked what he had, he replied, 'A boy of fourteen.'

At Hill's suggestion, he returned a little later with Williams, carrying a hamper containing the body of a boy, for which they agreed to accept nine guineas. One of the surgeons, being struck by the freshness of the body, suspected foul play and delayed the men until the arrival of the police.

The body was identified as that of Carlo Ferrari, an Italian boy who made a living by exhibiting white mice on the street. Bishop and Williams had enticed the boy to their lodgings where he was drugged and, while insensible, lowered head down into a well until suffocated. The boy's teeth were extracted as a by-product and sold to a dentist named Mills for twelve shillings, real teeth being the preferred replacement in that day. They had some difficulty finding a customer for the body, having been turned down at Guy's Hospital and three private schools before approaching Hill.

All three were tried, convicted, and sentenced to hang, but May was respited when Bishop and Williams confessed and exculpated him from a part in the murder. These two admitted two other murders, a woman named Fanny Pigburn and a boy named Cunningham. The broadside reproduces three attempts at likenesses of the culprits. It was evidently printed the day before the execution, for no mention is made of the commutation of May's sentence to transportation for life.

Once convicted, the sentence was carried out with appalling swiftness. The trial had been held on Friday and the hanging was on Monday, a regular practice in disposing of the previous week's cases. At the execution great excitement prevailed. Many persons were hurt in the tremendous crowds, and the *Weekly Dispatch* sold over 50,000 copies of the number which contained the confession of the murderers.

The crime had one notable social benefit. The tremendous publicity given the case proved the final impetus needed to effect the passage of the Anatomy Act, which provided a legalized means of procuring bodies for the study of anatomy. In August 1832, the bill became a law and with this act the trade of body-snatching, like that of the modern bootlegger, soon passed into oblivion.

Two factors brought to an end the publishing of gallows literature. First, the newspapers themselves began to publish more of the details of crime, a concession to the demands of the masses. Second, the passing of public executions. On August 13, 1868, the first 'private' execution was held in the Maidstone Jail and, since executions were no longer public events like horse races or auctions, the 'dying speeches' also passed out.

If the villains of the times have attracted more attention than the heroes, we need be neither critical nor cynical. The public has its right to be entertained, and who is to say what great universal compulsion in all of us is not purged in the murders we read of in our papers? As one of the running patterers said, 'There's nothing beats a stunning good murder, after all.'

Sob Sisters Emerge
EDMUND PEARSON

Maria Barberi had become angry with her lover. He still refused to marry her – although, by all the laws of God and man, he ought to have done that any time for more than a year. She got a razor, an unpleasant, jagged razor, which looked as if it had been used not only to sharpen pencils but to open tin cans.

The faithless one – his name was Domenico Cataldo – was sitting in a bar-room, playing cards with some friends. Maria crept up behind him, and very efficiently cut his throat. In doing this, as any newspaper reader knows, she observed the conventional limit of the gash – it was 'from ear to ear'.

Cataldo, thoroughly dismayed, rose from his chair and rushed into the street. Pausing in front of the bar-room, at the corner of Avenue A and Fourteenth Street, he remarked:

'I die!'

And, falling upon the pavement, he instantly made good his statement. The police led Maria away to prison.

With her family, a few years before, Maria had come to New York from southern Italy. She met Cataldo in the street. Her father warned her against the man, but his allure was great. He had four hundred dollars in the bank, and to this he added as much more – from what source I cannot tell you. He and Maria set up housekeeping (disregarding all omens) on Thirteenth Street.

From time to time, so said Maria, Cataldo uttered a promise of matrimony. But he said less and less about it, and finally, on the day of the throat-slitting, expressed the utmost contempt for the holy estate. His exact words were:

'Only pigs marry.'

This obviously incorrect assertion seemed to need no reply. Maria, however, found it exasperating. So she had recourse to the crushing rejoinder of the razor, and now Cataldo was in the morgue, and she was in the Tombs.

Three months later, in July 1895, Maria sat in court, wearing her usual bovine expression. On the bench, as in all proper murder trials of that period, was Recorder Goff. This old Irish gentleman, with his white beard and gentle voice, has gone down in tradition as a 'hanging judge'. This is because he had the idea – even then curiously antiquated – that the criminal law does not exist to be made into the likeness of a monkey.

The first trial of Maria Barberi was brief. There could be no denial of the killing. The character of Cataldo was discussed, but the Recorder simply told the jury that the question for them was not whether the dead man might have been a saint or a devil. It was: Had Maria deliberately murdered him? They conferred for one hour, and answered that she had.

Not long afterwards, Recorder Goff sentenced her to death. He was presently to learn that the law not only can be made into a monkey, it can be transformed into a three-ring circus, with a cageful of baboons.

The newspapers presently discovered that if Maria were executed in the electric chair, she would be the first woman so to suffer. Straightway, the founts of emotion were unseated; the sob sisters were gathered together; and for a year and a half there beat upon Sing Sing Prison, upon the Tombs, and upon the Criminal Courts, the rolling billows of a mighty ocean of mush.

The Governor might have chosen the expedient of commuting the sentence to a term of years in prison. But the law still held that Maria was a murderess; while to all the hysterical folk in the land, the death sentence had converted her into a heroine, a broken blossom, and a martyr of the tyrant Man. Nothing but complete exoneration would satisfy: to punish her original prosecutors, Maria must not only be set free, but walk on roses.

When she went into court for sentence, the *Tribune* noted the group of sympathizing women: her aunt; the Contessa di

Brazza Savargnon; and others. She – I think the *Tribune* means the aunt, and not the Contessa – was frisked as she entered court and found to be carrying a stiletto with a blade five inches long. During the second trial it would have been most unpopular to record that any of Maria's supporters went so well heeled.

The *Tribune*, however, coldly refrained from ecstasies about Maria Barberi, and even said something about 'sentimentality run wild'.

The Contessa di Brazza Savargnon announced that, for her part, she intended to leave no stone unturned in her efforts to secure justice for Maria. The Contessa's participation gratified the newspapers, and helped to lift the case out of the lowly atmosphere of Avenue A.

People began to send in petitions and write wrathfully to the newspapers. The story of Maria's blow for oppressed womanhood had rallied the advocates of 'Women's Rights' and inflamed the country. On the same day, groups of people as widely separated as 'the Italo-Americans of Texas' and the summer boarders at the Griswold Hotel, near New London, sent red-hot messages to the Governor of New York. Austin Corbin and Colonel Bob Ingersoll began to boil.

The sentence was denounced as a 'ferocious absurdity'. An indignant native American, resident of Connecticut, wrote in to say that as women had had no part in making the laws, they were not responsible to the laws – a theory which must have delighted the noble army of shoplifters. This gentleman added, as a clincher, that in writing his letter he had used an inkstand which once belonged to 'the great Garibaldi'.

One man, in Fort Scott, Kansas, sent to the Governor of New York demanding transportation to Sing Sing so that he could be electrocuted instead of Maria. Being about to die for her, he could not be expected to pay his fare too.

In August, the hot and silly season, the whole country seemed to be exploding with indignation towards that callous set of brutes, the male citizens of New York. Five or ten years were subtracted from Maria's age, and she was called 'this child of fifteen'. That she had voluntarily lived as Cataldo's mistress for more than a year was, of course, quite ignored, and she was described as a Lucrece, desperately striking in defence of her 'unsullied purity'.

The massed chivalry of Arkansas arose, and, in a petition signed by the Governor and all the state officials, apprised Governor Morton of New York as to the correct conduct of a man of honour.

Instead of some short cut, like a commutation of sentence, Maria was granted another trial, to which she came in November 1896 – two weeks after Mr McKinley's election to the Presidency. This trial is thought to have marked the first great emergence of the sob sisters. They were already in existence, but never before had they been given a chance to utter such a universal moan, or to compose so many columns of unmitigated tripe. It is to be admitted that some of the worst of the sob sisters, as well as those who directed it all, were really brothers.

The *Journal* and the *World* were contending for supremacy. The *Journal* had an artist, who, every Sunday, drew a picture of a nauseous boy in a yellow nightgown, and the *World* had an artist who also drew a nauseous boy in a yellow nightgown, and although the colour of those nightgowns was extended, in popular phrase, to cover both papers, there was still no decision as to which was the better. Each claimed ownership of the 'Yellow Kid'.

Both papers set out to convert into a great human tragedy a murder trial which contained neither mystery, nor romance, nor legal or social importance. The conduct of the lawyers was perhaps equally footling, and the result illustrated the ability of the public to go – for one month – perfectly cuckoo about something for which they do not care a solitary damn.

No reporter, no artist, could endow Maria with beauty. She was squat in face and in figure. The newspaper illustrations at that time could make even Mrs Langtry look like a scarecrow, and to little Signorina Barberi they did cruel justice. Nor was it discoverable – in spite of rumours – that 'the stork was hovering over the Tombs'. So the reporters had to content themselves with a lesser bird: Maria's canary, which was in a cage in her cell. His name was Cicillo, and he and the Contessa di Brazza Savargnon flutter in and out of the story.

After a few preliminary accounts of Maria in her dungeon (the solitary sunbeam that fell on the cold stones – tears of the lonely girl – the dawning of hope – 'a prayer and all is bright again') the newspapers allowed the trial to begin. Justice Goff was no longer presiding. Messrs McIntyre and Lauterbach were cast for the parts of First and Second Ruffian – that is, they represented the People – Messrs Friend, House and Grossman for the defence.

Maria had learned English in her sixteen months at Sing Sing. She was supported in court by the 'Tombs Angel', a being whom the newspaper artist made to look as gloomy as the gates of Tartarus. Her function was to restore Maria from time to time by means of 'peptonoids', of which she had a bottle in her pocket. Everybody who read the *Journal* or the *World* knew how often, and at what times, the Angel slipped Maria a peptonoid.

Maria had crocheted a silk purse, not out of the traditional sow's ear but from the orthodox material, and also a chatelaine bag. She ornamented them both with jet beads, and gave them to 'Lawyer Friend'. The *World* also showed large-scale views of Maria's ears. It discussed Lombroso's theories, and asked, *Is she a degenerate?*

The defence was 'psychical epilepsy'. Mr House described the prisoner's life, and her family history in Italy for three generations. Her ruin had been accomplished by means of drugs. In the 1890s no girl was ever ruined except by drugs. Sometimes the rascal put the drug into her soda water; in especially wicked instances, into beer. Maria had been ruined both ways.

A genealogical chart was produced: it showed that Maria was descended from the Barbellis on one side and Bonfantis on the other. Both families were full of insanity and epilepsy. The lawyer mentioned other allied families, all lunatics. Maria had an uncle who was an 'exhibitionist'; he used to take his friends to a tavern, treat them to drinks all round, get himself drunk, and then, tearing his clothes off, run down the street shouting.

Cataldo had 'insulted' the girl for days. Finally, everything 'went blank', and Maria killed him.

What these newspapers thought about her is undiscoverable. On the same page with articles recounting her sweetness, her prayers, her Christian kindliness, would be enlarged plans of the palms of her hands, with especial emphasis on her 'degenerate thumb' and her 'abnormal nail'.

Astrologer Bache cast her horoscope, and the papers reproduced it. The progressive Luna had reached the evil Uranus, while Mars and Neptune by transit were retrograde. So there was danger of 'ultimate collapse', but while her life would be spared, she would hardly escape 'a milder touch of the law'. This looked as if the stars in their courses were hedging, and even so they guessed wrong.

Maria's mother, a grim old lady in a mantilla, gave evidence. The headlines for that day were: *Tortured in Court, Mother Gives Way. 'Oh My Head!' She Moans.* This was because she was cross-examined.

Maria was a witness in her own behalf. The artists were waiting for this. She sat under the mural painting of the Three Fates, in the Supreme Court Room, and the pictures all showed the skull in that painting as ominously near Maria's head.

QUESTION (*by Mr House*): Maria, were you a good girl before you met Cataldo?

ANSWER (*in a whisper*): Yes.

'Don't cry, my dear,' said Mr House.

Maria had her handkerchief to her eyes, but wept very little.

That afternoon, Mr McIntyre, for the prosecution, refrained from cross-examination. So she kissed his hand and told him that, the very first night at Sing Sing, she had prayed for him. This was the first of many kissings, and the artists drew pictures of them all. Mr McIntyre, although a great, big, strong assistant district attorney wearing a bowler hat, was all broken up. He moved aside – thirty sob sisters marked him well – and 'something like a tear' glistened in his eye.

Next day, however, he questioned her at length. So she *Wept on Stand* and *Collapsed in Cell*. (Pictures of both the weeping and the collapsing.)

The high spot of the eighteenth day of the trial came as a surprise. Angelo Piscopo, friend and neighbour, was testifying as to Maria's infirmities. Nobody had suspected Mr Piscopo's accomplishments as an actor of the Grand Guignol school. When he was asked about the prisoner's fits, he suddenly uttered a dismal howl and gave such an imitation of epilepsy that two of the sob sisters became hysterical and had to be removed from court, while the Tombs Angel ran out of peptonoids.

The next day was given over to social pastimes and amenities. 'Lawyer Friend' had his forty-third birthday. Maria gave him a silver lead pencil and a letter full of gratitude. The other members of the bar – on both sides – united in buying him a fine luncheon and a large basket of red roses. All – as Captain Andy Hawks would say – all one big, happy family. Afternoon tea was served in the Tombs for Maria and other guests. Mrs Sarah Bird poured.

Around Mulberry Bend was being sold a street ballad:

'Tis not for me to speak aloud
On lofty themes. I tell
As one among the lowly crowd
How young Maria fell.

Swift as a flash a glittering blade
Across his throat she drew,
'By you,' she shrieked, 'I've been betrayed:
This vengeance is my due!'

Behold her now, a wounded dove:
A native of a clime
Where hearts are melted soon with love
And maddened soon to crime.

Meanwhile, greater days were preparing. The more costly methods of wasting time were yet to be employed. Outside, expert alienists were pawing the ground and shouting Ha! Ha! among the trumpets. There were five great doctors on each side. So all day long the noise of battle rolled.

Doctor Hrdlicka, one of Maria's doctors, was asked by Mr McIntyre if, when he measured Maria with Benedict's instruments, he knew that Professor Langer of Vienna had found them to be .07 of a centimetre short.

Said the Doctor: 'I didn't use Benedict's. I used the *compas d'épaisseur* of Glissière, the cephalometer of Anthelme, and the bregma indicator of Broca.'

'Oh,' said Mr McIntyre.

The following day, the lawyer put over a fast one and nearly evened the score. He showed the Doctor some unlabelled charts and plans of human craniums; and almost trapped the learned scientist into branding as 'abnormal' President Grover Cleveland, Senator David B. Hill, George Vanderbilt, and Judge Gildersleeve, who was presiding over the trial.

Finally, all topics of conversation having been exhausted, the lawyers and doctors were reduced to discussing whether baldness and premature grey hairs are signs of degeneracy.

After about a month of this solemn balderdash, at a public cost of two or three hundred dollars a day, the jury deliberated for one hour and acquitted the prisoner. There were more kissings and embracings.

'My dear, I never doubted for an instant that you were a good, honest girl,' said the prosecutor.

The *World* and the *Journal* each reproduced her autographed letters of thanks to the editors. She was offered five hundred dollars a week by two or three dime museums. Her return to the Tombs was a triumph.

'Let me in, let me in!' the girl cried, beating with her chubby hands against the grating. She laughed loudly. There was no ray of triumph, of jubilation in the laugh. She was a baby, free again, playing like a baby at going to prison. Keeper John Hurley opened the grating.

When she got in, all the warders had to be kissed. The

Contessa had been mislaid, but someone at last reached her by telephone. Maria greeted her over the wire.

'Hello, the Contessa!' she cried. 'I am so glad!'

Outside the Tombs, the crowd continued to cheer.

Cicillo, the canary, for some reason, did not get out that night. A day or two later, Maria, accompanied by 'Lawyer Friend' and a shoal of reporters and artists, made a special visit and recovered him.

Meanwhile – the papers recorded it, but drew no inferences – over in Brooklyn, one Mrs James Dockery had found Mr Dockery too tiresome. She cut his throat with a razor, and he was removed to an emergency hospital. According to later reports, Mr Dockery was in 'a highly critical condition'.

The Arran Murder

WILLIAM ROUGHEAD

The isle of Arran, as most readers know, lies in the estuary of the Clyde, between the pleasant shores of Carrick and Kintyre. To the north, beyond the Kyles of Bute, are the sea-lochs, moors, and mountains of Argyll; southward the Craig of Ailsa stands sentinel in the wider Firth. The first prospect of the island, whether from the Ayrshire coast or from the deck of some passing vessel in the fairway, is unforgettable – the majestic outline of the serrated peaks soaring out of the sea to pierce the rain clouds too often wreathed about their summits, the sunlight gleaming on their granite flanks, wet from some recent shower, and over all, austere and solitary, the great grey cone of Goatfell, 'the mountain of the winds'. Amidst these formidable giants are many glens, some bare and savage as themselves, others domesticated as it were by the kindly uses of man; while at their feet lie certain bays whose yellow sands, beloved by generations of children, are, alas! no 'undiscovered country' to the excursionist.

At the time of which we write, the moral and physical atmosphere of the island was above reproach; wickedness and manufactories were alike unknown. The larger villages boasted each its own constable, who embodied the law in some peaceful cottage, incongruously labelled 'Police Station'; but these officers led a life of ease and dignity among the blameless lieges, being only called upon to exercise their functions now and then on the person of an obstreperous tripper. Yet this fortunate isle was to become the scene of a crime, characterized at a later stage as 'unprecedented and incredibly atrocious'.

On the forenoon of Friday, 12th July 1889, the once

famous Clyde steamer *Ivanhoe*, in the course of her daily run to Arran from the upper reaches of the Firth, called at Rothesay, the 'capital' of Bute. Among the passengers who then joined the vessel was a party from Glenburn Hydropathic, including a young Englishman named Edwin Robert Rose, a clerk in the employment of a Brixton builder, then spending his fortnight's holiday in Scotland. He was thirty-two years of age, of light build, five feet seven in height, of athletic, active habits, and in the best of health and spirits. On the sail to Arran he struck up an acquaintance with a fellow-passenger, a young man who gave his name as Annandale, and they landed together at Brodick for an hour or so until the steamer's return from Whiting Bay. Apparently they had decided to take lodgings in the village, for shortly after the steamer's arrival Annandale presented himself at the house of Mrs Walker, Invercloy, and inquired for rooms. Invercloy is the name of the village, Brodick that of the district. It was then the Glasgow Fair week, and the limited accommodation available was taxed to its utmost limits. Mrs Walker, however, was able to offer a room with one bed, in a wooden structure adjoining her house, having a separate entrance from the outside. Annandale agreed to take it for a week, stating that he came from Tighnabruaich, and that his room would be shared by a friend who could not remain longer than the following Wednesday. It was arranged that they should occupy the room next day, and that Annandale was to take his meals there, while Rose got his at Mrs Woolley's tea-shop in the village. They returned together to Rothesay that afternoon, and Annandale accompanied Rose to the Hydropathic, where the latter introduced him to some of his friends.

Two of these named Mickel and Thom, who also intended spending the week-end at Brodick, left for Arran by the *Ivanhoe* on Saturday, the 13th, and were joined on board by Rose and Annandale. Mickel and Thom were unable to find rooms, and slept on a friend's yacht in the bay. From the Saturday to Monday the four men saw a good deal of each other, walking and boating together, and occasionally meeting at meals in Woolley's shop. Mr Mickel formed an unfavourable opinion of Annandale, who struck him as singularly silent and uncommunicative, and as he could neither find out who that young man was nor where he came from, Mickel more than once strongly advised Rose to get rid of him, even if he had to leave his lodgings, and in particular not to climb Goatfell in his company, as he had proposed to do. Rose promised accordingly, and at half-past three in the afternoon of Monday, 15th July, Mr Mickel and his friend left by the *Ivanhoe*, Rose and Annandale being on the pier to see them off.

Both Mickel and Thom spoke highly of Rose as a young fellow of agreeable manners, very frank and open, and 'ready to take up with strangers'. So far as they knew, he seemed to have plenty of money. He had a watch and chain, and carried a pocket-book, containing a return half-ticket to London, and his luggage consisted of a black leather Gladstone bag. His wardrobe included a chocolate and brown striped tennis-jacket, a grey felt hat, and a white serge yachting cap.

Mrs Walker saw nothing further of her lodgers that day, as, from the situation of their room, they could go out and in without her knowledge. At eleven o'clock on the Tuesday morning she knocked at their door. Getting no answer, she entered and found that the visitors had vanished, together with the two bags which they had brought with them when they came. The room appeared to have been occupied overnight by two persons. A straw hat, a pair of slippers, a waterproof, and a tennis racket had been left behind. Such incidents are probably not unknown to Arran landladies, and the worst that Mrs Walker anticipated was the loss of her rent. She did not report the matter to the police.

Rose's holiday expired on Thursday, 18th July, on which day his brother went to the station in London to meet him. His relatives, alarmed at his non-arrival, telegraphed to the Reverend Mr Goodman, the son of Rose's employer, who was staying at Glenburn Hydropathic, from whom they learned that Rose had gone to Arran with an acquaintance a few days before, and had not returned. On Saturday, the 27th, Rose's brother, accompanied by the Chief Constable of Bute, arrived at Brodick. They ascertained that, in spite of Mickel's warning, the missing man had gone up Goatfell on the Monday afternoon with the mysterious Annandale, who had been seen to leave Brodick alone next morning by the early steamer, and it was believed that Rose had never left the island.

On Sunday, the 28th, a search was organized, every able man willingly taking his share of the work, and various parties began systematically to beat the district. No one unacquainted with the nature of the ground can form any idea of the difficulties attending their efforts. Upon the north and west Goatfell is bounded by a congregation of jagged mountain ridges and fantastic peaks, with deep shadowy glens and grim ravines, the bleak sides of which are furrowed by innumerable gullies and abrupt watercourses – a scene in its awful solitude and grandeur so wild, dreary, and desolate as hardly to be matched in Britain. Day after day the search was continued among the barren screes and boulder-strewn corries, day after day the weary searchers returned unsuccessful to their homes, nor till the evening of the following Sunday, 4th August, was the object of their quest attained.

That day the search party, consisting of upwards of two hundred persons, was divided into three portions, one of which was scouring the east shoulder of Goatfell, at the head of Glen Sannox. Francis Logan, a Corrie fisherman, being high up on the mountain-side, near a place named Coire-na-fuhren, noticed an offensive odour which he traced to a large boulder some distance further up the slope. Built up about its face was a heap of smaller rocks and stones, with pieces of turf and heather inserted between the clefts. On examining this structure more closely, Logan saw among the stones part of a human arm. He at once raised a shout, and Sergeant Munro with others of the search party, including the lost man's brother, were quickly on the spot. When the stones, forty-two in number, were removed, in a cavity beneath the boulder was seen the dead body of a man. The screen of stones which had concealed it, the largest being over a hundredweight, was obviously the work of human hands. Dr Gilmour, Linlithgow, a summer visitor at Corrie, was sent for as the nearest medical man, and until his arrival the body, which was guarded by the police, remained untouched. When the doctor reached the boulder about eight o'clock, he first examined the position of the body, which lay at full length upon its face, and was fully clothed, the skirt of the jacket being turned back over the head, probably to conceal its ghastly appearance while the stones were piled around it. The body was then lifted from beneath the boulder, and having been identified by Mr Rose as that of his missing brother, a thorough examination was made by Dr Gilmour. Nothing was found upon the body; all the pockets were empty, and one of them was turned inside out. On examining the head and face, Dr Gilmour found both 'fearfully and terribly smashed'. Practically the whole of the face and left side of the head was destroyed and in an advanced stage of decomposition, but the body otherwise was uninjured, excepting a fracture of the top of the left shoulder-blade.

While those who found the body were awaiting the doctor's arrival, a search of the surrounding ground was made. Above the boulder the hill slopes steeply upward to the ridge, at an angle of about forty-five degrees, on the line of a deep gully and watercourse, often dry in summer, but in which there was then a small stream. The ground is composed of slabs of granite, rough heather, sand, and gravel, strewn with boulders and loose stones. The following articles, afterwards identified as Rose's property, were found higher up the gully at various distances from the boulder: a walking-stick, lying head downwards, as if dropped; a waterproof, split in two pieces, 'huddled together in a dub, as if they had been trampled upon'; a knife, pencil, and button; and a cap, folded in four, with a large heavy stone on the top of and almost completely concealing it, in the centre of the bed of the stream. On one side of the gully, above where the cap was found, was a clear drop of nineteen feet, while on the other side, lower down, above where the knife and pencil were found, was a similar fall of thirty-two feet.

About nine o'clock the body was placed in a box and taken to the coach-house of Corrie Hotel, where a post-mortem

144

examination was made next day by Dr Gilmour and Dr Fullarton of Lamlash, after which it was buried in the ancient and picturesque burying-ground of Sannox, at the entrance to the glen. On 27th September the body was exhumed by warrant of the Sheriff, to enable Sir Henry (then Dr) Littlejohn and Dr Fullarton to examine more particularly the condition of the internal organs. The conclusion arrived at in the various medical reports as to the injuries which caused death were that these had been produced by direct violence of repeated blows on the left side of the head, inflicted with some heavy, blunt instrument.

We shall now see what, so far as ascertained, were the movements of the mysterious Annandale on the day of the murder.

From the sea-level at the old inn of Brodick – now used in connection with the estate – on the north side of the bay, the way to Goatfell lies through the grounds of Brodick Castle, past the Kennels, and through the woods to the open moor, whence the climber has a clear view of the task before him. Two relatives of Mrs Walker, who knew her lodgers by sight, returning from Goatfell that afternoon, met Annandale and Rose in the Castle grounds about four o'clock. One of them noticed that Rose was wearing a watch-chain. Shortly thereafter the Reverend Mr Hind, with two other visitors from Lamlash, who had left Brodick about three o'clock to climb the fell, were overtaken on the open hill beyond the Castle woods by two young men. One of these (afterwards identified by a photograph as Rose) walked with the party for about half an hour. The other kept steadily some yards ahead, and spoke to no one. Rose mentioned that he came from London, and had been staying at Rothesay. A shower coming on, Mr Hind's party took shelter behind a boulder, but the others, who had waterproofs, continued the ascent. The party could see them going up in front, and when they themselves gained the top about six o'clock, they saw Rose and his companion standing upon the further edge of the plateau from the point at which they reached it. The view from the summit is one of the most extensive and magnificent in Scotland. After enjoying the prospect for about a quarter of an hour, Mr Hind's party descended the mountain by the way they came, reaching Brodick in time for the 8.30 steamer to Lamlash. They saw no more of the young men on the way down, and wondered what had become of them. Two brothers named Francis were photographing on the hill that day; one sat down to rest, while the other went on. After the first reached the top he was joined by his brother, following the two young men, walking in single file. Rose had some conversation with the brothers about the scenery. When they left the summit at six twenty-five they saw these young men standing on a boulder, with their backs to Ailsa Craig, and pointing in the direction of Glen Sannox, as if discussing the way down. This is the last that was seen of Rose alive. The brothers, we may here anticipate, at the trial identified the prisoner as his companion.

There are two recognized routes in descending Goatfell – the direct and comparatively easy one to Brodick, which is that usually taken; and the much longer and more arduous descent by 'The Saddle', the lofty ridge connecting Goatfell with its giant neighbour Cir-Mhor, and forming the head of the two great glens of Rosa and Sannox, which run almost at right-angles from each other. A third way, rarely taken by anyone before this case occurred, save by shepherds or others familiar with the hills, is to go straight down into Glen Sannox from the ridge of North Goatfell by the wild and lonely gully of Coire-na-fuhren. By either of these last routes the climber, having descended into Glen Sannox, follows that glen eastward to its entrance at Sannox Bay, three and a half miles from the ridge, returning to Brodick by the coast road and the village of Corrie, a further distance of seven and a half miles.

At half-past nine o'clock that Monday evening a shepherd named Mackenzie was talking to two servant girls near the old burying-ground of Sannox, when he saw a man coming out of the glen and going in the direction of Corrie. Mackenzie remarked at the time that the man was 'awful tired and worn-out like, and seemed to have had a heavy day's travelling on the hills'. This is the first that was seen of Rose's late companion after they were left together upon the mountain top shortly before half-past six. A few minutes after ten o'clock a visitor standing at the bar of Corrie Hotel was accosted by a stranger, who asked the visitor to order a drink for him, which he could·not get himself as it was after closing time. The barmaid supplied him with some spirits in a bottle, which he took away with him, remarking that he had to walk the six miles to Brodick. He was afterwards identified by his impromptu host.

Next morning (Tuesday, 16th July), Mary Robertson, who had been staying in Invercloy, went to Brodick pier at seven o'clock to take the early steamer to Ardrossan. Between the village and the pier she overtook a man, whom she later identified, carrying two bags, one black, the other brown, on his way to the boat. It happened that on the Saturday before the murder Mickel and Thom had introduced Rose and Annandale to a friend named Gilmour. By a curious chance, Mr Gilmour was returning to Glasgow that morning, and on going on board the *Scotia* at Brodick pier the first person he saw was Annandale, wearing a grey felt hat. They travelled to Greenock together, and Mr Gilmour offered to help Annandale to carry his luggage. He noticed particularly the black leather bag, which his companion took into the compartment with him when they left the steamer at Ardrossan. This, so far as the evidence goes, was the last that was seen of Rose's bag.

On Saturday, 6th July, ten days earlier, a young man, whose card bore the name of 'John Annandale', had taken a room for a fortnight in the house of Mrs Currie, in Iona Place, Port Bannatyne, Rothesay. His luggage consisted of a brown leather bag. On Friday, the 12th, he told his landlady that he was going to Arran for a few days, and left, wearing a straw hat and taking the brown bag with him. On the afternoon of Tuesday, 16th July, he reappeared at Port Bannatyne, wearing a grey felt hat and carying a paper parcel containing, as his landlady afterwards found, a white serge yachting cap and a chocolate and brown striped tennis jacket. These articles he wore during the remainder of his stay. He talked 'quite

147

pleasantly' to Mrs Currie about his visit to Arran, saying that he had been up Goatfell and had enjoyed himself. His time expiring on Saturday, the 20th, he asked her to have his bill and dinner ready at one o'clock. He went out, however, in the forenoon and never returned; all that Mrs Currie got for his fortnight's board and lodging was the yachting cap and a pair of tennis shoes, which were afterwards identified as Rose's property.

Even as Mrs Prig, on a certain historic occasion, boldly expressed her disbelief in the existence of the immortal Mrs Harris, so may the discerning reader have had his own misgivings regarding the genuineness of Mr Annandale. These may now be justified by the statement that this name had been temporarily adopted, for what reason does not appear, by a man named John Watson Laurie, twenty-five years of age, employed as a patternmaker at Springburn Works, Glasgow. Since 8th June of that year he had been living in lodgings at 106 North Frederick Street there, until he went to Rothesay on 6th July. While at Rothesay he met an acquaintance named Aitken, who knew him as Laurie. To him, Laurie pointed out Rose as a gentleman with whom he was going to Arran. Aitken saw him again on Saturday, the 20th, when Laurie was leaving Rothesay for Glasgow. He was then wearing a yachting cap which struck Aitken as very like the one he had seen Rose wear. Aitken asked, 'How did you and your friend get on at Brodick?' to which Laurie replied, 'Oh, very well.' He returned to his Glasgow lodgings and resumed his work as usual on 22nd July. He mentioned to a fellow-lodger that he had a return-half ticket to London. On Wednesday, 31st July, Aitken met him accidentally in Hope Street. That week the fact of Rose's disappearance had been published in the Glasgow newspapers, and Aitken accosted Laurie with the startling question, 'What do you know about the Arran mystery?' Laurie 'hummed and hawed'; and Aitken said, 'Dear me, have you not been reading the papers? Was not Rose the name of the gentleman with whom you went to Brodick?' Laurie said it could not be the same man, as his Mr Rose had returned with him and had since gone to Leeds. Aitken then strongly

148

advised him to communicate what he knew to the authorities, and asked him whose cap he was wearing when they last met at Rothesay. Laurie replied, 'Surely you don't think me a . . .' and did not complete the sentence. He excused himself for leaving Aitken at the moment, as he saw someone approaching whom apparently he wished to avoid, but at Aitken's request he agreed to meet him at his office that evening at six o'clock to give him further particulars. Laurie did not fulfil the engagement, and Aitken never saw him again. Four days later Rose's body was found, and Aitken, so soon as he learned the fact, gave information to the police.

Evidently realizing that Glasgow was now no place for one of his peculiar circumstances, Laurie that day applied to the foreman at the Springburn Works for his wages, saying that he was leaving to be a traveller in the grain trade. He also informed a fellow-worker that he was going to Leith as an engineer, that he had a return-half ticket to London, and that he had been spending his holiday at Brodick with a friend whom, he euphemistically added, 'he had left in Arran'. The same day he sold his patternmaker's tools to a broker in the Commercial Road for twenty-five shillings, and disappeared from Glasgow. His landlady there, more fortunate than those who had enjoyed his patronage at Brodick and Port Banna-tyne, received on 3rd August a letter from him, posted at Hamilton, enclosing a remittance for rent due. 'There are some people trying to get me into trouble,' he wrote, 'and I think you should give them no information at all. I will prove to them how they are mistaken before very long.' She after-wards communicated with the police, and delivered to them certain articles which Laurie had left in his room.

Laurie was next heard of at Liverpool, where, on Tuesday, 6th August, he took lodgings at 10 Greek Street, paying a week's rent in advance. On the morning of Thursday, the 8th, however, he informed his landlady that he was leaving that day, as he had got a situation in Manchester as a traveller in the cotton trade. He left behind him a box he had brought from Glasgow which, when taken possession of later by the authorities, was found to contain some white shirts, identified as Rose's property, having the name of 'John W. Laurie' impressed thereon with a stamp, also found in the box. It does not appear from the evidence led at the trial why Laurie left Liverpool so suddenly, but the *Liverpool Courier* that day published the fact of his identity with 'Annandale', together with an account of his recent movements, which plainly shewed that the police were upon his track.

Since the discovery of the body, the Glasgow newspapers had been full of 'The Arran Murder', and the hunt for the perpetrator had been followed with keen interest, so when the *North British Daily Mail* received and published a letter from the wanted man, the local excitement was intense. This letter was dated 10th August, and bore the Liverpool postmark. 'I rather smile,' he wrote, 'when I read that my arrest is hourly expected. If things go as I have designed them I will soon have arrived at that country from whose bourne no traveller returns, and since there has been so much said about me, it is only right that the public should know what are the real circumstances. . . . As regards Mr Rose, poor fellow, no one who knows me will believe for one moment that I had any complicity in his death. . . . We went to the top of Goatfell, where I left him in the company of two men who came from Loch Ranza and were going to Brodick.' He admitted that he himself returned by way of Corrie, and had been in the hotel there about ten o'clock.

The renewed outburst of newspaper articles and correspondence produced by the publication of this letter drew a further protest from the fugitive. In a second communication, dated 27th August and bearing to have been posted at Aberdeen, addressed to the *Glasgow Herald*, he complained of the 'many absurd and mad things' appearing about himself in the papers, which he felt it his duty to correct. 'Although I am entirely guiltless of the crime I am so much wanted for,' he wrote, 'yet I can recognize that I am a ruined man in any case, so it is far from my intention to give myself up. . . . When I saw from an evening paper that Mr Rose had not returned to his lodgings, I began to arrange for my departure, for I had told so many about him. Seemingly, there was a motive for doing away with poor Rose; it was not to secure his valuables. Mr Rose was, to all appearances, worse off than myself; indeed, he assured me that he had spent so much on his tour that he had barely sufficient to last till he got home. He wore an old Geneva watch with no gold albert attached, and I am sure that no one saw him wear a ring on his tour. . . . As I am not inclined to say any more, I hope this will be the last the public will hear of me.' Both letters were signed 'John W. Laurie', and were proved to be in his handwriting.

It is difficult to see what induced Laurie to write these letters. He seems to have lost his head at finding himself the subject of so much of the popular attention which, that August, was divided between himself, Mrs Maybrick, then on her trial at Liverpool, and 'Jack the Ripper', whose mysterious crimes were horrifying humanity. Be that as it may, the first letter enabled the police to get the box left by him at Liverpool; but they considered that the posting of the second at Aberdeen was intended as a blind, and that Laurie had returned to his old haunts, as he was reported to have been seen at Uddingston and also at Coatbridge. How much money Rose actually had upon him at the time of his death was never proved, but at least there must have been enough to enable his murderer so successfully to elude the vigilance of the police during the five weeks which elapsed between his absconding and apprehension.

On Tuesday, 3rd September, a man entered the railway station at Ferniegair, which is the first out of Hamilton on the Lesmanhagow branch of the Caledonian line. He was about to take a ticket, when he saw a police constable on the platform; he at once left the station and made for the Carlisle road. The constable followed, as the man resembled Laurie, whom he had previously known. Laurie, for it was he, realizing that he was being shadowed, began to run; crossing a field and the railway, he reached the Lanark road, and running along it till he came to a wood called the 'Quarry Plantation', near Bog Colliery, about three miles from Hamilton, was lost sight of by his pursuer. The constable, who had been joined by some of the workmen from the colliery, got them to surround the wood, which he himself began to search, and presently found Laurie lying under a bush, with an open razor beside him and a superficial wound in his throat. His hand had been less certain than at Coire-na-fuhren. He was then arrested, and having received the usual caution said, 'I robbed the man, but I did not murder him.' On the following day the prisoner was taken to Rothesay, where he was examined before the Sheriff on the charge of murdering Rose, upon which he was duly committed for trial, and was removed to Greenock prison. There on the 11th he was further examined before the Sheriff. In his first declaration the prisoner admitted his identity, adding, 'I have nothing to say to the charge in the meantime.' In his second, being shewn the cap, waterproof, and other things found near the boulder, he declared, 'I wish to say nothing about any of these articles.'

The trial of John Watson Laurie for the murder of Edwin Rose took place before the High Court of Justiciary at Edinburgh on Friday, the 8th, and Saturday, the 9th of November 1889. So greatly had the public interest been excited and sustained by the unusual and mysterious character of the crime, the circumstances in which the body was found, and the subsequent hue and cry after the murderer, that long before the opening of the doors the entrance to the Court was besieged by a crowd, estimated by the *Scotsman* of the day to consist of about two thousand people. Specially stringent regulations, however, had been made regarding admission to the Court-room, and only a privileged few were able to witness the proceedings when the Lord Justice-Clerk (Lord Kingsburgh) took his seat at ten o'clock. There appeared for the Crown the Solicitor-General, Mr (afterwards Lord) Stormonth-Darling, assisted by Mr Graham Murray (later Lord Dunedin) and Mr Dugald M'Kechnie, Advocates-Depute; the counsel for the defence were the Dean of Faculty, Mr John Blair Balfour (later Lord Kinross), and Mr Scott Dickson.

According to the theory of the prosecution, Laurie, who was familiar with the locality, having induced Rose to descend by Coire-na-fuhren, struck him down by a blow with a stone upon the left side of the head, delivered from above and behind, as they clambered down the steep incline; then, as he lay on the ground, his face and head were furiously battered so as to prevent recognition, the injury to the top of the shoulder-blade being caused by a blow which missed the head and struck the top of the shoulder. Laurie had thereafter rifled the body and buried it beneath the boulder, close to which the deed was done. Why he did not also conceal in the same hiding-place the cap and other articles found in the gully the Crown failed to explain. Possibly he overlooked them until he had finished building up the turf and stone dike about the body, when even he may have hesitated to reopen the cavity, preferring to place the cap under the large stone in the stream where it was found, and let the rest take their chance of discovery. The waterproof was split up the back into two pieces. No reason was given for this, but it looks as if it had been thus torn from the body (for Rose when last seen alive was wearing it) and then rolled up and trampled into the pool. The stick, knife, pencil, and button were either dropped, unnoticed by Laurie, during the assault, or thrown away by him after he had searched the pockets of his victim.

The theory of the defence was that all the injuries to the body were produced simultaneously as a result of a fall over one or other of the steep rocks before referred to, further up the gully. On the left side, above the place where the cap was found, as already mentioned, was the nineteen-feet drop, 156 yards beyond the boulder; the thirty-two-feet drop was on the other side, forty yards lower down, above where the knife and pencil were found. The former fall was that favoured by the defence. There was no indication on the body or clothes of its having been dragged from thence down to the boulder, which, looking to the nature of the ground, must, if done, have left unmistakable signs of the process. Indeed, the only injury to these, apart from the head, was that of the shoulder-blade, with corresponding damage to the flesh, the clothing, and the waterproof. If killed further up the gully, the body of Rose must therefore have been carried down to the boulder. The prisoner in his letter to the *Mail* had stated that he left

Rose on the top of the mountain with two men from Loch Ranza, and the defence maintained that Laurie never saw him again, alive or dead. Even if the death were the result of an accidental fall, the robbing and elaborate burial of the body and the folding and concealment of the cap proved the presence of another person, and the defence could do no more than deny, with the prisoner, that these acts were the work of his hands. The unlikelihood of any third party finding and robbing the dead body, and thereafter running the needless and fearful risk of burying it, is obvious, while the suggestion of the learned Dean that the stone (which, by the way, weighed between seven and eight pounds) might have been carried down by a freshet, was negatived by the witnesses who saw its position upon the folded cap.

On the first day of the trial the prosecution was mainly concerned to prove that Rose met his death by murder; on the second, they sought to establish the prisoner's connection with the crime. The members of the search party who had seen the body found, one and all denied that the descent was dangerous or specially difficult, or that a man going down by the left side of the gully, which was the natural way, would have any occasion to go near the steep rocks at all. In cross-examining the police witnesses, the Dean elicited the curious fact that, after the post-mortem examination on 5th August, the boots removed from the body were taken to the shore at Corrie and there buried below high-water mark. The constable who had done this was severely pressed by the Dean as to his reason for so disposing of them, the Dean holding that their condition as regards nails and heels was most important with reference to the question at issue, but the witness could give no more satisfactory answer than that he had been ordered by his superior officer 'to put them out of sight'. It has been said that the object of this irregular act was to prevent the dead man's spirit from 'walking', which, if true, would seem to imply some deficiency of humour on the part of the authorities.

The medical evidence as to the cause of death was the real battleground of the case. The skilled witnesses for the Crown were Drs Gilmour and Fullarton, who saw the body at the boulder and performed the post-mortem examination, and Sir Henry (then Dr) Littlejohn, who examined the body later, on its exhumation. Into the ghastly details of the injuries to the head and face it is unnecessary here to enter; it is sufficient to say that the three medical witnesses concurred in stating that these had been produced by direct violence, in the manner alleged by the prosecution. The limbs and extremities were free from fractures and dislocations, and there was no indication of blood either upon the body or clothes. The injured parts were horribly decayed, and the fact that the highest of the cervical vertebrae was lying loose when first seen by Dr Gilmour was attributed by that gentleman to the advanced decomposition of the neck. The whole of the upper jaw was detached in one piece. These injuries, in his opinion, must have been due to repeated impacts, whether by blows or falls. All the injuries were confined to the left side; and in the case of a sheer fall the injuries to the face would not, he said, be present. Dr Fullarton stated that the extent and severity of the fractures were the result of repeated blows with a blunt instrument; he had never seen a head so smashed except by a machinery accident. The injury to the shoulder confirmed his view, for any conscious person falling would have had his hands before him, and the injuries, which in this case were all localized on one spot, would have been different. He thought the first blow had been given while the man was standing, and the others when he was on the ground. Dr Littlejohn stated that the condition of the cranium as seen by him was at once suggestive of direct violence by blows. A heavy stone in the hand would be an instrument likely to have caused the injuries. The severity of the bruises would stop haemorrhage, and the absence of haemorrhage would account for the speedy decomposition. The detachment of the cervical vertebra, as described in the first medical report, might be consistent either with dislocation or decay of the tissues. A fall would not have inflicted such localized violence without producing severe injuries to the extremities and to the internal organs of the abdomen, which in this case were intact and uninjured, and the latter remarkably well preserved. He had considerable experience of falls from heights such as the Dean Bridge and the Castle Rock, Edinburgh, but he never saw injuries like these so caused. A fall of such severity must have implicated the liver, the condition of which was normal, and there would also be other injuries not present in this case.

The medical experts for the defence were Sir Patrick (then Dr) Heron Watson and Drs M'Gillivray and Alexis Thomson, none of whom had the advantage of seeing the body. They were therefore called to give their opinion solely upon the medical reports and evidence adduced for the Crown. Dr Heron Watson stated that the injuries which he had heard described were, in his view, more consistent with a fall than with repeated blows, and he considered that they had been produced instantaneously. All the probabilities were in favour of a fall upon the vertex. The vertebrae of the neck were probably broken, and there would be little bleeding, which, in the case of blows, would have been copious. The fact that the liver was not ruptured did not affect his opinion. He described, as the result of certain grisly experiments, the difficulty of fracturing the human skull by blows, so as to produce the extensive smashing present in that case. He suggested that Rose had slipped on the slope, and, turning round before he reached the edge, fell over the cliff headlong, backwards and leftwards. If the head alighted on a granite boulder on which there was a nodule of some size, this would account for the injuries to the face and shoulder. The other two medical witnesses for the defence concurred generally in the opinion of Dr Heron Watson as against that of the Crown doctors.

With regard to the conflict of medical testimony, it is noteworthy that upon cross-examination neither side absolutely negatived the possibility of the other's theory; and it occurs to the lay mind that perhaps, as Mr Mantalini remarked in another connection, they may 'both be right and neither wrong', in the sense that Laurie may have first pushed Rose over the rocks, and, having stunned him, then completed the deed with a stone.

The several chapters of the story which has here been briefly told were elicited from the various witnesses. The identity of the prisoner and 'Annandale' was clearly established; the property of the dead man found in his possession was duly identified by relatives and friends; and his movements, as well before as after the murder, were traced beyond all manner of doubt. It was proved that to go from the top of Goatfell to the boulder took half an hour, and that to walk at an ordinary pace from the boulder to Corrie Hotel took an hour and forty minutes, while the prisoner had spent four hours upon the way. In addition to their medical men the defence called only four witnesses: one, an Italian fisherman, to give expert evidence as a guide regarding the dangerous character of the descent by Coire-na-fuhren; another, a girl who had known Laurie at Rothesay, to say that she found him 'chatty and agreeable' on his return from the excursion to Arran. It appeared, however, on cross-examination, that the guide, who had only been three years in the island, had never been in Glen Sannox till after the body was found; while the girl admitted that on her asking Laurie how long he had taken to climb Goatfell he avoided the question and made no reply. The other two witnesses called upon were the servant girls who had been with Mackenzie at Sannox burying-ground. They did not remember Mackenzie's remark as to the man, but admitted that it might have been made.

At a quarter past five on the second day of the trial the Solicitor-General rose to address the jury on behalf of the Crown. After drawing their attention to the exceptional features of the case, he remarked that if this was a murder, it was undoubtedly one of a peculiarly atrocious character. The salient facts of the case were these: Two young men went up the hill together. Only one came down. The other was found, after an interval of weeks, with his body horribly mutilated, hidden away among the rocks of the hillside, and all his portable property removed. The survivor was seen within a few hours of the time when the death of his friend must have been accomplished. He returned to the place from which they both started, and gave no sign or hint of anything having happened to his friend, or that he had not returned with him. The next morning he left Arran and resumed his ordinary occupation, which he continued until the hue and cry arose. Then he fled, and when he was about to be arrested, attempted to cut his throat. The Solicitor-General then reviewed the evidence led for the crown bearing upon the movements of the prisoner, from his arrival at Rothesay under a false name and his subsequent association with Rose until his return to their Brodick lodgings alone. Laurie spent the night in the room which he and his friend had shared, and left next morning by the first available steamer, before the people of the house could see him, without paying his bill, and leaving the room in such a state as would suggest that it had been occupied by two persons. When he left, he obliterated every trace of Rose except the tennis racket, which, as it bore Rose's name, would have been awkward to take with him. He returned to Rothesay wearing Rose's hat and carrying other property of his in a parcel, while certain things which also had belonged to Rose were found in the trunk left by the prisoner at Liverpool. The watch and chain and pocket-book, which Rose was known to have upon him, were missing, and though they did not know how much money he had in his possession, it must have been sufficient to pay his way during the remainder of his holiday. The question was: Whose hand rifled the pockets and put the body under the boulder? He thought they would have little difficulty in coming to the conclusion that the prisoner was with Rose down to the end. The suggestion of the defence that these two parted on the top of the mountain was excluded by the facts of the case. If, then, the prisoner robbed and buried the body, was his the hand that caused the death? The supposition that Rose's death was the result of an accident, and that the robbery and secretion of the body was the work of the prisoner, was so inherently, so wildly improbable that, even apart from the medical evidence, the jury must hesitate to give it credence. If such were indeed the fact, it indicated a depravity of mind but little removed from that which led to murder. The Solicitor-General then discussed the nature of the *locus* and the character of the injuries to the body, and examined the conflict of medical testimony. The prisoner's own behaviour, he said, afforded the readiest solution of what had really happened. He asked them to apply to it the ordinary standard of human conduct, and to say if any man could have so acted who was not the murderer of Rose. As to motive, the prisoner probably expected to get more by the murder than he actually got, but having done it, he had to go through with it. Finally, counsel submitted that the prosecution had established beyond reasonable doubt that the prisoner at the bar was guilty of the crime with which he was charged.

The Dean of Faculty then addressed the jury for the defence. He agreed with the prosecutor that if the case were true, this was a murder unprecedented and incredibly atrocious. If so, the onus of proof was all the heavier upon the Crown. Every probability, he might say every possibility, was against it. Even if they came to the conclusion that murder had been committed, of which he hoped to shew there was no evidence, they must consider whether there was sufficient proof that the murder was committed by Laurie. They would bear in mind that suspicion was not proof. Before they could arrive at a verdict of 'Guilty', they must be clear in their minds upon these points. He then described the injuries to the body, and pointed out that there were no signs of any struggle or of the body having been dragged, nor was it suggested that any instrument had been found in the neighbourhood to which the infliction of the injuries could be attributed. All these were upon the left side. No right-handed man would have attacked Rose upon that side, and it was not suggested that the prisoner was left-handed. He argued that the fractures of the skull and the injury to the shoulder, involving as it did the clothing, together with the severance of the highest joint of the backbone, all supported the theory of the defence. Near the spot they had two declivities such as would bring about these results if a man fell over either of them. He did not know where the Crown said the murder was committed. If at the boulder, how came the various things at the places where they were found? Concealment could not have been the object, for they were left lying perfectly open, and their position was much more consistent with Rose's pitching over the rock and the things flying in all directions. His first point against the Crown was that they had failed to prove a murder, and that the probability on the medical testimony was that the injuries were due to causes other than wilful infliction of violence. With regard to the prisoner's conduct, the Dean remarked that there was nothing in Laurie having called himself 'Annandale' when he went to Rothesay; he was not then aware of Rose's existence, and he was seen and known as Laurie there by other persons. Their meeting was casual, and the visit to Brodick in company was, in the circumstances, quite natural. Laurie could then have had no murderous design. The reticence of the prisoner, as described by some of the witnesses, was due to his suffering from toothache. There was no evidence that Rose and Laurie were ever together in this world again from the time they were seen on top of Goatfell. Whoever removed the body, the jury would understand that their verdict must not proceed upon the suggestion of the Solicitor-General that it was the theory of the defence that the prisoner had done so. No one knew by whom it was done, but at Fair holidays there were plenty of other people on the island who might have robbed the body and put it where it was found. That the prisoner alone and unaided could have lifted, carried, and piled the heavy stones upon it was most unlikely; two men would be required to do that. When Laurie arrived at Corrie Hotel he had no appearance of being a red-handed murderer, but if the Crown case were true there must have been some traces of the deed upon him. He left the island next day, and it was proved that he improperly took away with him some things belonging to Rose. He made no secret of it, for he wore these things at Rothesay among people who knew them both. If this were a charge of theft, these circumstances might be important; but what connection had they with the murder of Rose? Not one article which Rose had with him on the day of his death had been traced to the prisoner. If he had murdered his friend would he have gone back among people who had seen them both together, and afterwards have quietly returned to his work? Not until Aitken shewed that he suspected him did Laurie realize that, having been seen with Rose in Arran, he might himself be held responsible for his disappearance. If he had expected this charge he would not have waited till 31st July before leaving Glasgow. He would realize later that his disappearance then had only tended further to compromise him, so he continued in hiding, and when about to be captured he attempted to cut his throat. When he said, 'I robbed the man, but I did not murder him,' it was certainly not a confession that he had rifled the body, but had reference to the things which he had taken away from the lodgings. In conclusion, the Dean maintained that the Crown had failed to prove, first, that there was any murder, and, secondly, if there had been, that Laurie was the murderer. He asked the jury to return a verdict which would acquit the prisoner of that most terrible and appalling charge.

At twenty mintues to nine o'clock the Lord Justice-Clerk began his charge to the jury. His Lordship described the case as one of the most remarkable that had ever come before a Court of Justice. Both the theories which had been set up presented points almost inconceivable to the ordinary mind. As this was a case of purely circumstantial evidence, he proposed in the first place to go over the facts as to which there was no doubt. His Lordship then reviewed the evidence as to the movements of Rose and Laurie till they were last seen together on the top of the mountain. It was proved that the deceased was then wearing his watch-chain, and they also knew that he had in his pocket-book a return-half ticket to London. It was quite certain that neither of them descended by the same way as they came up. They took a route which, though not the ordinary one, was proved not to be dangerous to any person taking reasonable care. Now, on the way down Rose unquestionably met his death by violence of some kind, and after death his body was carefully hidden by someone under the boulder. If he died by falling over one or other of the rocks further up the gully, it might have been a work of great labour and difficulty to bring the body down to the boulder and conceal it with the stones. His cap was found folded up, with a heavy stone placed upon it, his waterproof, cut in two, was rolled together near the burn, his pockets were rifled, his watch, money, and return ticket were gone. All that must have happened within a few hours of a summer evening. The prisoner was seen coming out of the glen at half-past nine, and again at Corrie Hotel about ten o'clock. He returned to Brodick, and, without any intimation to the people of the place, left the next morning, taking with him Rose's bag, and wearing his grey felt hat. On his return to Rothesay the prisoner was seen wearing Rose's tennis jacket and yachting cap. His Lordship then referred to the incident of the prisoner's conversation with the witness Aitken, to the fact that Laurie had stated to others that he had a return-half ticket to London, to the circumstances of his flight to Liverpool with a box containing property proved to have belonged to Rose, to the letters which he addressed to the newspapers, and finally, to his apprehension and attempted suicide. These were facts about which there could be no doubt, and the Crown said they all pointed to the prisoner as having committed the crime with which he was charged. The defence was that the death of Rose did not take place in presence of Laurie, that they, having gone up Goatfell together, did not descend together, although the one met his death on the way by Glen Sannox to Corrie, and the other reached Corrie by way of Glen Sannox. Laurie must have been surprised to find that his friend did not return to their lodgings, but the effect which Rose's non-arrival had upon him was that, without saying a word to anyone, he went off with his own and Rose's luggage. The defence maintained that Rose had fallen over one of the rocks at a considerable distance from the boulder, and that it would have been impossible for one man to have brought the body down and buried it. His Lordship was afraid there were two views as to that, for the Crown's contention was that Rose was done to death by blows with a stone, which could have happened close to the boulder. The Dean had asked if Rose was killed there, how came the various articles to be found below the rocks further up the gully? Again his Lordship was afraid that if Rose in fact was killed at the boulder, the person who put him to death might so have disposed of the articles as to suggest that Rose had fallen over a precipice. His Lordship pointed out that the hiding of the cap and the cutting-up of the waterproof must have been done by a human hand after Rose's death. The defence being that Laurie and Rose were never seen together after they left the top of the hill, it was extremely remarkable that the prisoner did not reach Corrie Hotel till ten, while the witnesses who left the top at the same time reached Brodick before half-past eight. The jury must consider if they could reconcile all these facts with the idea that Laurie was not present at Rose's death. If he was, there was no escape from the conclusion that his was the hand that folded the cap, cut off the waterproof, and hid the body; and then they would have to consider could these acts possibly have been done by a man who had witnessed a terrible and accidental death. With regard to Laurie's possession of a return ticket to London, it was in evidence that Rose had such a ticket in his pocket-book. It had been urged for the defence that the prisoner openly wore the coat and hats of Rose, and that no person anxious to conceal a crime would have done so, but it was his duty to point out that such rashness on the part of criminals often formed the very threads of the web of justice. They must take the whole facts of the case together, and say whether it led to a conclusion that was reasonable and just. His Lordship then reviewed the medical evidence, and observed that those who saw all the details and examined them were necessarily in a better position to give their evidence and opinions than those who merely based their statements upon evidence which they heard. It was not the province of the jury to decide between the medical opinions, but to find what, taking the whole facts and incidents along with that evidence, was the most probable cause of death. If they came to the conclusion that the prisoner was present and that his hand buried the body, that would tend very much against the theory of the defence. The case was purely one of facts, and it was the jury who had the responsibility and duty of coming to a conclusion on those facts which would commend itself to their consciences as reasonable and experienced men.

At a quarter to ten, on the conclusion of the Judge's charge, the jury retired to consider their verdict, and after an absence of forty minutes they returned to Court, when the Foreman announced that their verdict was 'Guilty, by a majority.' It was afterwards ascertained that the verdict was arrived at by a majority of one, eight voting for Guilty and seven for Not Proven. So soon as the Lord Justice-Clerk had pronounced sentence of death the prisoner, who stood up to receive judgement, turned round in the dock, and facing the crowded benches, said in a clear, firm voice, 'Ladies and gentlemen, I am innocent of this charge!' His Lordship at once intimated that the prisoner could not be allowed to make a speech. Laurie was then removed to the cells below, and the Court rose at twenty minutes to eleven o'clock.

No one who witnessed the closing act of this famous trial can forget the impressive character of the scene. Without, in the black November night, a great crowd silently awaited the issue of life or death. The lofty, dimly-lighted Court-room, the candles glimmering in the shadows of the Bench, the imposing presence of the Justice-Clerk in his robes of scarlet and white, the tiers of tense, expectant faces, and in the dock the cause and object of it all, that calm, commonplace, respectable figure, the callous and brutal murderer whom Justice had tardily unmasked.

On Monday, the 11th, the convict was conveyed from Edinburgh to Greenock, where the sentence was to be executed on 30th November. This was a distinction which the magistrates and citizens of that town viewed with anything but satisfaction, for since its creation as a burgh of barony in 1675, only four executions had taken place there, the last being in 1834, and it was hoped and expected that the sentence would be carried out in Edinburgh.

A movement was at once set on foot in the Coatbridge district, where Laurie's relatives were well known and respected, to obtain a commutation of the death sentence. Various meetings were held, and a petition to Lord Lothian, the Scottish Secretary, was adopted. Apart from the stereotyped objections to the verdict common to such documents, the petitioners stated that there had been, and then was, insanity in the convict's family; that he himself had shewn from infancy decided symptoms of mental aberration, which accounted for the extraordinary and eccentric character of his conduct both prior and subsequent to the 15th of July; and that the petitioners were prepared to adduce proof of such aberration if required. This petition, which was widely signed in Glasgow and the West of Scotland, was duly despatched to Dover House on Friday, 22nd November. Meanwhile, pending the result of this application, the Greenock magistrates proceeded to make the necessary arrangements for carrying out the sentence, and thriftily borrowed the Glasgow scaffold. Laurie, who still maintained the cool and calm demeanour which he had preserved throughout the trial, was said to be confident that his life would be spared.

On Saturday, the 23rd, on the appointment of Lord Lothian, the convict was visited by Sir Arthur Mitchell, K.C.B., Dr Yellowlees, of Glasgow Royal Asylum, and Professor (afterwards Sir William) Gairdner, of Glasgow University, with a view to examining and reporting upon his mental condition. It was stated in the newspapers at the time that Laurie had himself written a letter to Lord Lothian to the effect that Rose was killed in his presence by an accidental fall from a rock, and that his (Laurie's) subsequent actions arose from his dread that he would be charged with murder, and, owing to the absence of witnesses, might be unable to prove his innocence. This was at least a more plausible explanation than that afforded by the defence at the trial; but it is understood that the line of argument then taken was the prisoner's deliberate choice, and was adopted by his counsel at his own request.

On Thursday, the 28th, two days before that fixed for the execution, the local authorities were informed by telegraph that in consequence of the Medical Commission having reported that the convict was of unsound mind, the Secretary for Scotland had felt justified in recommending a respite. The terms of the commissioners' report were not disclosed.

The death sentence having been formally commuted to penal servitude for life, Laurie was removed on 2nd December to Perth Penitentiary, the scaffold was returned to Glasgow, and the Greenock magistrates were left to pay the bill.

The *Glasgow Herald* of 3rd December 1889 published an interesting account of the unfavourable impression made by Laurie upon those who were in close contact with him during his confinement, from which the following passage may be quoted: 'His references to Rose were not marked by any exhibition of sympathy for that unfortunate gentleman. On the contrary he spoke of him as a vain, proud man, always boastful of his money, and desirous of making his hearers believe that he was wealthy. The significance of Laurie's comment upon this point is striking; with singular callousness he added that Rose had not very much after all.'

Four years elapsed before public attention was again directed to the Arran murderer. On 24th July 1893 Laurie, who had been removed to Peterhead Convict Prison, made a bold bid for freedom. He was employed as a carpenter, his behaviour had been exemplary, and, having a good voice, he was, as a newspaper reporter records, 'the mainstay of the Presbyterian choir, leading the praise with great enthusiasm'. But the old Adam was not wholly eradicated. That morning a gang of convicts under a civil guard was early at work upon an addition which was being made to the warders' houses outside the prison walls, and Laurie was carrying planks for the scaffolding. There was a dense sea fog; so, seizing his opportunity, he leapt a fence and made for the public road. He was then seen by the civil guard, but before the latter could fire the fugitive had disappeared in the fog. An alarm was instantly raised, and guard and warders started in pursuit. One warder, mounted on a bicycle, speedily overtook the running man. He struggled violently, but other warders arriving on the scene, he was quickly handcuffed and marched back to prison. On the way, says our reporter, 'Laurie characterized his captors in language wholly inconsistent with the ecclesiastical office which he fills.' Human nature was too strong for the precentor.

In 1909, on the completion of twenty years of his sentence, echoes of the old story were heard in the Press, and persistent rumours were circulated that the convict was about to be released. But on 28th April 1910 Laurie was removed from

Peterhead to Perth Criminal Asylum, where he died on 4th October 1930, forty-one years from the date of his first imprisonment.

In the ancient burying-ground of Sannox, briers and brambles have striven to conceal the granite boulder which, with a somewhat painful propriety, marks the resting-place of Edwin Rose; and year by year the tourists visiting that beautiful and lonely spot leave, with better intention than taste, their calling-cards upon the stone.

Mrs Snyder and Mr Gray

DAMON RUNYON

Long Island City, New York, 19 April 1927

A chilly looking blonde with frosty eyes and one of those marble, you-bet-you-will chins, and an inert, scare-drunk fellow that you couldn't miss among any hundred men as a dead set-up for a blonde, or the shell game, or maybe a gold brick.

Mrs Ruth Snyder and Henry Judd Gray are on trial in the huge weatherbeaten old court house of Queens County in Long Island City, just across the river from the roar of New York, for what might be called, for want of a better name, The Dumbbell Murder. It was so dumb.

They are charged with the slaughter four weeks ago of Albert Snyder, art editor of the magazine *Motor Boating*, the blonde's husband and father of her nine-year-old daughter, under circumstances that for sheer stupidity and brutality have seldom been equalled in the history of crime.

It was stupid beyond imagination, and so brutal that the thought of it probably makes many a peaceful, home-loving Long Islander of the Albert Snyder type shiver in his pyjamas as he prepares for bed.

They killed Snyder as he slumbered, so they both admitted in confessions – Mrs Snyder has since repudiated hers – first whacking him on the head with a sash weight, then giving him a few whiffs of chloroform, and finally tightened a strand of picture wire around his throat so he wouldn't revive.

This matter disposed of, they went into an adjoining room and had a few drinks of whiskey used by some Long Islanders, which is very bad, and talked things over. They thought they had committed 'the perfect crime', whatever that may be. It was probably the most imperfect crime on record. It was cruel, atrocious and unspeakably dumb.

They were red-hot lovers then, these two, but they are

168

strangers now. They never exchanged a glance yesterday as they sat in the cavernous old court room while the citizenry of Long Island tramped in and out of the jury box, and the attorneys tried to get a jury of twelve men together without success.

Plumbers, clerks, electricians, merchants, bakers, butchers, barbers, painters, salesmen, machinists, delicatessen dealers, garage employees, realtors and gardeners from the cities and the hamlets of the County of Queens were in the procession that marched through the jury box, answering questions as to their views on the death penalty, and their sympathies toward women, and other things.

Out of fifty men, old and young, married and single, bald and hairy, not one was found acceptable to both sides. Forty-three were excused, the State challenged one peremptorily, the attorneys for Mrs Snyder five, and the attorneys for Gray one. Each defendant is allowed thirty peremptory challenges, the State thirty against each defendant.

At this rate they may be able to get a jury before the Long Island corn is ripe. The State is asking that Mrs Snyder and her meek-looking Lothario be given the well-known 'hot seat' in Sing Sing, more generally known as the electric chair, and a lot of the talesmen interrogated today seemed to have a prejudice against that form of punishment.

Others had opinions as to the guilt or innocence that they said they couldn't possibly change. A few citizens seemed kindly disposed toward jury service, possibly because they haven't anything at hand for the next few weeks, but they got short shrift from the lawyers. The jury box was quite empty at the close of the day's work.

Mrs Snyder, the woman who has been called a Jezebel, a lineal descendant of the Borgia outfit, and a lot of other names, came in for the morning session of court stepping along briskly in her patent-leather pumps, with little short steps.

She is not bad looking. I have seen much worse. She is thirty-three and looks just about that, though you cannot tell much about blondes. She has a good figure, slim and trim, with narrow shoulders. She is of medium height and I thought she carried her clothes off rather smartly. She wore a black dress and a black silk coat with a collar of black fur. Some of the girl reporters said it was dyed ermine; others pronounced it rabbit.

They made derogatory remarks about her hat. It was a tight-fitting thing called, I believe, a beret. Wisps of her straw-coloured hair straggled out from under it. Mrs Snyder wears her hair bobbed, the back of the bobbing rather ragged. She is of the Scandinavian type. Her parents are Norwegian and Swedish.

Her eyes are blue-green, and as chilly looking as an ice cream cone. If all that Henry Judd Gray says of her actions the night of the murder is true, her veins carry ice water. Gray says he dropped the sash weight after slugging the sleeping Snyder with it once and that Mrs Snyder picked it up and finished the job.

Gray's mother and sister, Mrs Margaret Gray, and Mrs Harold Logan, took seats in the court room just behind Mrs Snyder. At the afternoon session, Mrs Gray, a small, determined-looking woman of middle age, hitched her chair over so she was looking right into Mrs Snyder's face.

There was a rather grim expression in Mrs Gray's eyes. She wore a black hat and a black coat with a fur collar, a spray of artificial flowers was pinned to the collar. Her eyelids were red as if she had been weeping.

The sister, Mrs Logan, is plump and pleasant looking. Gray's wife has left him flat, in the midst of his troubles, and gone to Norwalk, Conn., with their nine-year-old daughter. She never knew her husband was playing that Don Juan business when she thought he was out peddling corsets. That is she never knew it until the murder.

Gray, a spindly fellow in physical build, entered the court room with quick, jerky little steps behind an officer, and sat down between his attorneys, Samuel L. Miller and William L. Millard. His back was to Mrs Snyder who sat about ten feet distant. Her eyes were on a level with the back of his narrow head.

Gray was neatly dressed in a dark suit, with a white starched collar and subdued tie. He has always been a bit to the dressy side, it is said. He wears big, horn-rimmed spectacles and his eyes have a startled expression. You couldn't find a meeker, milder looking fellow in seven states, this man who is charged with one of the most horrible crimes in history.

He occasionally conferred with his attorneys as the examination of the talesmen was going forward, but not often. He sat in one position almost the entire day, half slumped down in his chair, a melancholy looking figure for a fellow who once thought of 'the perfect crime'.

Mrs Snyder and Gray have been 'hollering copper' on each other lately, as the boys say. That is, that they have been telling. Gray's defence goes back to old Mr Adam, that the woman beguiled him, while Mrs Snyder says he is a 'jackal', and a lot of other things besides that, and claims that he is hiding behind her skirts.

She will claim, it is said, that while she at first entered into the conspiracy to kill her husband, she later tried to dissuade Gray from going through with it, and tried to prevent the crime. The attorneys will undoubtedly try to picture their respective clients as the victims of each other.

Mrs Snyder didn't want to be tried with Gray, but Gray was very anxious to be tried with Mrs Snyder. It is said that no Queens County jury ever sent a woman to death, which is what the State will ask of this jury, if it ever gets one. The relations among the attorneys for the two defendants are evidently not on the theory of 'one for all and all for one'. Probably the attorneys for Gray do not care what happens to Mrs Snyder, and probably the attorneys for Mrs Snyder feel the same way about Gray.

Edgar Hazelton, a close-trimmed dapper looking man, with a jutting chin and with a pince-nez balanced on a hawk beak, who represents Mrs. Snyder, did most of the questioning of the talesmen for the defence. His associate, Dana Wallace, is a former district attorney of Queens County, and the pair are said to be among the ablest lawyers on Long Island. It is related that they have defended eleven murder

171

cases without a conviction going against them.

Supreme Court Justice Townsend Scudder is presiding over the court room, which has a towering ceiling with a stained-glass skylight, and heavy dark oak furniture with high-backed pews for the spectators. Only no spectators were admitted today because the room was needed for the talesmen.

The court room is so huge it was difficult to hear what was going on at any distance from the bench. I believe it is the largest court room in the country. It was there that the trial scene in the picture *Manslaughter* was filmed.

In the court room on the floor below was held the trial of Mrs Nack in the famous Guldensuppe murder thirty years ago, when the reporters used carrier pigeons to take their copy across the river to Park Row.

Microphones have been posted on the tables, and amplifiers have been rigged up on the walls, probably the first time this was ever done in a murder trial, but the apparatus wasn't working any too well today, and one hundred and twenty newspaper writers scattered around the tables listened with their hands cupped behind their ears.

Here is another record, the number of writers covering the trial. We have novelists, preachers, playwrights, fiction writers, sports writers and journalists at the press benches. Also we have nobility in the persons of the Marquis of Queensberry and Mrs Marquis. The Marquis is a grandson of the gent whose name is attached to the rules governing the manly art of scrambling ears, but the young man wore a pair of fancy-topped shoes yesterday that surprised me. It isn't done you know, really!

The Reverend John Roach Straton was present, wearing a Buster Brown necktie that was almost unclerical. A Catholic priest was on hand, but he carried no pad or pencil to deceive us. Some of the writers came attended by their secretaries, which shows you how far we have gone since the days of the carrier pigeons at the Guldensuppe trial.

There were quite a number of philosophers. I have been requested by my Broadway constituency to ascertain if possible what, if anything, philosophy suggests when a hotsy-totsy blonde with whom a guy is enamoured tells him to do thus and so. But then a philosopher probably never gets tangled up with blondes, or he wouldn't be a philosopher.

Mrs Snyder showed signs that might have been either nervousness or just sheer impatience during the day. Her fingers constantly toyed with a string of black beads at her throat. Her entire set-up suggested mourning. She has nice white hands, but they are not so small as Gray's. His hands are quite effeminate.

In fact, the alienists who examined Gray and pronounced him quite sane say he is effeminate in many ways. Gray showed no signs of nervousness or any particular animation whatever. He just sat there. It must be a strain on a man to sit for hours knowing the eyes of a woman who is trying to get him all burned up are beating against the back of his neck and not turn around and give her at least one good hot glare.

27 April 1927

Some say Mrs Ruth Snyder 'wept silently' in court yesterday. It may be so. I could detect no sparkle of tears against the white marble mask, but it is conceivable that even the very gods were weeping silently as a gruff voice slowly recited the blonde woman's own story of the murder of her husband by herself and Henry Judd Gray.

Let no one infer she is altogether without tenderness of heart, for when they were jotting down the confession that was read in the court room in Long Island City, Peter M. Daly, an assistant district attorney, asked her:

'*Mrs Snyder, why did you kill your husband?*'

He wanted to know.

'Don't put it that way,' she said, according to his testimony yesterday. 'It sounds so cruel.'

'Well, that is what you did, isn't it?' he asked, in some surprise.

'Yes,' he claims she answered, 'but I don't like that term.'

A not astonishing distaste, you must admit.

'Well, why did you kill him?' persisted the curious Daly.

'To get rid of him,' she answered, simply, according to Daly's testimony; and indeed that seems to have been her main idea throughout, if all the evidence the State has so far developed is true.

She afterward repudiated the confession that was presented yesterday, with her attorneys trying to bring out from the State's witnesses that she was sick and confused when she told her bloody yarn five weeks ago.

The woman, in her incongruous widow's weeds, sat listening intently to the reading of her original confession to the jury, possibly the most horrible tale that ever fell from human lips, the tale of a crime unutterably brutal and cold-blooded and unspeakably dumb.

Her mouth opened occasionally as if framing words, and once she said no quite distinctly, an unconscious utterance, which may have been a denial of some utterance by the lawyer or perhaps an assurance to her soul that she was not alive and awake.

This is a strange woman, this Mrs Ruth Brown Snyder, a different woman to different men.

To the inert Henry Judd Gray, her partner in crime, sitting at the table just in front of her, as soggy looking as a dummy in his loose hanging clothes, she was a 'woman of great charm', as he said in his confession which was outlined in court by a police officer yesterday.

To big, hale and hearty George P. McLaughlin, former police commissioner of New York City, who heard her original statement of the butchery, she was a 'woman of great calm', as he said on the witness stand yesterday.

To the male reporters who have been following the trial she is all that, anyway, though they construe her calm as more the chill of the icy Northland, whence came her parents.

The attorneys for Mrs Snyder, the nimble Dana Wallace and Edgar Hazelton, indicated yesterday clearly that part of their line of defence, in this devil-take-the-hindmost scramble between Ruth and Henry Judd, is to be an attempted impeachment of the confession, and Gray's attorneys showed the same thought.

174

Samuel L. Miller, representing Gray, charged that the confession of the corset salesman was secured while he was under duress and by intimidation and threats.

Gray sat with his chin in his hands, his eyes on the floor, scarcely moving a muscle as Mrs Snyder's confession, damning him in almost every word, was read. I have never seen him show much animation at best, but yesterday he seemed completely sunk. He occasionally conferred in whispers through his fingers with one of his attorneys, but with not the slightest show of interest.

It was Gray who slugged poor Albert Snyder with the five-pound sash weight as the art editor lay asleep in his bed, so Mrs Snyder's confession relates, while Mrs Snyder stood outside in the hall, seeing, by the dim light thrown into the chamber of horror by an arc in the street, the rise and fall of the paper-wrapped weight in Gray's hand.

What a scene that must have been!

Twice she heard her husband groan. Roused from an alcoholic stupor by that first thump on his head, he groaned. Then groaned again. Silence. Out came Henry Judd Gray, saying: 'Well, I guess that's it.'

But the confessions do not jibe here. The outline of Gray's confession, which will be read today, indicates Gray says he dropped the weight after whacking Snyder once, and that Ruth picked it up 'and belaboured him'.

'Those were Gray's words – "belaboured him",' ex-Commissioner McLaughlin said yesterday.

District Attorney Newcombe overlooked an opportunity for the dramatic yesterday that old David Belasco, sitting back in the crowd, probably envied, in the reading of Ruth's confession. This was first identified by Peter M. Daly, the assistant mentioned above, after Ruth's attorneys had failed in a hot battle against its admission.

Newcombe stood before the jury with the typewritten sheets in one hand and talked off the words without elocutionary effort, the microphone carrying his voice out over the silent court room. The place was jammed. Women again. At the afternoon session they almost tore the buttons off the uniforms of the coppers on guard at the doors, trying to shove past them. The cops gallantly repulsed the charge.

The first paragraphs of the confession, made to Daly soon after the murder and under circumstances that the defence is attacking, were given over to a recital of Ruth's early life – born on Manhattan Island thirty-three years ago, a schoolgirl, an employee in the same magazine office with Snyder, then an artist when she married him.

The thing has been told so often before that I here go over it sketchily. Soon she was unhappy with her husband, fourteen years older than herself. He constantly belittled her. He threatened to blow out her brains. He was a good provider for herself and their nine-year-old daughter, but wouldn't take her out – so she took to stepping out, as they say. An old, old yarn – Friend Husband a non-stepper, Friend Wife full of go.

She met Henry Judd Gray, the corset salesman, in Henry's restaurant in the once-throbbing Thirties in New York, and the first thing anybody knew she and Henry were thicker than is meet and proper. She told Henry of her matrimonial woes, and Henry, himself a married man, with a young daughter, was duly sympathetic.

But let's get down to the murder.

She wrote Henry and told him how Albert Snyder had threatened her life. She wrote in a code they had rigged up for their own private use, and Henry answered, saying the only thing to do was to get rid of Albert. They had talked of ways and means, and Gray gave her the famous sash weight and went out to Queens Village one night to wipe Albert Snyder out.

They got cold feet that night and Albert lived. Then Snyder again threatened her, the confession said, and told her to get out of his house, so she wrote to Henry once more, and Henry wrote back, saying, 'We will deliver the goods Saturday.' That meant Saturday, March 19. They arranged all the details by correspondence.

Henry arranged his alibi in Syracuse and came to New York the night she and her husband and child were at the

Fidgeons' party. She left a door unlocked so Henry could get in the room of her mother, Mrs Josephine Brown, who was away for the night. Ruth saw him there and talked with him a moment when she came back from the party with her husband and child.

Henry had the sash weight which she had left under the pillow in Mrs Brown's room for him. He had chloroform, some cheesecloth and a blue cotton handkerchief. Also, she had hospitably left a quart of liquor for him of which he drank about half. She put her child to bed, then went into her husband's room and waited until he was asleep, then returned to the waiting Henry.

They talked briefly, and Henry kissed her and went into Albert Snyder's room. She stood in the hallway and saw Gray pummel the sleeping man with the sash weight as related. Then Gray tied Snyder's hands and feet, put the handkerchief, saturated with chloroform, over his face, besides stuffing his mouth and nostrils with the gauze, also soaked with chloroform. Then Henry turned Snyder over so the art editor's face would be buried in a pillow and rejoined Ruth.

Henry Judd wore rubber gloves at his sanguinary task, the confession said, and he went to the bathroom to wash his hands. He found blood on his shirt, so Ruth went into the room where the dead man lay, got one of Albert Snyder's shirts and gave it to Henry Judd. Then they went into the cellar and burned the bloody shirt and put the sash weight into a tool box after rubbing it with ashes.

Now, they returned to the sitting room, this pair, and Henry Judd suddenly thought of some picture wire he had brought along, presumably to tie Snyder's hands and feet. At least, he had two pieces, Ruth said. One he had lost, so he took the other and went into the death chamber and wrapped the wire around Albert Snyder's throat, tightening it with his fingers.

Then he went around and upset the premises generally, to bear out the robbery idea, then sat and gossiped, talking of this and that until daybreak, when Henry Judd tied his sweetheart's hands and feet and left to return to Syracuse. She first went out and got a wallet out of Albert Snyder's pocket and gave it to Henry Judd. She does not know how much it contained.

After Henry's departure, she rolled out of her mother's bed, whereon he had placed her, and aroused her little daughter, telling her to get a neighbour.

Such, in substance and briefly, was the story of that night in Queens Village.

There was a supplemental statement with reference to some letters, including one from Gray, sent from Syracuse after he had departed for New York to join with her in the slaughter. Peter M. Daly asked her, at a time when Gray had not yet been definitely hooked with the crime, how she reconciled the postmark with her statement of the murder and she said it was part of Henry's alibi.

Thus Ruth was 'hollering copper' on Henry, even before she knew Henry was 'hollering copper' on her. They didn't stand hitched a minute after the showdown came.

Wallace wanted to know if Mrs Snyder hadn't said she was confused and sick while making the statement, but Daly said no. He admitted Mrs Snyder had a crying spell and that a physician was called in. Wallace mentioned it as a fainting spell, but Daly wouldn't concede it was such. It seems to be agreed it was some kind of a spell, however.

28 April 1927

Right back to old Father Adam, the original, and perhaps the loudest 'squawker' among mankind against women, went Henry Judd Gray in telling how and why he lent his hand to the butchery of Albert Snyder.

She – she – she – she – she – she – she – she. That was the burden of the bloody song of the little corset salesman as read out in the packed court room in Long Island City yesterday.

She – she – she – she – she – she. 'Twas an echo from across the ages and an old familiar echo, at that. It was the same old 'squawk' of Brother Man, whenever and wherever he is in a jam, that was first framed in the words:

178

'She gave me of the tree, and I did eat.'

It has been put in various forms since then, as Henry Judd Gray, for one notable instance close at hand, put it in the form of eleven long typewritten pages that were read yesterday, but in any form and in any language it remains a 'squawk'.

'She played me pretty hard.' . . . 'She said, "You're going to do it, aren't you?"' . . . 'She kissed me.' . . . She did this. . . . She did that. . . . Always she – she – she – she – she ran the confession of Henry Judd.

And 'she' – the woman-accused, how did she take this most gruesome squawk?

Well, on the whole, better than you might expect.

You must remember it was the first time she had ever heard the confession of the man who once called her 'Momsie'. She probably had an inkling of it, but not its exact terms.

For a few minutes her greenish blue eyes roared with such fury that I would not have been surprised to see her leap up, grab the window sash weight that lay among the exhibits on the district attorney's table and perform the same offices on the shrinking Gray that he says she performed on her sleeping husband.

She 'belaboured him', Gray's confession reads, and I half expected her to belabour Gray.

Her thin lips curled to a distinct snarl at some passages in the statement. I thought of a wildcat and a female cat, at that, on a leash. Once or twice she smiled, but it was a smile of insensate rage, not amusement. She once emitted a push of breath in a loud 'phew', as you have perhaps done yourself over some tall tale.

The marble mask was contorted by her emotions for a time, she often shook her head in silent denial of the astounding charges of Gray, then finally she settled back calmly, watchful, attentive, and with an expression of unutterable contempt as the story of she – she – she – she ran along.

Contempt for Henry Judd, no doubt. True, she herself squawked on Henry Judd, at about the same time Henry Judd was squawking on her, but it is a woman's inalienable right to squawk.

As for Henry Judd, I still doubt he will last it out. He reminds me of a slowly collapsing lump of tallow. He sat huddled up in his baggy clothes, his eyes on the floor, his chin in hand, while the confession was being read. He seems to be folding up inch by inch every day.

He acts as if he is only semi-conscious. If he was a fighter and came back to his corner in his present condition, they would give him smelling salts.

29 April 1927

There was little breathing space left in the yellowish-walled old court room when the morning session opened.

In the jam I observed many ladies and gents with dark circles around their eyes which indicated loss of sleep, or bad livers. I identified them as of the great American stage, playwrights, producers, actors, and even actresses.

They were present, as I gathered, to acquire local colour for their current or future contributions to the thespian art, and the hour was a trifle early for them to be abroad in the land. They sat yesterday writing through the proceedings and perhaps inwardly criticizing the stage setting and thinking how unrealistic the trial is as compared with their own productions.

Among the other spectators comfortably chaired, or standing on tired feet, were ladies running from a couple of inches to three yards wide. They were from all parts of Long Island, and the other boroughs of the large and thriving City of New York, the inmates of which are supposed to be so very blasé but who certainly dearly love their murder cases.

A big crowd waited in the hallways and outside the court house. Tearful females implored the obdurate cops guarding the stairs and the court room doors to ease them through somehow.

It was a strange gathering. Solid-looking citizens found a morning to waste. They would probably have felt greatly inconvenienced had they been requested to spend the same amount of time on a mission of mercy. Several preachers and some of our best known public 'pests' were scattered around the premises. What a fine commentary, my friends, on what someone has mentioned as our vaunted intelligence.

Peggy Hopkins, Countess Morner and what not, Joyce, the famous grass-widow, came again to dazzle all the beholders with the magnificence of her display. It was Peggy's second visit. Probably she didn't believe her eyes and ears on her first visit that a lady had seemed to have some difficulty in getting rid of her husband. Peggy never did, you can bet on that. She wore a suit of a distressing green and a red fox collar and arrived at the court house in a little old last year's Rolls-Royce.

Now the woman and the crumpled little corset salesman, their once piping-hot passion colder than a dead man's toes, begin trying to save their respective skins from the singeing at Sing Sing, each trying to shove the other into the room with the little green door.

'What did Mrs Snyder say about the confession of Gray's – that squawk?' I asked her attorneys yesterday.

'Well, let's see, she said he – ' began Dana Wallace, the buzzing, bustling little man who sits at Mrs Snyder's side in the court room when he isn't on his feet, which is seldom.

'She said – Well, wait now until I recall what she said,' put in Edgar Hazelton, the other attorney for the woman.

They seemed at a loss for words. I suggested: 'Did she say he is a rat?'

'Well I suppose it would amount to that in your language,' replied Wallace. (What did he mean 'my' language?) 'Only she didn't use that term.'

'No, no,' chimed in Hazelton, 'not rat.'

'She said, in substance, "and to think I once loved that – that –" Well, I think she used a word that means something like coward,' Wallace concluded.

'Do you think she will keep her nerve on the stand?' I asked.

'Yes,' they both answered in unison.

I am inclined to think so, too.

Whatever else she may lack, which seems to be plenty, the

woman appears to have nerve. Or maybe she hasn't any nerves. It is about the same thing.

In any event, she has never for a moment cowered like her once little pal of those loving days before the black early morning of 20 March. She has been cold, calm, comtemptuous, gusty, angry, but never shrinking, save perhaps in that little walk to and from the court between the recesses. She then passes before the hungry eyes of the spectators.

That seems to be her most severe ordeal. She grips her black corded-silk coat in front with both hands, and seems to hasten, her eyes straight ahead. However, we shall see about that nerve now.

30 April 1927

We were, in a manner of speaking, in the chamber of horrors with Mrs Ruth Brown Snyder yesterday afternoon, mentally tiptoeing along, goggle-eyed and scared, behind her, when the blonde woman suddenly gulped, and began weeping.

She had taken us, just before the tears came, step by step to a bedroom in her little home in Queens Village. We were standing there, you might say, all goose-pimply with the awfulness of the situation as we watched, through the medium of the story she told on the witness stand, the butchery of her husband by Henry Judd Gray.

Maybe the ghost of the dead art editor suddenly popped out on her as she got us into that room and was showing us the picture of the little corset salesman at his bloody work while she was trying to stay his murderous hand. Anyway, the tears came, welling up into the frosty eyes of the blonde and trickling down over that marble mask of a face.

Plump Mrs Irene Wolfe, the grey-haired matron of the Queens County jail, hurried to Mrs Snyder's side and put her arms around the weeping woman. A few sips from a glass of water, and Mrs Snyder was again composed sufficiently to go on with the fearful tale of the killing of her husband that she started early in the afternoon and by which she hopes to save herself from the electric chair.

She blamed it all on Gray, even as he will blame it all on her. The baggy little man sitting inertly, as always, in the chair just a few feet from her listened to the woman with only an occasional glance at her.

Yet it would be interesting to know his thoughts. This was his old Momsie. This was the woman he once thought he loved with a great consuming love – this woman who was trying to consign him to the electric juices. He seemed to stagger slightly as he walked out of the court room at the close of the session, whereas before he had tried to put a little snap into his tread.

This woman broke down twice while she was on the witness stand, once when she had us in that death chamber, with Henry Judd Gray pounding the life out of her husband, as she claims, and again when she mentioned the name of her nine-year-old daughter, Lorraine.

But in the main she was as cold and calm sitting there with a thousand people staring at her as if she were at her dinner table discoursing to some guests. She kept her hands folded in her lap. She occasionally glanced at the jury, but mostly kept her eyes on Edgar Hazelton, one of her lawyers who examined her on direct examination.

This examination was not concluded when Court took a recess at 4.30 until Monday morning. It is the custom of Queens County courts to skip Saturday.

It was difficult to tell just what effect Mrs Snyder's tale had on the jury, of course. In fact it would be unfair to make a guess until her tale is finished. It certainly had some elements of plausibility, despite the confession she now says was obtained under duress, and despite the motive of Albert Snyder's life insurance that is advanced by the prosecution.

Mrs Snyder's attorneys attempted to show today that she had tried to have the insurance reduced to cut down the premium, but their evidence on that point did not seem particularly strong. She insisted in her testimony that this had been the purpose.

She smiled just once with any semblance of joy, which was

when Justice Scudder admitted, over the objections of the State, the bank books showing that Albert Snyder and Ruth had a joint account. It is by this account that the defence expects to show that Albert Snyder had full cognizance of his wife's payment of the premiums on the policies.

She says Gray always referred to Albert Snyder as 'the governor'. Once she accidentally tripped over a rubber gas tube in the house and pulled it off the jet. She went out and when she came back her husband was out of doors and said he had nearly been asphyxiated. She wrote Gray of the incident, and he wrote back:

'It was too damn bad the hose wasn't long enough to shove in his nose.'

When she testified in just that language there was something in her manner and way of speaking out the word that caused a distinct stiffening among the women in the court room.

'Brazen!' some of them whispered.

This gas jet incident, by the way, was alleged by the State to have been one of the times when Mrs Snyder tried to murder her husband.

She says Gray threatened to kill himself and her if she didn't do what he told her. She was afraid of Gray, she said, although the drooping little man in front of her didn't seem to be anything to be afraid of. She tried to break off with him, she said, and he threatened to expose her.

She said Gray sent her sleeping powders to give 'the governor' on the night of the party at the Fidgeons', which was Albert Snyder's last night on earth. Moreover, Gray announced in the letter accompanying the powders, according to her testimony, that he was coming down Saturday to finish 'the governor'.

He came down all right.

'My husband was asleep. I went to my mother's room, where I met Mr Gray. We talked several minutes. He kissed me and I felt the rubber gloves on his hands. He was mad. He said, "If you don't let me go through with this, I'll kill us both." He had taken my husband's revolver. I grabbed him

184

by the hand and took him down to the living-room.

'I pleaded with him to stop when we got downstairs, then I went to the bathroom. I said to Mr Gray, "I'll bring your hat and coat down to you." I heard a terrific thud. I rushed to my husband's room. I found Gray straddling my husband. I pulled the blankets down, grabbing him, and then I fainted. I don't remember anything more.'

That's her story and I presume she will stick to it.

3 May 1927

For five hours and a half yesterday questions went whistling past that marble chin of Mrs Ruth Brown Snyder's, but she kept on sticking it out defiantly from under the little brim of her black hat, like a fighter that can't be hurt.

At a pause just before recess in the old court room with the sickly yellow walls in Long Island City she reached out a steady hand, picked up a glass of water from the table in front of her, took a big swig, and looked at Charles F. Froessel, the assistant district attorney, who had been cross-examining her, as much as to say, 'Well, come on.'

But Froessel seemed a bit fagged out, and mopped a steaming brow with a handkerchief as Justice Townsend Scudder granted a motion by one of Mrs Snyder's attorneys for a recess until tomorrow morning.

The dialogue between Froessel and Mrs Snyder toward the close of the day was taking on something of the aspect of a breakfast table argument between a husband and the little woman, who can't exactly explain certain matters that the old boy wants to know.

She is a magnificent liar, if she is lying. You must give her that. She stands out 'mid keen competition these days, if she is lying. And if a liar she is a game liar, one of those 'that's my story and I'll stick to it' liars, which is the mark of the able liar.

And I regret to report that she seems to impress many of her listeners in the light of a wonderful liar rather than as a poor widowed soul falsely accused. The men were rather softening up toward the blonde woman at the close yesterday in sheer admiration of her as a possible liar, and even the women who leer at her all day long had stopped hating her. They seemed to be commencing to think that she was reflecting credit to femininity just as a prodigious liar.

Even Henry Judd Gray, the baggy-looking little corset salesman who was on trial with her for the murder, and who has been sitting inert and completely befogged since the case began, sat up yesterday as if they had suddenly puffed air into him.

He had a fresh haircut and clean linen and looked all sharpened up. He half started when she fairly shrilled 'no' at Froessel when he was asking her about the life insurance on Albert Snyder. Perhaps Gray had heard her say 'no' in that same voice before.

It was about the life insurance for $53,000 on Snyder's life that the assistant district attorney was most curious in his cross-examination, and about which Mrs Ruth Brown Snyder was the least convincing. It was to double in the event of her husband's death by accident, and the State claims that Albert Snyder didn't know his wife had taken it out.

It was a very bad session for her on that particular point. Her answers were at times vague and evasive, but her voice never lost its snap. She said the only motive Gray could have had for killing her husband was to get the life insurance money, and when it was suggested to her that she was the beneficiary, she argued: 'Well, he knew he would get it away from me just as he got money from me before.'

'Isn't it a fact that you and Gray planned to spend that insurance money together?' she was asked.

'No,' she said quickly.

Most of her answers were sharp yesses, or noes. In fact, Froessel insisted on yes-or-no answers, though sometimes she whipped in a few additional remarks to his great annoyance.

He hectored and badgered the blonde at times until her counsel objected and the Court admonished him. Froessel, a plump-built man of medium height, in the early forties, has a harsh voice and a nagging manner in cross-examination. He wears spectacles and is smooth-shaven and persistent, and there is no doubt that Mrs Snyder at times wished she had a sash weight handy.

That scared-rabbit looking little man, Henry Judd Gray, the corset salesman, is now engaged in what the cops would describe as 'putting the finger' on Mrs Ruth Brown Snyder, only such a short time back his ever-loving, red-hot Momsie.

He seems to be a fairly expert 'finger man', so far. Perhaps his proficiency goes back to his early youth and much practice pointing the accusatory digit and saying, 'Teacher, he done it.'

He lugged us through many a rendezvous in many a different spot with Mrs Snyder yesterday afternoon, while the lady, who had done a little 'fingering' herself for three days, sat looking daggers at Henry Judd, and probably thinking arsenic, mercury tablets, chloroform, picture wire and sash weights.

This was after she had come out of a spell of weeping when her little daughter, Lorraine, was on the stand. That was a spectacle, my friends – the child in the court room – to make the angels shed tears, and men hide their faces in shame, that such things can be.

Henry Judd had scarcely gotten us out of the hotels which he and Mrs Ruth Brown Snyder infested in the days – ah, yes, and the nights – when their heat for each other was up around 102 Fahrenheit, when a recess was taken until this morning.

It is likely that the case will go to the jury by Friday. It has taken two weeks to try a murder that the citizens of Pueblo County, Colorado, could have settled in two minutes under any cottonwood tree on the banks of the Arkansas, if all the State of New York has developed is true. But the citizens of Pueblo County are forehanded and forthright gents.

6 May 1927

Mankind at last has a clue, developed by the Snyder-Gray trial, as to the approximate moment when a blonde becomes very, very dangerous.

Gentlemen, if she asks you to try out a few sleeping powders,

187

that is the instant you are to snatch up the old chapeau and take the air.

Henry Judd Gray gave this valuable tip to his fellow citizens from the witness stand yesterday, when he was under cross-examination.

He said that not until Mrs Ruth Brown Snyder induced him to serve as a sort of guinea pig of experimentation with sleeping powders, which she purposed using on her husband, did he realize he was completely under the spell of her magnetism that caused him to later join hands with her in the slaughter of her husband, Albert Snyder.

It was in May, a year ago, that he inhaled the powders for her so she might see how they would work. He had knocked around with her quite a bit up to that time, but it seemed the old spell hadn't got down to business. After that, he said, he knew he would do anything she wanted.

He was in her power. Narrowly did I escape writing it powder. It wasn't fear, he said; no, not fear. She had never threatened him. It was more magnetism than anything else.

This remains the best show in town, if I do say so, as I shouldn't. Business couldn't be better. In fact, there is some talk of sending out a No. 2 company and 8,000,000 different blondes are being considered for the leading female role. No one has yet been picked for Henry Judd Gray's part but that will be easy. Almost any citizen will do with a little rehearsal.

7 May 1927

The Snyder-Gray murder trial – you instinctively put the woman first in this instance – is about over, and the twelve good men and true, who have been stolidly listening to the horrible tale for two weeks will decide soon what shall be done with this precious pair, the cheaters who tried to cheat the laws of God and man and wound up trying to cheat each other.

At about three o'clock yesterday afternoon, all hands rested as they say when they have dug up all the testimony they think will do any good, or any harm, either. If the Sabbath peace

and quiet of any neighbourhood is offended by loud sten-
torian voices, that will be the lawyers warming up for a lot of
hollering Monday.

Court has taken a recess until then. Dana Wallace will open
in defence of Mrs Snyder. William L. Millard will follow
Wallace, in an effort to talk Gray out of the chair.

Richard S. Newcombe, the grave district attorney of
Queens County, will do most of the arguing for the State of
New York.

And what, think you, do the blonde woman and the little
corset salesman expect from the twelve good men and true?

Gray – nothing. Gray's attorneys say he now has a clean
conscience, since relieving it of the details of the butchery of
Albert Snyder, and he thinks the jury will believe his story of
how the woman wound her insidious blonde coils about his
life until he couldn't help doing anything she desired.

I gather from the statement that he expects no clemency.
Blessed be he who expects nothing, for mayhap he will not be
disappointed. I suppose that deep down Gray is hoping for
mercy.

And the blonde? You can always look for a blonde to say
something unique. Mrs Ruth Brown Snyder says, through
her attorneys, Dana Wallace and Edgar Hazelton, that she
doesn't see how 'any red-blooded men' can believe Gray's
story – that hers was the heavy hand in the hammering and
chloroforming and wiring to death of her husband.

He seemed to be red-blooded himself, this Albert Snyder,
whose ghostly figure has stalked in the background of this
horrible screen presentation of human life and death for two
weeks. Much of that red blood is still on a pillow on which his
head rested when Gray first beat down upon it with the sash
weight, and which was still lying on the district attorney's
table along with the other horrible exhibits of the crime after
Court took a recess yesterday afternoon.

Two hundred men and women gathered about the table,
pushing and struggling with each other for a mere peek at the
exhibits. Several hundred others had gone into the street
outside to pull and haul for a view of Olga Petrova, as she

stood beside her Rolls-Royce, being photographed, and of Leon Errol, the comedian, and other celebrities who honoured us with their presence yesterday.

That scene in the court was one that should give the philosophers and psychologists pause. The women were far more interested in the bloody pillow than they would have been in a baby buggy. It was the last thrill left to them after Gray and Mrs Snyder walked out of the court, the woman passing rows of the leering eyes of her sisters with her head down, but with a dangerous gleam in the greenish blue eyes.

Henry Judd started off the day with a good big jolt of water from the glass on the table in front of the witness stand. He imbibed water while he was on the stand at the same rate at which he used to drink whisky, if he was the two-handed whisky-wrestler that his story would indicate.

Wallace touched briefly on Gray's whisky drinking again as he went into the corset salesman's finances. He wanted to know if Henry Judd always paid for the drinks. Henry said he did, a statement which interested all the bootleggers present. They wondered how he could do so much elbow-bending on his income.

9 May 1927

If you are asking a medium-boiled reporter of murder trials, I couldn't condemn a woman to death no matter what she had done, and I say this with all due consideration of the future hazards to long-suffering man from sash weights that any lesser verdict than murder in the first degree in the Snyder-Gray case may produce.

It is all very well for the rest of us to say what *ought* to be done to the blonde throwback to the jungle cat that they call Mrs Ruth Brown Snyder, but when you get in the jury room and start thinking about going home to tell the neighbours that you have voted to burn a woman – even a blonde woman – I imagine the situation has a different aspect. The most astonishing verdict that could be rendered in this case, of course, would be first degree for the woman and something else for the man. I doubt that result. I am inclined to think that the verdict, whatever it may be, will run against both alike – death or life imprisonment.

Henry Judd Gray said he expects to go to the chair, and adds that he is not afraid of death, an enviable frame of mind, indeed. He says that since he told his story to the world from the witness stand he has found tranquillity, though his tale may have also condemned his blonde partner in blood. But perhaps that's the very reason Henry Judd finds tranquillity.

He sat in his cell in the county jail over in Long Island yesterday, and read from one of the epistles of John.

'Marvel not, my brethren, if the world hates you. We know that we have passed from death unto life, because we love the brethren. He that loveth not his brother abideth in death. Whosoever hateth his brother is a murderer: and ye know that no murderer hath eternal life abiding in him.'

A thought for the second Sunday after Pentecost.

In another cell, the blonde woman was very mad at every-body because she couldn't get a marcel for the bobbed locks, one hair of which was once stronger with Henry Judd Gray than the Atlantic Cable.

Also she desired a manicure, but the cruel authorities would not permit the selected one to attend the lady.

Thus Mrs Snyder will have to go into court today with hang-nails and just those offices that she can give her bobbed bean herself. I fear that this injustice will prove another argument of sinister persecution when the folks start declaiming against burning the lady, if such should chance to be the verdict of the jury.

However, with all her troubles about her fingernails and the marcel, Mrs Snyder did not forget Mother's Day. She is herself a mother as you may remember, though the fact seemed to skip her mind at times when she was all agog over Henry Judd. Also she has a mother, who spent the Sabbath very quietly in the house of horror in Queens Village with Mrs Snyder's little daughter, Lorraine.

From the old jail Mrs Snyder sent her mother this:

Mother's Day Greeting – I have many blessings and I want you to know how thankful I am for all that you have done for me.

191

Love to you and kiss Lorraine for me.   Ruth

Henry Judd Gray, although calm yesterday, declined his breakfast. Moreover, he scarcely touched his lunch. Mrs Snyder, on the other hand, is reported to have breakfasted well and was longing for some of the good Signor Roberto Minotti's spaghetti and roasted chicken at noon.

They both attended divine services at the jail in the afternoon. Mrs Snyder seems quite calm, though at similar services last week she was all broken up. As between the two, the blonde seems to be rallying for the last round better than her former sweet daddy of the days before the murder.

Judge Scudder, the tall, courtly, dignified man, who has impressed all beholders of this proceeding as one of the ablest jurists that ever wrapped a black robe around himself, will charge the jury at some length because he must outline what consists of four different degrees of homicide. He will undoubtedly devote much time to the conspiracy charge in the indictment.

The jurors are men of what you might call average intelligence, I mean to say there are no intellectual giants in the box. They are fellows you might meet in any club or cigar store or speakeasy. A good jury, I call it. I doubt if they will be influenced by any psychological or philosophical twists that the lawyers may attempt to offer them, if any.

10 May 1927

Mighty short shrift was made of Mrs Ruth Brown Snyder and Henry Judd Gray by that jury of Long Islanders – the verdict being murder in the first degree for both, the penalty death in the electric chair.

The twelve men went out at 5.20 yesterday afternoon and were back in the box ready to deliver their verdict at 6.57, an hour and thirty-seven minutes. They took off their coats as they entered the jury room, hoisted the windows for a breath of air, and took two ballots.

The first was ten to two for first degree murder, so I understand, the second was unanimous. Justice moved on the gallop against the murderers once the jury got hold of the case.

Mrs Snyder, standing up to hear the verdict, dropped in her chair and covered her face with her hands. Henry Judd Gray, standing not far from her, held himself stiffly erect for a moment, but more like a man who had been shot and was swaying ever so slightly for a fall. Then he sat down, pulled a prayer book out of his pocket and began reading it.

He kept on reading even while the lawyers were up at Justice Scudder's bench arguing with the Court against immediate sentence. Mrs Snyder sat with her face buried between her hands. Justice Scudder finally fixed the time of sentence for Monday morning at ten o'clock.

Gray finally put the prayer book back in his pocket and sat looking straight ahead of him, as if he had found some comforting passage in the word of the Lord. He said to his guard on his way to his cell, 'I told the truth and my conscience is clear. My mother is glad I told the truth and God Almighty knows I told the truth.'

'Oh, I thought they'd believe me – I thought they'd believe me,' moaned Mrs Snyder to Father Patrick Murphy when she met him in the hallway going back to the jail. But before she left the court room there was a flash of the old defiance that marked her demeanour until the late stages of the trial.

'I haven't lost my nerve. My attorneys know that I have not had a fair trial, and we will fight this verdict with every ounce of strength.'

They have a curious custom in New York State of taking the prisoners before the clerk of the court after a verdict is returned and setting down their 'pedigree' – age, occupation, habits and the like. John Moran, the clerk of the Queens County Court, sits in a little enclosed booth like a bank teller's cage, just in front of the judge's bench, and Mrs Snyder was asked to step up there. Mrs Irene Wolfe, the matron of the county jail, and a guard supported her, the man putting his arm around the blonde woman as if he was afraid the black-gowned figure would crumble and fall.

The law is a harsh institution. It would have seemed more merciful to take the woman away at once to some quiet place, where she could allow the tears she was choking back with difficulty to fall as they might.

But they stood her up there and asked her a lot of questions that seemed fatuous in view of what is already known of her, and she answered in a low voice – Ruth Brown Snyder, thirty-two years old, born in New York and all that sort of thing. Married? A widow. The tears began trickling down the marble-white cheeks.

Then they finally took her out of the court room by the same path she had trod so often the last couple of weeks. She was pretty thoroughly licked at that moment, and small wonder, for she had just heard twelve men tell her she must die.

Gray stood up before Moran, still holding himself stiffly, but did not weep. In answer to one of the set questions as to whether he is temperate or otherwise, he said temperate, which sounded somewhat ironical in view of Gray's testimony during the trial as to the prodigious amounts of liquor he consumed.

He, too, was finally taken away, still walking as if he had put a ramrod down the back of his coat to hold himself so. Henry Judd Gray had said he expected such a sentence, and he was not disappointed.

The pair probably knew they were gone when they received word to make ready to return to the court room in such a short time after the jury retired. Rumour had tossed the verdict pretty well around Long Island City and the court room when the announcement came that the jury was ready to report and the verdict was a foregone conclusion.

A few hours' delay might have produced hope for one or the other of the man and woman that fate tossed together with such horrible results. It was still daylight over Long Island City, although the yellowish-walled old court room was vaguely lighted by electric lamps, which shed less illumination than any lights I ever saw.

There was a painful stage wait, and in came Mrs Snyder and Gray, the former between two matrons, Mrs Wolfe and another, and Gray between two guards. Attorney Edgar Hazelton came in with her. He had evidently gone out to steel her for the verdict. He knew what it was, no doubt of that. She walked in with her little quick, short steps, but her face was grey – not white-grey, a dull, sickening grey.

The man walked firmly, too, but you could see by the expression in his eyes he felt what was coming. He seemed to be holding himself together with a strong effort.

Now a stir told of the coming of Justice Scudder, a lean, stooping figure in his black robe, bobbing his head to the right and left with little short bows like an archbishop. The crowd always rises at the entrance of the judge, then sits down again in some confusion, but this time everyone seemed to adjust himself in his seat noiselessly.

Justice Scudder peered around from under the green-shaded stand lamp on his desk with an inquiring expression, and, as the roll of the jurors was called, they answered in very low voices. Only one said 'here' rather loudly, almost defiantly, it seemed.

The clerk of the court motioned the jurors to stand and then Mrs Snyder and Henry Judd Gray were also told to rise. They stood there, Mrs Snyder just behind Gray, leaning against the table. Gray had no support. They could not see each other.

Ten women fainted in the court room in the course of the day, such was the pulling and hauling and the general excitement of the occasion, but Mrs Ruth Brown Snyder remained as cool as the well-known old cucumber, even when she heard herself termed enough different kinds of animals to populate the zoo.

She was mentioned as a serpent by William L. Millard. Also as a tigress. Still, Millard gave her a back-handed boost, at that, when he called her a sinister, fascinating woman. Perhaps Mrs Snyder would have been just as well pleased if he had left off the sinister.

Cruel, calculating and cunning, he said she was. She kept her eyes closed while Millard was berating her, supporting her head on her right hand, an elbow leaned on the table. Her left hand was across her breast. Once she dabbed her eyes with a little kerchief, as if she might be mopping away a few tears.

But all that Millard said about Mrs Snyder was just a few sweet nothings compared with what Dana Wallace said about Gray. He was 'human filth', 'diabolical fiend', 'weak-minded', 'despicable creature', 'falsifier', and finally a 'human anaconda', which is interesting if true, and ought to get Harry Judd a job in any side show.

The little corset salesman just stared straight ahead while Wallace was blasting him. However, he was upright and alert and heard everything Wallace said, probably figuring it sounded libellous. His mother and sister sat near by and comforted him.

There was much talk of the Deity on all sides. Both Millard and Wallace appealed to Him, and so, too, did the district attorney, when he came to summing up for the State. Newcombe was brief, and omitted brickbats for the defendants. He did compare Mrs Snyder to a jungle cat, possibly just to make sure that no animals had been left out.

The district attorney was in what you may call a soft spot, anyway, with the defendants at loggerheads, and each trying to push the other into the electric chair. However, from the beginning Newcombe has conducted this case with singular simplicity of method, and without any attempt at red fire.

Millard's argument for Gray was as expected, that Henry Judd was a poor fool, a dupe, and a lot of other things that mean a chump, who was beguiled by the woman.

However, he astonished the populace by advancing the theory that Mrs Snyder slipped Henry Judd a dose of poison the night of the murder, expecting her little playmate in blood would fold up and die also after he had assisted in dispatching Snyder. The poison didn't work, Millard said.

Furthermore, Millard made the first open suggestion of abnormality in Mrs Snyder. I heard hints that Gray's attorneys intended trying to show that the lady wasn't altogether normal, during the trial, but all that junk was kept out – by agreement, as I understand it – and only in his argument yesterday did Millard mention the abnormality.

For Mrs Snyder, the defence was she was the victim of Henry Judd, 'the human anaconda', and he was but 'hiding

196

behind the woman's skirts'. This caused Lieutenant McDermott, of the Police Department, to suggest mildly to me that it was a great phrase and true, in the old days, but now a woman's skirts are nothing to hide behind if a gent wishes to be really concealed.

Both Millard and Wallace were in favour of their clients being acquitted. Millard's was something of an appeal for pity, but Wallace said, in the spirit of Mrs Snyder's defiance throughout this trial, that she was not asking for pity, she was asking for justice.

In some ways it was a disheartening spectacle, if one happened to think how many spectators would have been attracted to Long Island City to hear a few pleas for the Mississippi Flood sufferers. In another, it was something of a tribute to the power of good old publicity. It pays to advertise. We have been three-sheeting Henry Judd and Ruth to good purpose.

Editor's comment: *Though the respective ingenious lawyers of Ruth Snyder and Henry Judd Gray did their best (or, to those who believe in ethics, worst) to persuade judges to grant new trials, then to sway politicians towards the belief that they would benefit were the sentences to be commuted to life imprisonment, the executions were carried out soon after eleven o'clock on the morning of Friday, 13 January 1928. The woman was seated first. Her final words, not original (they had been spoken in a similar situation by, among others, Johann Hoch, an American 'bluebeard'), were: 'Father, forgive them, for they know not what they do.' Making the case squalid to the end, a photographer for the New York* Daily News *gained admittance to the death chamber by posing as a reporter and, using an 'ankle camera', took a photograph of Mrs Snyder as the electricity pulsed through her body. A couple of minutes after the body had been wheeled into the autopsy room, Gray was strapped into the chair. He remained silent.*

Incidentally, Damon Runyon declined his invitation to the double event.

More Authors Cover the Snyder Trial
JAMES THURBER

I

WHO DID WE DID DID WE WE DID, SAYS MISS STEIN!
By Gertrude Stein

This is a trial. This is quite a trial. I am on trial. They are on trial. Who is on trial?

I can tell you how it is. I can tell you have told you will tell you how it is.

There is a man. There is a woman. There is not a man. There would have been a man. There was a man. There were two men. There is one man. There is a woman where is a woman is a man.

He says he did. He says he did not. She says she did. She says she did not. She says he did. He says she did. She says they did. He says they did. He says they did not. She says they did not. I'll say they did.

II
JOYCE FINDS SOCKSOCKING IS BIG ELEMENT IN MURDER CASE!
By James Joyce

Trial regen by trialholden Queenscountycourthouse with tumpetty taptap mid socksocking with sashweights by jackals. In socksocking, the sashwiring goes: guggengaggleoggogg-snukkkk. . . . To corsetsale is to alibi is to meetinloven-killenlove. *Rehab des arbah sed drahab!* Not a quart of papa's booze had poison booze vor the killparty for the snuggle-snuggle. . . .

Editor's comment: *There is a third parody, of the style of Ty Cobb, the sports reporter; but I have omitted this, not because some of the baseball terms would be pretty meaningless, and the rest quite meaningless, to most non-American readers, but because about a quarter of the piece relates to a then topical but now virtually forgotten incident, an explanation of which would need a footnote dwarfing the pastiche.*

The page of The New Yorker *on which the parodies appeared is, I think, the most variedly entertaining one that I have seen in any periodical. At the foot of the left-hand column, filling the inch or so of space below the parodies, is a report taken from the* Auburn (Alabama) News *which no one on that paper realized was funny, and the rest of the page is filled by an advertisement for a joyful shampoo, which reads, in part:*

. . . Glad news to women who have hated ordinary shampoos for the trouble they cause.

Your bob, once so chic, is . . . well, impossible! But what a different story after Taroleum! . . . Nothing beautifies a woman's hair as much as just the right amount of fluffiness – enough to let the light steal softly through the locks, adding colour, sheen, luster. Perhaps you will also be glad to know that Taroleum cleans quickly and thoroughly with oodles and oodles of snowy white suds. You'll find that a shampoo can be joyful! . . .

Your druggist has large bottle for 50 cents.

The Importance of Spelling

F. TENNYSON JESSE

England is, perhaps more than any country in the world, possessed of ultra-respectable seaside 'resorts'. They ooze respectability. Their neat villas, their pine trees, their old people in bathchairs, their often somewhat somnolent climate, very seldom are connected with crime. Yet Bournemouth, probably the most respectable and exclusive 'Queen of the Watering Places', can boast of one of the most unaccountable murders of all. This was the murder of a young woman called Irene May Wilkins who lived in a suburb of London. She was the daughter of a barrister and had served in the first World War in the Women's Army Auxiliary Corps. She was a nice-looking, strong and healthy girl of good character, anxious to help her widowed mother and not afraid of hard work, so she put an advertisement in the *Morning Post*, a very reputable paper, which ran as follows:

> Lady Cook, 31, requires post in a school. Experienced in school with forty boarders. Disengaged. Salary £65. Miss Irene Wilkins, 21 Thirlmere Road, Streatham, S.W.16.

Before noon on the day that this advertisement was published, 22 December 1921, Irene Wilkins received a telegram from Bournemouth, sent to her suburban home in Streatham, London. It read:

> Morning Post. Come immediately 4.30 train Waterloo. Bournmouth Central. Car will meet train. Expence no object. Urgent. Wood, Beech House.

Now, there are two things to be remarked at once about this telegram. Bournemouth is spelt without the *e* which should be in the middle and expense is incorrectly spelt with a *c* instead of an *s*. However, even if Irene Wilkins and her mother and sister noticed these little oddities, it is probable that they thought that the girl in the post office may have been responsible for the mis-spelling. Irene at once wired to Bournemouth that she would come down for an interview, and that afternoon at about 3 o'clock she left home to catch the 4.30 express from Waterloo, London. Some time after she had left, the telegram she had sent to Bournemouth was returned to Thirlmere Road as the post office said that there was no such name and address as Wood, Beech House, Bournemouth. Mrs Wilkins was a little upset by this, but not unduly so.

Early on the morning of Friday the twenty-third of December, the dead body of a young woman was found between Bournemouth and Christchurch in rather a desolate spot, no longer farmland but only partly under construction. It is now covered with villas but was not then a built-up area. A labourer found the body at daybreak as he walked to work. The labourer's attention had been drawn by the sight of two cows nosing at something on the ground. He got over into the field and found the body lying on its back; the face was covered with blood. He betook himself to the nearest telephone and called the police. They found that in the roadway was the track of an automobile running on Dunlop Magnum tyres, and by the extra deepness of the tread it was to be seen that the car had pulled up beside the point where the body was found.

There was not the smallest doubt that the girl had been murdered, and most brutally murdered. Her head and face were bruised and battered as by a fist driven violently into it, so that her eyelids were swollen and her teeth driven into her lower lip. Added to these comparatively superficial injuries, her skull had been penetrated by three distinct strokes of some very heavy instrument, one on the hairline of the forehead, one through the left cheek bone and one on the level of the right ear, lacerating the brain. Each of these three wounds was alone enough to cause death. It was obvious that she had fought desperately for her life. Her right arm, the fist clenched, was thrown above her head; her left arm was flung straight out at the side, the fist also clenched; and her hands were covered with blood and deeply scratched. There were many bruises on her lower arms and on her hips and thighs. Her clothes were pulled up round her waist, but the attempt at criminal assault had failed and she was still *virgo intacta*.

Some man had lured Irene Wilkins to Bournemouth, and there she had striven to save herself and been savagely killed whilst in almost every house in Bournemouth the knitting needles clicked and the teacups tinkled and bridge-cards were laid out for the evening's amusement. The ordinary life of a seaside town went on unknowing, because whoever the murderer had been he had known his way well enough to select this deserted spot for his purpose. Already a description of the missing girl had been given to the police by her now frantically anxious family so that identification had been immediate, but Irene had known nobody in or near Bournemouth.

The 4.30 train from Waterloo was due at Bournemouth Central Station at 6.45, but had not come in till 7.03 on the evening of the twenty-second of December. To drive at a moderate speed from the station to the scene of the murder was found to take a little over ten minutes in a direct line. Rain had fallen during the early evening but at 8.45 it had ceased and had given place to a strong drying wind. Yet Irene's clothes were still damp with rain, particularly the under part of her overcoat. It could fairly be assumed that the assault had taken place before 8.45 and after 7.30. A cottager had come placidly walking along the path at some time soon after 8.30 to change the tethering place of his goats and had seen the silhouette of an empty car standing with dimmed lights in the lane on his journeys both to and from his cottage. It is possible that it was he, though all unaware, who had interrupted the final spoliation which Irene Wilkin's attacker had evidently intended but had failed to accomplish. The tracks of the car continued along the lane and rejoined the road to Bournemouth by another partially constructed driveway.

The police came to the conclusion that in all probability the driver of the car which had brought Irene Wilkins from Bournemouth Station to the point where she met her death knew the locality well and was still in the neighbourhood, and the local evening paper bore the story of the finding of the body. There was a roundup of all cars in the district and the order was given that every chauffeur and every owner-driver were to report to the police for questioning. Particular attention was paid to their movements between 7 and 9 o'clock on the evening in question and particular notice was taken of all vehicles using Dunlop Magnum tyres or those with a similar tread.

Now, a Mr Frank Humphris, consulting engineer and designer, had also travelled down by the 4.30 train from Waterloo on the twenty-second of December, and he had noticed Irene on the platform at Bournemouth Central Station where they and a great many others had got out. She was standing beside him at the barrier and her hat caught his eye; it was of pale brown suede with a trimming of red suede threaded through slits in the crown, the ends crossing at the left. He had seen her asking a porter where to go, as if she were uncertain what to do. He came out of the station expecting to find his car waiting for him but it was not there and while he was looking for it a gust of wind picked up some newspapers from a pile just outside the entrance and scattered them into the road where four cars were parked. Mr Humphris darted forward to intercept the newspapers and in doing so almost ran into a man who was standing in the shadow of a car. This man was dressed in chauffeur's uniform without an overcoat. He wore a double-breasted short coat, black breeches, black boots, and a peaked cap. There was, alas, nothing to show that his heart and mind were as black as his outer coverings. Mr Humphris, who was a noticing sort of man, observed the chauffeur; he saw that the car was a greenish-grey touring car with a peculiar top and that the lights were not on; he strolled a few yards beyond the station approach, still looking for his own car, and he saw the grey-green car, driven by the chauffeur he had nearly collided with, drive past him at a good speed. In the front seat of the car beside the chauffeur was the girl he had already observed on the platform: her brown suede hat with the red insertion was silhouetted clearly against the lighted wall of the station entrance. The car itself attracted his attention for several reasons. The lamps, he afterwards said in evidence, were excessively brilliant and their position was unique – considerably more forward than is usual. The body of the car had peculiar lines, the hood extremely long, and there was an odd second windshield designed for the benefit of passengers in the back seat. In particular, the luggage carrier so struck him that he thought of fitting it or something like it on one of his own cars.

Mr Humphris did not see the local paper on the evening it was first published but when he read of the discovery of Irene's body he immediately communicated with the police. He had no doubt whatever that the girl he had seen on the platform and in the grey-green car was the girl who had been murdered. On the twenty-fifth of December he wrote a full statement of what he knew while his Christmas dinner spoiled in the oven. The police now knew the appearance of the car to look for, besides looking for one with Dunlop Magnum tyres. Mr Humphris's evidence was corroborated two days later by a commercial traveller who had also been struck by the long sloping hood of the car in the station yard and had happened to notice that its lights were switched off as soon as it was parked. He, too, remembered the newspapers whirling in the wind. He had examined one of the car's wheels, which were wire wheels, and had taken particular notice of the hub as he was curious to know the make of the car, but though he peered closely at it he had not then been able to make out the lettering. Later, owing to this close scrutiny, he recognized the car again with absolute confidence as a Mercedes.

One of the first things the police followed up was the matter of the telegram which had been despatched from Bournemouth to Streatham on December twenty-second. In investigating this, two other such telegrams were found to have been sent off with similar spelling mistakes in them. These had been despatched on the seventeenth and on the twentieth of that month but mercifully the girls to whom they had been addressed had not been able to answer the summons in person. In the first telegram, that of the seventeenth of

December, the word *advertisement* was spelt *advertisment* and the word *immediate* was spelt *immidiate; Bournemouth* was spelt without its medial *e, if* was spelt *iff* and *expense* was spelt *expence*. In the second telegram, sent off on the twentieth of December, the word *pleasant* was spelt *plesent* and, due to the curious structure of the *c's car* looked like *ear*. In the third telegram, the one sent to Irene on the twenty-second of December, mistakes and oddities in the first were repeated; *car* again looked like *ear*, and although the writer was presumably copying the address from the advertisement in the *Morning Post, Thirlmere Road* had been spelt *Thirlmear Road*.

These three telegrams were now used by the police to try to determine the identity of their sender by his handwriting and spelling peculiarities. Therefore each person who was interviewed in respect of the tyres was also told to write down from dictation the three telegrams, and the resulting efforts were scrutinized for similiarities of form and style and closely compared with the originals. This ought to have caught the murderer at once but, owing to a slip-up amongst the papers, it did not do so till much later, though in the long run the telegrams hanged the murderer.

Days passed and the Wilkins family got through their unhappy Christmas and poor Irene was duly buried and there was still no arrest. No one in Bournemouth, that blameless resort, spoke of anything else. The place became full of amateur detectives and the usual dozens of people volunteered information to the police, most of it completely useless. Then on the thirty-first of December, nine days after the murder, an attaché-case containing among other personal possessions an envelope filled with testimonials to Miss Wilkins, which she had taken with her from London and which was missing when the body was found, was discovered among rhododendron bushes in Branksome Wood at the other end of Bournemouth. It was mildewed and had evidently been lying there some days and it confirmed Superintendent Garrett, who was in charge of the case, in his belief that, no matter how the Press might scream for Scotland Yard to be called in, the murderer was resident in the neighbourhood and had charge of a car; how otherwise account for a body being found at one extremity of the town and the attaché-case eight miles away in the opposite direction?

The police toiled on, something like 22,000 documents were filed in relation to the case, and the weeks dragged into months. By April, Superintendent Garrett was convinced that he knew the guilty man but had nothing like enough evidence to arrest him. He had the deepest suspicion of a man called Thomas Henry Allaway, a chauffeur in good private employment with wealthy people in one of the best parts of Bournemouth. Mr Garrett resolved to go through every document again in relation to the case and this laborious task was rewarded by the discovery of a report which had been dealt with and filed away as irrelevant by a subordinate. This was no less than a second report from Mr Frank Humphris, this time giving the licence number of the car which he had seen in the station yard on the night of the murder. He and his son had seen the car once again when hurrying to catch a train to London on January fourth, but Mr Humphris had had time to tell his son to scribble the number down. The car had been sent for by the police at that time and its driver questioned and made to write out the three telegrams from dictation, but his replies were disarming and his handwriting vertical, whereas the original telegrams were in a sloping hand, and so the whole report had been relegated to the limbo of a closed file. We will pass over what must have been Superintendent Garrett's feelings when he realized that this document had been all this time in the possession of the police and had not been placed in front of him, but it is easy to imagine that he felt like doing quite a little murdering himself. The number of the car was LK 7405 and proved to be a Mercedes, the property of Mr and Mrs Sutton of Barton Close, Bournemouth, who employed as their chauffeur the same Thomas Henry Allaway whose behaviour and record had earlier brought him under suspicion. Garrett now concentrated upon this man.

Thomas Henry Allaway was not an attractive person. During the war he had been a driver in the R.A.S.C. and had deserted. On recapture, owing to a civil offence in London, he had been sent back to drive in France and later on the Rhine. He had a heavy sullen face and a somewhat sharklike mouth, squared at the corners, which he kept slightly open. But people cannot be arrested because they are unattractive, or even because they have mouths like sharks. All the handwriting Garrett had been able to get hold of was entirely different from that of the decoy telegrams; so far the police had nothing in Allaway's handwriting written before the murder, only since, and these few specimens were in an upright hand. Garrett set about obtaining some specimen of the man's handwriting of an earlier date, and it is likely that Allaway became aware of the concentration of attention upon himself for he seemed to grow more and more uneasy. He was now betting desperately on horse races but never winning. His employer had lately secured for him, instead of the lodgings he had been occupying, a nice little flat, and he had taken his furniture out of storage and had settled in his new home with his wife and small daughter. Yet he decided to run away. On Thursday, the twentieth of April of the year following Irene's death, while engaged in the odd jobs which he often performed in his employer's house before the car was required in the morning, he stole a cheque book, filled in several cheques, forging Mr Sutton's name, and passed them off on various tradesmen who knew him as the Suttons' chauffeur. In this way he got hold of £20-odd in cash, and with this money he fled, despatching his family to his wife's parents' home in Reading. Garrett was delighted. He sent an officer to London to look for Allaway in his known haunts but he also told the Reading police to keep a watch on Allaway's wife's home and to arrest him if he should appear there. For it was now possible to apprehend Allaway for forgery and, holding him on that charge, to pursue all the enquiries necessary to bring in the murder charge.

On the twenty-eighth of April Garrett received a telephone message from the officer in London, where Allaway had been hiding under an assumed name, that his quarry was lost to sight. Garrett thereupon telephoned the Reading Police. That evening Allaway was arrested in Reading. He ran away when he saw the waiting policeman as he approached the house, but a passer-by tripped him up and he spent that night in a police cell at Reading and next day was taken back to Bournemouth. Betting slips had been found on him when he was examined at Reading and these, written in London when he was not bothering to change his writing, were in the same hand as the decoy telegrams.

Mrs Allaway came down at the request of the police to Bournemouth and, thinking the charge was merely one of forgery, handed over some postcards and a long letter written to her by her husband while he was in the R.A.S.C., driving in Germany. The letter was not only in the slanting hand of the three telegrams but bore many of the characteristic misspellings. Allaway had treated his wife badly and at one time she had wanted a separation; he had contracted syphilis while in Germany and she may not have minded too much the idea of his spending some months in prison. But she was horrified when she found what the charge hanging over her husband was. She did her best for him in the witness box at the trial, but by then there was very little that could be done. Allaway denied that the long letter from Germany, signed 'your loving husband Tom', was in his handwriting, saying that he had had an injured wrist at the time and a friend had written it for him. He gave the name of a man who had had one name in the army and another in civil life, but this man was found in Birmingham and Allaway's statement was quickly seen to be the futile lie it was.

Mrs Sutton of Barton Close told Superintendent Garrett that on the twenty-ninth of December last Allaway had driven her out to take tea with her sister, who lived at Branksome Wood. The entrance to the house faced the wood and it was here, among the rhododendron bushes that the attaché-case belonging to Irene Wilkins had been found on the thirty-first of December. Tea parties are apt to be lengthy affairs, especially when two sisters meet, and Allaway had had plenty of time and opportunity to dispose of the case, for he had remained with the car till Mrs Sutton wanted to go home, some one and a half hours later.

208

A week after he had been brought back to Bournemouth from Reading, Allaway was put in the 'line-up' for identification. The parade contained some nine or ten chauffeurs and taximen, and Allaway was allowed to place himself wherever he pleased. A newsagent picked him out as the man who had bought a copy of the *Morning Post* from him on the twenty-second of December. Three post office girls were brought: one failed to pick anyone out; one first picked out a man very like the prisoner and then picked out Allaway; the third was the most convincing. She had taken the second of the three telegrams at the Bournemouth post office and had queried the word 'car'. She remembered his voice as well as his face. She picked him out at once and then stood with her back to the parade listening while each man in turn repeated the words 'car . . . car will meet', which Allaway had read to her at the time of sending off the telegram. He had altered his position in the row when she turned her back, but no sooner had he spoken than she said: 'That is the man.' He had the hoarse voice of the syphilitic and its tone had impressed itself on her memory.

Mr Frank Humphris was another of the witnesses called to the parade and he had no hesitation whatsoever in picking out Allaway, by his open rectangular mouth, as the man he had almost bumped into in the station yard near the green-grey car in which he had driven Miss Wilkins away.

The third telegram, it must be remembered, that which Irene had received and which had been signed: 'Wood, Beech House', had been returned the same afternoon to the Wilkins' house at Streatham, but not before the post office had done their best to find for whom it was intended by taking it to Beech Hurst, Beechwood Avenue. At that house, Mr Sutton's son, an invalid, lived, and Allaway had often driven Mr Sutton there. It is difficult for anyone to think of entirely strange and unknown names at random, and particularly so for an ignorant and illiterate man, so it is worthy of note that place-names with a half-familiar ring to Allaway's ears should have been chosen as the place from which the decoy telegram originated.

After the identification parade, Garrett asked Allaway if he would care to make a statement. Allaway decided to write his statement instead of dictating it, and to write it in the artificial vertical handwriting he had been building up. It was probably a recapitulation of what he did with his time most nights in the week and it spread over as much of the important evening as possible, but even so there was the best part of an hour unaccounted for between 7.30 and 8.15, in which he said he was reading alone in his lodgings while his wife was at the cinema. Most of the witnesses, when called upon to corroborate at what hour he made his appearance at the Salisbury Hotel to drink and chat with friends till his wife should join him, were of the opinion that it was nearer nine than 8.15. And it had been estimated that the assault upon Irene must have occurred between 7.30 and 8.45. It would have been wiser if Allaway had risked giving a bad impression and refused to make any statement at all; or if he had risked the pitfalls his tongue might have slipped into had he dictated one. For the remarkable thing about the statement he wrote was that the handwriting, which began in the acquired fashion – upright, tending even to backward – gradually relapsed as it went on into the slanting hand in which all the telegrams had been written.

Later he was asked to take down the three telegrams again from dictation. When he had done this early in January, he had scrawled down his answers, using the mudguard of the Mercedes as a desk, in such a way that they bore no resemblance to any of his handwritings. This time he was exceedingly careful to maintain his upright hand but once again the spelling errors were there: he spelt *pleasant plesent*, *Bournemouth* without the medial *e*, *Thirlmere Thirlemar*, and *expense* with a *c* instead of an *s*. If there be a moral in this, it is that a murderer should learn how to spell.

The evidence now began to pile up. A signalman had seen Allaway meeting the train that had brought Irene and had answered some question as to the arrival of the down-train. Mr Humphris was ready with his evidence and his son could testify as to the number of the car. From among hundreds of hats presented for his selection Mr Humphris had promptly picked out the brown suede hat trimmed with red. Then there were the various witnesses present at the identification parade. The commercial traveller was able to identify Mr Sutton's Mercedes as the car whose hub he had examined in the station yard. A tea salesman who kept two vans in the same garage as the Mercedes, a public garage in Portland Mews, came forward to say that at nine o'clock on the morning of December twenty-fourth, following the police announcement in connection with vehicles with Dunlop Magnum tyres, he had seen Allaway changing a Dunlop Magnum tyre on a rear wheel of the Mercedes for a Michelin. In addition to Mrs Sutton's evidence as to the tea party at Branksome Wood, it was elicited from her that on numerous occasions in the past Allaway had driven her through the district where the murder had occurred, so that its secluded character was certainly known to him. A screw-hammer had been found in the flat from which Allaway had fled which would exactly account for the size and nature of the wounds inflicted on Irene Wilkins's face and head. Mr Sutton had engaged a successor to Allaway, who he must have devoutly hoped was less handy with a screw-hammer, and this man had moved into Allaway's flat and had found a key to the inner door of the garage in Portland Mews, hence the owner's previous testimony that Allaway could not have moved his car out unknown to him after garaging it as usual at 6 p.m became valueless. Specimens of Allaway's handwriting now in the hands of the police for expert comparison with the decoy telegrams ranged from betting slips and his application for a driver's licence, to the post cards and letters sent to his wife from Germany, and finally to the dictated telegrams and the statement with its conflicting styles.

Thomas Henry Allaway stood his trial for murder at Winchester Assizes on 3 July 1922 before Mr Justice Avory, one of the greatest, fairest and least sentimental of judges. It is not the responsibility of the prosecution in an English trial to prove motive. If motive is there, well and good, but it is quite unnecessary if the evidence is sufficient without it. It is, however, very interesting to ponder on what Allaway's motive could have been. He was a lustful man and a dour man. Three times he had sent off decoy telegrams to women whom he did not know, with the end in view of having sexual connection with them whether they consented or not. Irene, as we know, put up a hard fight, and Allaway may have stolen the few shillings that were in her bag or he may not. Murder has been committed for tiny sums, but I think we can say that the murder of Irene Wilkins was not committed for money. This strange, dark, brooding man, who could only be satisfied by intercourse with someone he did not know, had planned such an encounter again and again and had probably been strangely excited each time he had sent off his telegram. Each time he anticipated meeting and overpowering a strange woman. Yet there must have been many women in Bournemouth who were not known to him and who would have gone with him for the evening – but then there would always have been the danger, had they not been willing to submit to rape, that he would have been easily traced afterwards. The telegrams to London seem to show that he always intended both to murder and to rape, though it is impossible to guess in what order he envisaged it. Why otherwise should he seek so far afield?

He had been a bad husband and a bad citizen, but his measure as a murderer is something more than this; it is that he was a monster. There is a nightmare quality in the thought of this man, planning with a hideous excitement that no one but a monster could have known, the sequence of events that at the third attempt unfortunately fulfilled its inevitable pattern. How the murder actually took place must always be a matter for conjecture. Whether he opened the car door in that dark and empty lane and invited her to get out or whether he attacked her while still in the car and she fought back there, can only be a matter of surmise. That she fought from the first moment there is no doubt, nor that he attacked her with extreme ferocity.

Mr Justice Avory summed up very clearly and fairly, and

the all-male jury only took an hour to consider their verdict, which was one of 'Guilty'. In spite of the conclusive mass of evidence which established his guilt, there were those in England who preferred to think that Allaway was only a catspaw for some wealthy roué, but they had not seen what the jury had seen, the expression of the prisoner in the box when he was attempting to deny that it was his handwriting in the letter from Germany signed: 'your loving husband Tom.' Recognizing the utter futility of that denial, he paused, and in that one flashing moment he looked a beaten and a guilty man before all eyes.

Allaway lost his appeal and was hanged on an August morning in 1922. Without wishing to be vindictive, I yet feel it impossible to be sorry that for once an execution did not go altogether smoothly; the noose shifted and Allaway died from strangulation, thrashing around in the brick pit, instead of from a broken neck. The world is better off without him. The tragedy is that it needed the life of a good and honest girl to make that plain.

His death was still much more merciful than the one he had meted out to Irene Wilkins.

A Massacre in Massachusetts

HENRY DAVID THOREAU

Written in 1839

On the thirty-first day of March, one hundred and forty-two years before this, probably about this time in the afternoon, there were hurriedly paddling down this part of the river, between the pine woods which then fringed these banks, two white women and a boy, who had left an island at the mouth of the Contoocook before daybreak. They were slightly clad for the season in the English fashion, and handled their paddles unskilfully, but with nervous energy and determination, and at the bottom of their canoe lay the still-bleeding scalps of ten of the aborigines. They were Hannah Dustan, and her nurse, Mary Neff, both of Haverhill, eighteen miles from the mouth of this river, and an English boy, named Samuel Lennardson, escaping from captivity among the Indians. On the 15th of March previous, Hannah Dustan had been compelled to rise from childbed, and half dressed, with one foot bare, accompanied by her nurse, commence an uncertain march, in still inclement weather, through the snow and the wilderness. She had seen her seven elder children flee with her father, but knew not of their fate. She had seen her infant's brains dashed out against an apple tree, and had left her own and her neighbours' dwellings in ashes. When she reached the wigwam of her captor, situated on an island in the Merrimack, more than twenty miles above where we now are, she had been told that she and her nurse were soon to be taken to a distant Indian settlement, and there made to run the gauntlet naked. The family of this Indian consisted of two men, three women, and seven children, besides an English boy, whom she found a prisoner among them. Having determined to attempt her escape, she instructed the boy to inquire of one of the men how he should dispatch an enemy in the quickest manner, and take his scalp. 'Strike 'em there,' said he, placing his finger on his temple, and he also showed him how to take off the scalp. On the morning of the thirty-first she arose before daybreak, and awoke her nurse and the boy, and taking the Indians' tomahawks, they killed them all in their sleep, excepting one favourite boy, and one squaw who fled wounded with him to the woods. The English boy struck the Indian who had given him the information on the temple, as he had been directed. They then collected all the provision they could find, and took their master's tomahawk and gun, and scuttling all the canoes but one, commenced their flight to Haverhill, distant about sixty miles by the river. But after having proceeded a short distance, fearing that her story would not be believed if she should escape to tell it, they returned to the silent wigwam, and taking off the scalps of the dead, put them into a bag as proofs of what they had done, and then, retracing their steps to the shore in the twilight, recommenced their voyage.

Early this morning this deed was performed, and now, perchance, these tired women and this boy, their clothes stained with blood, and their minds racked with alternate resolution and fear, are making a hasty meal of parched corn and moose meat, while their canoe glides under these pine roots whose stumps are still standing on the bank. They are thinking of the dead whom they have left behind on that solitary isle far up the stream, and of the relentless living warriors who are in pursuit. Every withered leaf which the winter has left seems to know their story, and in its rustling to repeat it and betray them. An Indian lurks behind every rock and pine, and their nerves cannot bear the tapping of a wood-pecker. Or they forget their own dangers and their deeds, in conjecturing the fate of their kindred, and whether, if they escape the Indians, they shall find the former still alive. They do not stop to cook their meals upon the bank, nor land, except to carry their canoe about the falls. The stolen birch forgets its master and does them good service, and the swollen current bears them swiftly along with little need of paddle, except to steer and keep them warm by exercise. For ice is floating in the river; the spring is opening; the muskrat and the beaver are driven out of their holes by the flood; deer gaze at them from the bank; a few faint-singing forest birds, perchance, fly across the river to the northernmost shore; the fish hawk sails and screams overhead, and geese fly over with a startling clangour; but they do not observe these things, or they speedily forget them. They do not smile or chat all day. Sometimes they pass an Indian grave surrounded by its paling on the bank, or the frame of a wigwam, with a few coals left behind, or the withered stalks still rustling in the Indian's solitary cornfield on the interval. The birch stripped of its bark, or the charred stump where a tree has been burned down to be made into a canoe – these are the only traces of man, a fabulous wild man to us. On either side, the primeval forest stretches away uninterrupted to Canada, or to the 'South Sea'; to the white man a drear and howling wilderness, but to the Indian a home, adapted to his nature, and cheerful as the smile of the Great Spirit.

While we loiter here this autumn evening, looking for a spot retired enough, where we shall quietly rest tonight, they thus, in that chilly March evening, one hundred and forty-two years before us, with wind and current favouring, have already glided out of sight, not to camp, as we shall, at night, but while two sleep one will manage the canoe, and the swift stream bear them onward to the settlements, it may be, even to old John Lowell's house on Salmon Brook tonight.

According to the historian, they escaped as by a miracle all roving bands of Indians, and reached their homes in safety, with their trophies, for which the General Court paid them fifty pounds. The family of Hannah Dustan all assembled alive once more, except the infant whose brains were dashed out against the apple tree, and there have been many who in later times have lived to say that they had eaten of the fruit of that apple tree.

A Sort of Genius

JAMES THURBER

1937

On the morning of Saturday, the 16th of September, 1922, a boy named Raymond Schneider and a girl named Pearl Bahmer, walking down a lonely lane on the outskirts of New Brunswick, New Jersey, came upon something that made them rush to the nearest house in Easton Avenue, around the corner, shouting. In that house an excited woman named Grace Edwards listened to them wide-eyed and then telephoned the police. The police came on the run and examined the young people's discovery: the bodies of a man and a woman. They had been shot to death and the woman's throat was cut. Leaning against one of the man's shoes was his calling card, not as if it had fallen there but as if it had been placed there. It bore the name Rev. Edward W. Hall. He had been the rector of the Protestant Episcopal Church of St John the Evangelist in New Brunswick. The woman was identified as Mrs Eleanor R. Mills, wife of the sexton of that church. Raymond Schneider and Pearl Bahmer had stumbled upon what was to go down finally in the annals of our crime as perhaps the country's most remarkable mystery. Nobody was ever found guilty of the murders. Before the case was officially closed, a hundred and fifty persons had had their day in court and on the front pages of the newspapers. The names of two must already have sprung to your mind: Mrs Jane Gibson, called by the avid press 'the pig woman', and William Carpender Stevens, once known to a hundred million people simply as 'Willie'. The pig woman died eleven years ago but Willie Stevens is alive. He still lives in the house that he lived in fourteen years ago with Mr and Mrs Hall, at 23 Nichol Avenue, New Brunswick.

It was from that house that the Rev. Mr Hall walked at

around 7.30 o'clock on the night of Thursday, the 14th of September 1922, to his peculiar doom. With the activities in the house after Mr Hall's departure the State of New Jersey was to be vitally concerned. No. 23 Nichol Avenue was to share with De Russey's Lane, in which the bodies were found, the morbid interest of a whole nation four years later, when the case was finally brought to trial. What actually happened in De Russey's Lane on the night of September 14th? What actually happened at 23 Nichol Avenue the same night? For the researcher, it is a matter of an involved and voluminous court record, colourful and exciting in places, confused and repetitious in others. Two things, however, stand out as sharply now as they did on the day of their telling: the pig woman's story of the people she saw in De Russey's Lane that night, and Willie Stevens's story of what went on in the house in Nichol Avenue. Willie's story, brought out in cross-examination by a prosecutor whose name you may have forgotten (it was Alexander Simpson), lacked all the gaudy melodrama of the pig woman's tale, but in it, and in the way he told it on the stand, was the real drama of the Hall-Mills trial. When the State failed miserably in its confident purpose of breaking Willie Stevens down, the verdict was already written on the wall. The rest of the trial was anticlimax. The jury that acquitted Willie, and his sister, Mrs Frances Stevens Hall, and his brother, Henry Stevens, was out only five hours.

A detailed recital of all the fantastic events and circumstances of the Hall-Mills case would fill a large volume. If the story is vague in your mind, it is partly because its edges, even under the harsh glare of investigation, remained curiously obscure and fuzzy. Everyone remembers, of course, that the minister was deeply involved with Mrs Mills, who sang in his choir; their affair had been for some time the gossip of their circle. He was forty-one, she was in her early thirties; Mrs Hall was past fifty. On the 14th of September, Mr Hall had dinner at home with his wife, Willie Stevens, and a little niece of Mrs Hall's. After dinner, he said, according to his wife and his brother-in-law, that he was going to call on Mrs Mills. There was something about a payment on a doctor's bill. Mrs Mills had had an operation and the Halls had paid for it (Mrs Hall had inherited considerable wealth from her parents). He left the house at about the same time, it came out later, that Mrs Mills left her house, and the two were found murdered, under a crab apple tree in De Russey's Lane, on the edge of town, some forty hours later. Around the bodies were scattered love letters which the choir singer had written to the minister. No weapons were found, but there were several cartridge shells from an automatic pistol.

The investigation that followed – marked, said one New Jersey lawyer, by 'bungling stupidity' – resulted in the failure of the Grand Jury to indict anyone. Willie Stevens was questioned for hours, and so was Mrs Hall. The pig woman told her extraordinary story of what she saw and heard in the lane that night, but she failed to impress the Grand Jurors. Four years went by, and the Hall-Mills case was almost forgotten by people outside of New Brunswick when, in a New Jersey court, one Arthur Riehl brought suit against his wife, the former Louise Geist, for annulment of their marriage. Louise Geist had been, at the time of the murders, a maid in the Hall household. Riehl said in the course of his testimony that his wife had told him 'she knew all about the case but had been given $5,000 to hold her tongue'. This was all that Mr Philip Payne, managing editor of the *Daily Mirror*, nosing around for a big scandal of some sort, needed. His newspaper 'played up' the story until finally, under its goading, Governor Moore of New Jersey appointed Alexander Simpson special prosecutor with orders to reopen the case. Mrs Hall and Willie Stevens were arrested and so was their brother, Henry Stevens, and a cousin, Henry de la Bruyere Carpender.

At a preliminary hearing in Somerville the pig woman, with eager stridency, told her story again. About 9 o'clock on the night of September 14th, she heard a wagon going along Hamilton Road near the farm on which she raised her pigs. Thieves had been stealing her corn and she thought maybe they were at it again. So she saddled her mule, Jenny (soon to become the most famous quadruped in the country), and set off in grotesque pursuit. In the glare of an automobile's headlights in De Russey's Lane, she saw a woman with white hair who was wearing a tan coat, and a man with a heavy moustache, who looked like a coloured man. These figures she identified as Mrs Hall and Willie Stevens. Tying her mule to a cedar tree, she started toward the scene on foot and heard voices raised in quarrel: 'Somebody said something about letters.' She now saw three persons (later on she increased this to four), and a flashlight held by one of them illuminated the face of a man she identified first as Henry Carpender, later as Henry Stevens, and it 'glittered on something' in the man's hand. Suddenly there was a shot, and as she turned and ran for her mule, there were three more shots; a woman's voice screamed, 'Oh, my! Oh, my! Oh, my!' and the voice of another woman moaned, 'Oh, Henry!' The pig woman rode wildly home on her mule, without investigating further. But she had lost one of her moccasins in her flight, and some three hours later, at 1 o'clock, she rode her mule back again to see if she could find it. This time, by the light of the moon, she saw Mrs Hall, she said, kneeling in the lane, weeping. There was no one else there. The pig woman did not see any bodies.

Mrs Jane Gibson became, because of her remarkable story, the chief witness for the State, as Willie Stevens was to become the chief witness for the defence. If he and his sister were not in De Russey's Lane, as the pig woman had shrilly insisted, it remained for them to tell the detailed story of their whereabouts and their actions that night after Mr Hall left the house. The Grand Jury this time indicted all four persons implicated by the pig woman, and the trial began on November 3rd, 1926.

The first persons Alexander Simpson called to the stand were 'surprise witnesses'. They were a Mr and Mrs John S. Dixon, who lived in North Plainfield, New Jersey, about twelve miles from New Brunswick. It soon became apparent that they were to form part of a net that Simpson was preparing to draw around Willie Stevens. They testified that at about 8.30 on the night of the murders Willie had appeared at their house, wearing a loose-fitting suit, a derby, a wing collar with bow tie, and, across his vest, a heavy gold chain to which was attached a gold watch. He had said that his sister had let him out there from her automobile and that he was trying to find the Parker Home for the Aged, which was at Bound Brook. He stuttered and he told them that he was an epileptic. They directed him to a trolley car and he went stumbling away. When Mrs Dixon identified Willie as her visitor, she walked over to him and took his right hand and shook it vigorously, as if to wring recognition out of him. Willie stared at her, said nothing. When she returned to the stand, he grinned widely. That was one of many bizarre incidents which marked the progress of the famous murder trial. It deepened the mystery that hung about the strange figure of Willie Stevens. People could hardly wait for him to take the stand.

William Carpender Stevens had sat in court for sixteen days before he was called to the witness chair, on the 23rd of November, 1926. On that day the trial of Albert B. Fall and Edward L. Doheny, defendants in the notorious Teapot Dome scandal, opened in Washington, but the nation had eyes only for a small crowded courtroom in Somerville, New Jersey. Willie Stevens, after all these weeks, after all these years, was to speak out in public for the first time. As *The New York Times* said, 'He had been pictured as "Crazy Willie", as a town character, as an oddity, as a butt for all manner of jokes. He had been compared inferentially to an animal, and the hint of an alien racial strain in his parentage had been thrown at him.' Moreover, it had been prophesied that Willie would 'blow up' on the stand, that he would be trapped into contradictions by the 'wily' and 'crafty' Alexander Simpson, that he would be tricked finally into blurting out his guilt. No wonder there was no sound in the courtroom except the heavy tread of Willie Stevens's feet as he walked briskly to the witness stand.

Willie Stevens was an ungainly, rather lumpish man, about five feet ten inches tall. Although he looked flabby, this was only because of his loose-fitting clothes and the way he wore them; despite his fifty-four years, he was a man of great physical strength. He had a large head and a face that would be hard to forget. His head was covered with a thatch of thick, bushy hair, and his heavy black eyebrows seemed always to be arched, giving him an expression of perpetual surprise. This expression was strikingly accentuated by large, prominent eyes which, seen through the thick lenses of the spectacles he always wore, seemed to bulge unnaturally. He had a heavy, drooping, walrus moustache, and his complexion was dark. His glare was sudden and fierce; his smile, which came just as quickly, lighted up his whole face and gave him the wide, beaming look of an enormously pleased child. Born in Aiken, South Carolina, Willie Stevens had been brought to New Brunswick when he was two years old. When his wealthy parents died, a comfortable trust fund was left to Willie. The other children, Frances and Henry, had inherited their money directly. Once, when Mrs Hall was asked if it was not true that Willie was 'regarded as essential to be taken care of in certain things', she replied, 'In certain aspects.' The quality of Willie's mentality, the extent of his eccentricity, were matters the prosecution strove to establish on several occasions. Dr Laurence Runyon, called by the defence to testify that Willie was not an epileptic and had never stuttered, was cross-examined by Simpson. Said the doctor, 'He may not be absolutely normal mentally, but he is able to take care of himself perfectly well. He is brighter than the average person, although he has never advanced as far in school learning as some others. He reads books that are above the average and makes a good many people look like fools.' 'A sort of genius, in a way, I suppose?' said Simpson. To which the doctor quietly replied, 'Yes, that is just what I mean.'

There were all sorts of stories about Willie. One of them was that he had once started a fire in his back yard and then, putting on a fireman's helmet, had doused it gleefully with a pail of water. It was known that for years he had spent most of every day at the firehouse of the Engine Company No. 3 in Dennis Street, New Brunswick. He played cards with the firemen, ran errands for them, argued and joked with them, and was a general favourite. Sometimes he went out and bought a steak, or a chicken, and it was prepared and eaten in the firehouse by the firemen and Willie. In the days when the engine company had been a volunteer organization, Willie was an honorary member and always carried, in the firemen's parades, a flag he had bought and presented to the firehouse, an elaborate banner costing sixty or seventy dollars. He had also bought the black-and-white bunting with which the front of the firehouse was draped whenever a member of the company died.

After his arrest, he had whiled away the time in his cell reading books on metallurgy. There was a story that when his sister-in-law, Mrs Henry Stevens, once twitted him on his heavy reading, he said, 'Oh, that is merely the bread and butter of my literary repast.' The night before the trial opened, Willie's chief concern was about a new blue suit that had been ordered for him and that did not fit him to his satisfaction. He had also lost a collar button, and that worried him; Mrs Henry Stevens hurried to the jail before the court convened and brought him another one, and he was happy. At the preliminary hearing weeks before, Simpson had declared with brutal directness that Willie Stevens did indeed look like a coloured man, as the pig woman had said. At this Willie had half risen from his chair and bared his teeth, as if about to leap on the prosecutor. But he had quickly subsided. All through the trial he had sat quietly, staring. He had been enormously interested when the pig woman, attended by a doctor and a nurse, was brought in on a stretcher to give her testimony. This was the man who now, on trial for his life, climbed into the witness chair in the courtroom at Somerville.

There was an immense stir. Justice Charles W. Parker rapped with his gavel. Mrs Hall's face was strained and white; this was an ordeal she and her family had been dreading for weeks. Willie's left hand gripped his chair tightly, his right hand held a yellow pencil with which he had fiddled all during the trial. He faced the roomful of eyes tensely. His own lawyer, Senator Clarence E. Case, took the witness first. Willie started badly by understating his age ten years. He said he was forty-four. 'Isn't it fifty-four?' asked Case. Willie gave the room his great, beaming smile. 'Yes,' he chortled, boyishly, as if amused by his slip. The spectators smiled. It didn't take Willie long to dispose of the Dixons, the couple who had sworn he stumbled into their house the night of the murder. He answered half a dozen questions on this point with strong emphasis, speaking slowly and clearly: he had never worn a derby, he had never had epilepsy, he had never stuttered, he had never had a gold watch and chain. Mr Case held up Willie's old silver watch and chain for the jury to see. When he handed them back, Willie, with fine nonchalance, compared his watch with the clock on the courtroom wall, gave his sister a large, reassuring smile, and turned to his questioner with respectful attention. He described, with technical accuracy, an old revolver of his (the murders had been done with an automatic pistol, not a revolver, but a weapon of the same calibre as Willie's). He said he used to fire off the gun on the Fourth of July; remembering these old holidays, his eyes lighted up with childish glee. From this mood he veered suddenly into indignation and anger. 'When was the last time you saw the revolver?' was what set him off. 'The last time I saw it was in the courthouse!' Willie almost shouted. 'I think it was in October, 1922, when I was taken and put through a very severe grilling by – I cannot mention every person's name, but I remember Mr Toolan, Mr Lamb, and Detective David, and they did everything but strike me. They cursed me frightfully.' The officers had got him into an automobile 'by a subterfuge', he charged. 'Mr David said he simply wanted me to go out in the country, to ask me a very few questions, that it would not be very long.' It transpired later that on this trip Willie himself had had a question to ask Detective David: would the detective, if they passed De Russey's Lane, be kind enough to point it out to him? Willie had never seen the place, he told the detective, in his life. He said that Mr David showed him where it was.

When Willie got to the night of September 14th, 1922, in his testimony his anger and indignation were gone; he was placid, attentive, and courteous. He explained quietly that he had come home for supper that night, had gone to his room afterward, and 'remained in the house, leaving it at 2.30 in the morning with my sister'. Before he went to bed, he said, he had closed his door to confine to his own room the odour of tobacco smoke from his pipe. 'Who objected to that?' asked Mr Case. Willie gave his sudden, beaming grin. 'Everybody,' he said, and won the first of several general laughs from the courtroom. Then he told the story of what happened at 2.30 in the morning. It is necessary, for a well-rounded picture of Willie Stevens, to give it here at some length. 'I was awakened by my sister knocking at my door,' said Willie, 'and I immediately rose and went to the door and she said, "I want you to come down to the church, as Edward has not come home; I am very much worried" – or words to that effect. I immediately got dressed and accompanied her down to the church. I went through the front door, followed a small path that led directly to the back of the house past the cellar door. We went directly down Redmond Street to Jones Avenue, from Jones Avenue we went to George Street; turning into George Street we went directly down to Commercial Avenue. There our movements were blocked by an immense big freight automobile. We had to wait there maybe half a minute until it went by, going toward New York.

'I am not at all sure whether we crossed right there at Commercial Avenue or went a little further down George Street and went diagonally across to the church. Then we stopped there and looked at the church to see whether there were any lights. There were no lights burning. Then Mrs Hall said, "We might as well go down and see if it could not be possible that he was at the Mills's house." We went down there, down George Street until we came to Carman Street, turned down Carman Street, and got in front of the Mills's house and stood there two or three minutes to see if there were any lights in the Mills's apartment. There were none.' Willie then described, street by street, the return home, and ended with, 'I opened the front door with my latchkey. If you wish me, I will show it to you. My sister said, "You might as well go to bed. You can do no more good." With that I went upstairs to bed.' This was the story that Alexander Simpson had to shake. But before Willie was turned over to him, the witness told how he heard that his brother-in-law had been killed. 'I remember I was in the parlour,' said Willie, 'reading a copy of *The New York Times*. I heard someone coming up the steps and I glanced up and I heard my aunt, Mrs Charles J. Carpender, say, "Well, you might as well know it – Edward has been shot." ' Willie's voice was thick with emotion. He was asked what happened then. 'Well,' he said, 'I simply let the paper go – that way' (he let his left hand fall slowly and limply to his side) 'and I put my head down, and I cried.' Mr Case asked him if he was present at, or had anything to do with, the murder of Mr Hall and Mrs Mills. 'Absolutely nothing at all!' boomed Willie, coming out of his posture of sorrow, belligerently erect. The attorney for the defence turned, with a confident little bow, to Alexander Simpson. The special prosecutor sauntered over and stood in front of the witness. Willie took in his breath sharply.

Alexander Simpson, a lawyer, a state senator, slight, perky, capable of harsh tongue-lashings, given to sarcasm and innuendo, had intimated that he would 'tie Willie Stevens into knots'. Word had gone around that he intended to 'flay' the eccentric fellow. Hence his manner now came as a surprise. He spoke in a gentle, almost inaudible voice, and his attitude was one of solicitous friendliness. Willie, quite unexpectedly, drew first blood. Simpson asked him if he had ever earned his livelihood. 'For about four or five years,' said Willie, 'I was employed by Mr Siebold, a contractor.' Not having anticipated an affirmative reply, Simpson paused. Willie leaned forward and said, politely, 'Do you wish his address?' He did this in good faith, but the spectators took it for what the *Times* called a 'sally', because Simpson had been in the habit of letting loose a swarm of investigators on anyone whose name was brought into the case. 'No, thank you,' muttered Simpson, above a roar of laughter. The prosecutor now set about picking at Willie's story of the night of September 14th: he tried to find out why the witness and his sister had not knocked on the Mills's door to see if Mr Hall were there. Unfortunately for the steady drumming of questions, Willie soon broke the prosecutor up with another laugh. Simpson had occasion to mention a New Brunswick boarding house called The Bayard, and he pronounced 'Bay' as it is spelled. With easy politeness, Willie corrected him. '*Biyard*,' said Willie. 'Biyard?' repeated Simpson. Willie smiled, as at an apt pupil. Simpson bowed slightly. The spectators laughed again.

Presently the witness made a slip, and Simpson pounced on it like a swooping falcon. Asked if he had not, at the scene of the murder, stood 'in the light of an automobile while a woman on a mule went by', Willie replied, 'I never remember that occurrence.' Let us take up the court record from there. 'Q. – You would remember if it occurred, wouldn't you? A. – I certainly would, but I don't remember of ever being in an automobile and the light from the automobile shone on a woman on a mule. Q. – Do you say you were not there, or you don't remember? A. – I say positively I was not there. Q. – Why did you say you don't *remember*? A. – Does not that cover the same thing? Q. – No, it don't, because you might be there and not remember it. A. – Well, I will withdraw that, if I may, and say I was not there positively.' Willie assumed an air of judicial authority as he 'withdrew' his previous answer, and he spoke his positive denial with sharp decision. Mr Simpson abruptly tried a new tack. 'You have had a great deal of experience in life, Mr Stevens,' he said, 'and you have read a great deal, they say, and know a lot about human affairs. Don't you think it sounds rather fishy when you say you got up in the middle of the night to go and look for Dr Hall and went to the house and never even knocked on the door – with your experience of human affairs and people that you met and all that sort of thing – don't that seem rather fishy to you?' There was a loud bickering of attorneys before Willie could say anything to this. Finally Judge Parker turned to the witness and said, 'Can you answer that, Mr Stevens?' 'The only way I can answer it, Your Honour,' said Willie scornfully, 'is that I don't see that it is at all "fishy".' The prosecutor jumped to something else: 'Dr Hall's church was not your church, was it?' he asked. 'He was not a *Doctor*, sir,' said Willie, once more the instructor. 'He was the Reverend

Mister Hall.' Simpson paused, nettled, 'I am glad you corrected me on that,' he said. The courtroom laughed again.

The prosecutor now demanded that Willie repeat his story of what happened at 2.30 a.m. He hoped to establish, he intimated, that the witness had learned it 'by rote'. Willie calmly went over the whole thing again, in complete detail, but not one of his sentences was the same as it had been. The prosecutor asked him to tell it a third time. The defence objected vehemently. Simpson vehemently objected to the defence's objection. The Court: 'We will let him tell it once more.' At this point Willie said, 'May I say a word?' 'Certainly,' said Simpson. 'Say all you want.' Weighing his words carefully, speaking with slow emphasis, Willie said, 'All I have to say is I was never taught, as you insinuate, by any person whatsoever. That is my best recollection from the time I started out with my sister to this present minute.' Simpson did not insist further on a third recital. He wanted to know now how Willie could establish the truth of his statement that he was in his room from 8 or 9 o'clock until his sister knocked on the door at 2.30 a.m. 'Why,' said Willie, 'if a person sees me go upstairs and does not see me come downstairs, isn't that a conclusion that I was in my room?' The court record shows that Mr Simpson replied, 'Absolutely.' 'Well,' said Willie expansively, 'that is all there was to it.' Nobody but the pig woman had testified to seeing Willie after he went up to his room that night. Barbara Tough, a servant who had been off during the day, testified that she got back to the Hall home about 10 o'clock and noticed that Willie's door was closed (Willie had testified that it wouldn't stay closed unless he locked it). Louise Geist, of the annulment suit, had testified that she had not seen Willie that night after dinner. It was Willie's story against the pig woman's. That day in court he overshadowed her. When he stepped down from the witness chair, his shoulders were back and he was smiling broadly. Headlines in the *Times* the next day said, 'Willie Stevens Remains Calm Under Cross-Examination. Witness a Great Surprise.' There was a touch of admiration, almost of partisanship, in most of the reporters' stories. The final verdict could be read between the lines. The trial dragged on for another ten days, but on the 3rd of December, Willie Stevens was a free man.

He was glad to get home. He stood on the porch of 23 Nichol Avenue, beaming at the house. Reporters had followed him there. He turned to them and said, solemnly, 'It is one hundred and four days since I've been here. And I want to get in.' They let him go. But two days later, on a Sunday, they came back and Mrs Hall received them in the drawing room. They could hear Willie in an adjoining room, talking spiritedly. He was, it came out, discussing metallurgy with the Rev. J. Mervin Pettit, who had succeeded Mr Hall as rector of the Church of St John the Evangelist.

Willie Stevens, going on seventy, no longer visits the firehouse of No. 3 Engine Company. His old friends have caught only glimpses of him in the past few years, for he has been in feeble health, and spends most of his time in his room, going for a short ride now and then in his chauffeur-driven car. The passerby, glancing casually into the car, would not recognize the famous figure of the middle 1920s. Willie has lost a great deal of weight, and the familiar beaming light no longer comes easily to his eyes.

After Willie had been acquitted and sent home, he tried to pick up the old routine of life where he had left it, but people turned to stare after him in the street, and boys were forever at his heels, shouting, 'Look out, Willie, Simpson is after you!' The younger children were fond of him and did not tease him, and once in a while Willie could be seen playing with them, as boisterously and whimsically as ever. The firemen say that if he encountered a ragged child he would find out where it lived, and then give one of his friends the money to buy new clothes for it. But Willie's adventures in the streets of the town became fewer and farther apart. Sometimes months would elapse between his visits to the firehouse. When he did show up in his old haunts, he complained of headaches, and while he was still in his fifties, he spent a month in bed with a heart ailment. After that, he stayed close to home, and the firemen rarely saw him. If you should drop by the firehouse, and your interest in Willie seems friendly, they will tell you some fond stories about him.

One winter Willie took a Cook's tour to Hawaii. When he came back, he told the firemen he had joined an organization which, for five dollars, gave its subscribers a closer view of the volcanoes than the ordinary tourist could get. Willie was crazy about the volcanoes. His trip, however, was spoiled, it came out, because someone recognized and pointed him out as the famous Willie Stevens of the Hall-Mills case. He had the Cook's agent cancel a month's reservation at a hotel and rearrange his schedule so that he could leave on the next ship. He is infuriated by any reference to the murders or to the trial. Some years ago a newspaper printed a paragraph about a man out West who was 'a perfect double for Willie Stevens'. Someone in the firehouse showed it to Willie and he tore the paper to shreds in a rage.

Willie still spends a great deal of time reading 'heavy books' – on engineering, on entomology, on botany. Those who have seen his famous room at 23 Nichol Avenue – he has a friend in to visit him once in a while – say that it is filled with books. He has no use for detective stories or the Western and adventure magazines his friends the firemen read. When he is not reading scientific tomes, he dips into the classics or what he calls the 'worth-while poets'. He used to astound the firemen with his wide range of knowledge. There was the day a salesman of shaving materials dropped in at the engine house. Finding that Willie had visited St Augustine, Florida, he mentioned an old Spanish chapel there. Willie described it, and gave its history, replete with dates, and greatly impressed the caller. Another time someone mentioned a certain kind of insect which he said was found in this country. 'You mean they used to be,' said Willie. 'That type of insect has been extinct in this country for forty years.' It turned out that it had been, too. On still another occasion Willie fell to discussing flowers with some visitor at the firehouse and reeled off a Latin designation – *crassinae carduaceae*, or something of the sort. Then he turned, grinning, to the listening firemen. 'Zinnias to you,' he said.

Willie Stevens's income from the trust fund established for him is said to be around forty dollars a week. His expenditures are few, now that he is no longer able to go on long trips. The firemen like especially to tell about the time that Willie went to Wyoming, and attended a rodeo. He told the ticket-seller he wanted to sit in a box and the man gave him a single ticket. Willie explained that he wanted the whole box to himself, and he planked down a ten-dollar bill for it. Then he went in and sat in the box all alone. 'I had a hell of a time!' he told the firemen gleefully when he came back home.

De Russey's Lane, which Detective David once pointed out to Willie Stevens, is now, you may have heard, entirely changed. Several years ago it was renamed Franklin Boulevard, and where the Rev. Mr Edward W. Hall and Mrs Eleanor Mills lay murdered there is now a row of neat brick and stucco houses. The famous crab apple tree under which the bodies were found disappeared the first weekend after the murders. It was hacked to pieces, roots and all, by souvenir-hunters.

Editor's comment: *Willie Stevens died on 30 December 1942.*

The Bloomsbury Horror

RICHARD WHITTINGTON-EGAN

In a swift and bloody moment one wild December night, twenty-seven-year-old Harriet Buswell ceased to exist. It was she herself who brought death in out of the darkness and, all unknowingly, made it welcome in the poor little room which she occupied in Great Coram Street, Bloomsbury.

Like Harriet, Great Coram Street no longer exists. The dreary thoroughfare of out-at-elbows Victorian hotels and fly-blown lodging-houses, that ran straight as a dagger through the seedy heart of Bloomsbury, has vanished beneath the breakers' hammers. If Harriet's outraged ghost walks, it walks the concrete ways of the new Brunswick shopping precinct.

Even Harriet's only other memorial, a shrivelled, half-eaten apple, which lay for many years beside the other relics – the guns, the knives, the poison phials – in the Black Museum at Scotland Yard, has disappeared. But let us go back to the time when the apple – and Harriet – were glossy . . . back to the terrible and mystifying events of December 1872.

Harriet Buswell, who also went by the name of Clara Burton, was a young and not very successful actress, who, in the quaint phrase of our great-grandfathers was 'no better than she ought to have been'. Not to put too fine a point on it, when she could find no berth in the theatre, she played out her romances on the streets. She sought accommodating gentlemen friends at such haunts of pleasure as the Alhambra, the Argyll Rooms and Cremorne Gardens, and whisked them home to her second-floor back at No. 12 Great Coram Street – a discreet lodging-house presided over by an equally discreet landlady, Mrs Wright.

Some eight years before, in the tragic shadows of her unchartered past, there had been a baby, which had had to be farmed out. Free of encumbrances, and perilously alone, Harriet had resumed the battle for existence.

The close of 1872, a year of tempests which cost London £2,000,000 in damage, found Harriet in no better position than at its beginning. In fact, on the night of 24 December, Christmas Eve, the cupboard was bare. Painting a smile on her wan face, putting on her prettiest skirt and most pert bonnet, and borrowing a pathetic shilling from a fellow-lodger at No. 12, the desperate young woman stepped out into the wintry darkness of the shrouded Bloomsbury streets and headed for the gas flare and warmth of the golden-paved West End.

It was about midnight when she returned to Great Coram Street, escorted by a gentleman. Mrs Wright, who saw their arrival, was afterwards to say that the man appeared to her to be a foreigner. Harriet, she observed, was in excellent spirits, and was talking more loudly than usual. She was childishly pleased with a bundle of apples, oranges and nuts which her companion had bought for her on the way back at a fruiterer's in Compton Street, and showed them to Mrs Wright.

She was even more pleased with the shiny half-sovereign which he gave her, and came running downstairs to press it into Mrs Wright's not unwilling hand for overdue rent. The last time the landlady saw her, the last time anyone saw her alive, was when she emerged to ask for some stout to be brought up. It could not be done, as by then all the public houses were closed. Disappointed, Harriet withdrew up the gloomy stairs, and into the long darkness of oblivion.

Slowly, the noises of the late revellers in the streets died away. The house in Great Coram Street stood gaunt and silent under the frosty glitter of the stars. But, stealthily, in that black pool of silence, a murderer's hand moved. . . then, swiftly, slashed two deep gashes in the sleeping girl's throat. There was no struggle. No scream. The surface of the pool remained unruffled.

As the first grey light of the Christmas dawn filtered dustily into the shabby room, the assassin wiped his knife on a towel.

233

He drew down the blind over the closed window. Then, leaving a half-eaten apple with his teeth marks in it on the wash-stand, he fled the scene of his ferocious pleasure. Locking the door, to delay the discovery of the thing he left behind him on the bloodied bed, and pocketing the key, he tiptoed down the creaking stairs and softly let himself out of the house.

The sun rose. The church bells rang. All over Victorian England Christmas gifts were being exchanged, and the festive lunches being prepared. But up in the second-floor back in Bloomsbury, Harriet Buswell slept on.

Towards midday, Mrs Wright, thinking it strange that there was no sign of her lodger, sent her eight-year old son up to knock and ask her if she wanted any breakfast. The boy could get no reply, and other lodgers, called to the locked and silent room, at length broke down the door – and made their appalling discovery:

Superintendent Thompson, of E Division, took charge of the murder investigation. His task was unenviable, for, as every policeman knows, the casual Romeo of the 'Juliet of a night' is the proverbial Anonymous Man.

The case was not entirely hopeless, however. There was the apple. A careful cast of it and its indentations was made, and the marks were compared with the dead girl's teeth. They did not correspond. Clearly, then, they were the teeth marks of the killer.

And there were witnesses. Mrs Harriet Wright had seen her lodger's visitor. She thought he was a German. George Fleck, the Compton Street fruiterer, remembered selling the man the apples, oranges and nuts. William Stalker, a waiter, remembered serving the couple at the Cavour Restaurant. Like Mrs Wright, both men had thought him a foreigner, possibly a German.

Following these slender clues, Superintendent Thompson's inquiries about aliens led him to Ramsgate, where a German brig, the *Wangerland*, had been becalmed since two weeks before Christmas, after running on to the Goodwin Sands. She had been carrying 163 German emigrants bound for Brazil.

Very soon Superintendent Thompson had a suspect in his

spyglass. It seemed that one of the crew, a surgeon's assistant named Karl Whollebe, had been behaving suspiciously. After spending Christmas in London, he had returned to Ramsgate on 4 January 1873, sent his luggage back to the *Wangerland*, and announced his intention of spending the night at Hiscock's Royal Hotel. Then, unexpectedly, he decamped at two o'clock in the morning and rejoined the ship.

Superintendent Buss, of Ramsgate, arrested Whollebe on 18 January, and Thompson sent down two of his witnesses to attend an identification parade. Great was the embarrassment of the police when both Fleck and Stalker picked out the *Wangerland's* chaplain, the Reverend Gottfried Hessel, from the line-up of the ship's personnel.

Whollebe was released – and the horror-struck Pastor Hessel arrested. Hessel had, it transpired, accompanied Whollebe to London on 22 December, together with Mrs Hessel and a ship-owner, Mr Hermes. They had all stayed at Kroll's Hotel in the City. Things looked black for the Reverend Mr Hessel at Bow Street Magistrates' Court on 29 January, when Stalker confirmed that he was the man he had served at the Cavour.

Fleck, the fruiterer, also stuck to his identification, although his assistant was equally sure that Hessel was not the right man. A maid-servant, who lived across the street from No. 12, hazarded that Hessel certainly looked like a man she had seen leaving the murder house on Christmas morning.

Meanwhile, the police had obtained fresh evidence against Hessel. Jane Somers, a housemaid at Hiscock's Royal Hotel, where the Pastor had stayed when he returned from his London trip a few days after Christmas, said that he had asked for turpentine and a brush to clean his clothing. Even worse was to follow. Hessel had sent half a dozen bloodstained handkerchiefs to the laundry.

The head waiter at Hiscock's, John Popkin, had a weird conversation to recount. When Hessel heard of Whollebe's arrest, he said: 'I am very sorry for my friend. He is no more a murderer than you are. I will go to the station and console him. I will leave my boots off and my friend shall wear his.

My wife can prove that I was with her on Christmas Eve, but I am afraid they will not take my wife's word.'

At the next day's hearing, Mr Vaughan, the magistrate, *did* believe what amounted to Hessel's alibi. Whollebe testified that when he and Mr Hermes had gone out at 10 p.m. on 24 December, he had seen Hessel in the dining-room of Kroll's Hotel looking very unwell. Mr Kroll, the hotel proprietor, said that Hessel was heard coughing in his room during the night. Moreover, his boots, the only pair he had with him in London (so he said), were seen outside his bedroom door.

The magistrate freed the Pastor. 'To my mind,' he said, 'It has been conclusively shown that Dr Hessel was not the companion of the murdered woman that evening.'

The alibi had effectively cancelled out the identification parade, and the police, again somewhat embarrassed, had not got round to comparing Hessel's teeth with the marks in the apple.

Since then, modern forensic experts in America have done a great deal of work on teeth marks at the scene of a crime, and this clue would have been a gift. The Bloomsbury apple could have been a classic *pièce de-conviction*. Instead, the withered exhibit in the Black Museum was a memento not of a triumph of detection, but of a lost opportunity.

Pastor Hessel left the court something of a public hero. An appeal fund to compensate him for his sufferings raised £1,225.8s.11d., Queen Victoria herself contributing £30. Her Prime Minister, Mr Gladstone, wrote a letter which was really tantamount to an official apology to Hessel.

And so the German chaplain slipped away from our shores, leaving behind a mystery which has never been officially solved. But there were those who were convinced that he was a very lucky man. . . .

By the Rude Bridge

ALEXANDER WOOLLCOTT

1934

Let me begin by admitting that through the years I have
become a more and more spasmodic newspaper reader. This
may be due to a conviction that by faithfully absorbing the
imparted wisdom of the two Walters (Lippmann and Win-
chell) I can learn all I really care to know about what is going
on in the world. But, occasionally, through this failure of
attention to the news columns, I lose the final chapter of some
tale that has really interested me.

These sombre reflections were induced one day when a
chance remark brought to mind the Bennett killing which
enlivened Kansas City some years ago, and with a start I
realized that although it had involved four shots heard round
the world, I never did know what happened afterwards.
Wherefore I moved about among my neighbours, as might an
inquiring reporter, only to find that, one and all, they too had
lost track of the case. Yet at the time there was probably not a
literate household in Europe or the three Americas of which
the emotional seismograph had not recorded its tremors.

The Bennett killing, which occurred on the night of 29
September 1929, was usually spoken of, with approximate
accuracy, as the Bridge-Table Murder. The victim was a
personable and prosperous young salesman whose mission, as
representative of the house of Hudnut, was to add to the
fragrance of life in the Middle West. He had been married
eleven years before to a Miss Myrtle Adkins, originally from
Arkansas, who first saw his photograph at the home of a
friend, announced at once that she intended to marry him,
and then, perhaps with this purpose still in mind, recognized
and accosted him a year later when she happened to encounter
him on a train. That was during the war when the good points

of our perfume salesman's physique were enhanced by an officer's uniform. They were married in Memphis during the considerable agitation of 11 November 1918. The marriage was a happy one. At least, Senator Jim Reed, who represented Mrs Bennett in the trying but inevitable legal formalities which ensued upon her bereavement, announced in court – between sobs – that they had always been more like sweethearts than man and wife.

On Mr Bennett's last Sunday on earth, these wedded sweethearts spent the day playing a foursome at golf with their friends, Charles and Mayme Hoffman, who had an apartment in the Park Manor on Ward Parkway, which is, I think, a shiny new part of the town that was just forlorn, uncropped meadowland in the days when the great Dr Logan Clendening, the late Ralph Barton, and your correspondent were all sweet-faced tots together in dear old K.C. After dark and after an ice-box supper at the Bennetts', the men folk professed themselves too weary to dress for the movies, so the four settled down to a more slatternly evening of contract bridge. They played family against family at a tenth of a cent a side. With a pretty laugh, Mayme Hoffman on the witness stand referred to such a game as playing for 'fun stakes', though whether this was a repulsive little phrase of her own or one prevalent in the now devitalized society of a once rugged community, I do not know.

They played for some hours. At first the luck went against the Hoffmans and the married sweethearts were as merry as grigs. Later the tide turned and the cross-table talk of the Bennetts became tinged with constructive criticism. Finally, just before midnight, the fatal hand was dealt by Bennett himself and he opened the bidding with one spade. Hoffman hazarded two diamonds. Mrs Bennett leaped to four spades. Discreet silence from Mrs Hoffman. Stunned silence from Bennett. Hoffman doubled. That ended the bidding and the play began.

Mrs Bennett put down her hand. At her trial it was the policy of the defence, for strategic reasons, to minimize the part the bridge game had played in the ensuing drama, but the jury could not be confused on this point and three of the jurors went so far as to learn bridge in the long leisure of the jury room. Nor could the mind of that stern realist, Mayme Hoffman, be befogged. When summoned as a witness by Senator Reed, she knew she was really coming to the defence of Mrs Bennett as a bridge player.

'Myrtle put down a good hand,' she said staunchly, 'it was a perfectly beautiful hand.'

In any event, while she was dummy, Mrs Bennett retired to the kitchen to prepare breakfast for her lord and master, who would be leaving at the crack of dawn for St Joe. She came back to find he had been set two and to be greeted with the almost automatic charge that she had overbid. Thereupon she ventured to opine that he was, in her phrase, 'a bum bridge player'. His reply to that was a slap in the face, followed by several more of the same – whether three or four more, witnesses were uncertain. Then while he stormed about proclaiming his intention to leave for St Joe at once and while Mr Hoffman prudently devoted the interval to totting up the score, Mrs Bennett retired to the davenport to weep on the sympathetic bosom of Mayme Hoffman, saying many things, through her tears, including one utterance which, in my opinion, should give the Bennett case a permanent place in the files of such fond annalists as Wiliam Roughead of Edinburgh and Edmund (Whatever became of the Lester?) Pearson of New York. Mrs Bennett's sentiments were expressed as follows:

'No one but a cur would strike a woman in the presence of friends.'

I have not as yet been able to learn whether the game was ever settled, but when Mr Hoffman had completed his work as accountant, he ventured to reproach the host for unseemly behaviour, to which comment Bennett replied with a strong suggestion that it was time for the guests to go home. Mrs Hoffman – one can imagine her bridling a good deal and saying that she considered the source – had got into her wraps and Mr Hoffman was tidying up in the bathroom, when he saw his hostess advancing through the den, revolver in hand.

'My God, Myrtle,' he cried. 'What are you going to do?'

He soon learned.

There were four shots, with a brief interval after the second. The first went through the hastily closed bathroom door. The second was embedded in the lintel. The next two were embedded in Mr Bennett, the fourth and fatal shot hitting him in the back.

The next day the story went round the world. In its first reverberations, I noticed, with interest, that after her visit to the mortuary chapel Mrs Bennett objected plaintively to her husband's being buried without a pocket-handkerchief showing in his coat. To interested visitors, she would make cryptic remarks such as 'Nobody knows but me and my God why I did it,' thus leaving open to pleasant speculation the probable nature of her defence.

It would be difficult to explain to a puzzled Englishman, brought up as he is to think of America as a country of breathless speed, how seventeen months could be allowed to pass before Mrs Bennett was called upon to stand trial. By that time I myself had lost track. Wherefore, when the aforesaid Clendening called at Wit's End one Sunday, I asked what, if anything, had ever happened in the Bennett case.

'Oh!' the good doctor replied, 'she was acquitted. It seems it was just an unfortunate accident.'

For corroborative detail I have since consulted the files of the *Kansas City Star*, one of the three or four newspapers left in this country of which the staff still preserves, like the guarded secret of some medieval guild, the lost art of reportorial writing. The *Star* accounts of the trial are in the finest tradition of our craft. I cannot hope in so small a space to reproduce the flavour of Senator Reed's more than adequate performance. It seems the dutiful Mrs Bennett had merely gone for the revolver because her husband wanted to take it with him to St Joe; that in stumbling over a misplaced chair in the den she fired the first two shots unintentionally and that her husband (pardonably misreading her kind intentions) had sought to disarm her. In the ensuing Apache dance of their struggle for the gun, it had gone off and wounded him fatally.

The defence was materially aided by the exclusion, on technical grounds, of crucial testimony which would have tended to indicate that at the time Mrs Bennett had told a rather different story. It was also helped no little by the defendant herself who, in the course of the trial, is estimated to have shed more tears than Jane Cowl did in the entire season of *Common Clay*. Even the Senator was occasionally unmanned, breaking into sobs several times in the presence of the jury. 'I just can't help it,' he replied, when the calloused prosecutor urged him to bear up.

The Reed construction of the fatal night's events proved subsequently important to Mrs Bennett, in whose favour her husband had once taken out a policy to cover the contingency of his death through accident. Some months after the acquittal a dazed insurance company paid her thirty thousand dollars.

It was Harpo Marx who, on hearing the doctor's hasty but spirited résumé of the case, suggested that I make use of it for one of my little articles. He even professed to have thought of a title for it. Sceptically I inquired what this might be and he answered: 'Vulnerable.'

Protesting as I do against the short-weight reporting in the *Notable British Trials* series, it would ill become me to hoard for my private pleasure certain postscripts to the Bennett case which have recently drifted my way. It looked for a time as if we all might be vouchsafed the luxury of reading Myrtle's autobiography, but this great work has been indefinitely postponed. I understand she could not come to terms with the local journalist who was to do the actual writing. That ink-stained wretch demanded half the royalties. Mrs Bennett felt this division would be inequitable, since, as she pointed out, she herself had done all the work.

Then it seems she has not allowed her bridge to grow rusty, even though she occasionally encounters an explicable difficulty in finding a partner. Recently she took on one unacquainted with her history. Having made an impulsive bid, he put his hand down with some diffidence. 'Partner,' he said, 'I'm afraid you'll want to shoot me for this.' Mrs Bennett, says my informant, had the good taste to faint.

Editor's comment: *To say that one is cured of bridgeomania is as suspect as to claim smugly that one gave up smoking three years, seventeen weeks, five days, twelve hours and forty-five minutes ago; but I honestly believe that I shall never play another rubber of bridge – if only because, after studying all the advice according to Elwell, Culbertson and Goren, and playing what must have been thousands of hands, I still lacked finesse, a deficiency that lowered my self-esteem. Still, as I always try to be unselfish, especially in bad causes, let me diminish the desperation of bridge-addicted readers by giving details of 'the Bennett murder hand'.*

The cards were dealt like this:

North (*Myrtle Bennett*)
♠ A 10 6 3
♡ 10 8 5
♢ 4
♣ A 9 8 4 2

West (*Charles Hoffman*)
♠ Q 7 2
♡ A J 3
♢ A Q 10 9 2
♣ J 6

East (*Mayme Hoffman*)
♠ 4
♡ Q 9 4
♢ K J 7 6 3
♣ Q 7 5 3

South (*John Bennett*)
♠ K J 9 8 5
♡ K 7 6 2
♢ 8 5
♣ K 10

After John Bennett had opened the bidding with one spade, the western Hoffmann bid two diamonds, Myrtle Bennett bid four spades, and the eastern Hoffman passed.

West's opening lead of the ace of diamonds won the trick. John Bennett also lost to the ace of hearts, the queen of spades, and the queen of hearts, so he went down by one trick. An expert tells me that Bennett's worst mistakes were that he did not finesse for the queen of spades through west and that he did not set up the club suit so that he could discard his (sad term in the circumstances) heart losers; the expert adds that, for complicated reasons relating to the scoring, the Hoffmans really should have played the hand (something to do with their making a sacrifice bid of five diamonds which would have lost them only 100 points instead of exposing them to the risk of losing 820 points if the four-spade contract had been made).

True
ACCOUNT
OF A
Bloody Murther
Committed by three Foot-Padders in
FIG-LANE,
NEAR
St. Pancrafs-Church,
On the Wife of
Phillip Stanton,
AS
She was comeing with her Husband out of the Country on
Tuefday the 2*d* of *March* Inftant.

Tis obferved and Dayly experienced, that the frequent Examples of publick Juftice have not hitherto been fufficient to deter fome Perfons from committing very foul Crimes; yea even the worft of Sins, Murder it felf not excepted; many accuftoming themfelves to a whole courfe of Sin all their Life; till at length they become deftitute of Gods preventing Grace, and fo harden their own hearts, by indulging themfelves in all manner of Sin, not fticking at any thing to fulfil their Lufts; an Example of which too late an experience offers us.

For one *Philip Stanton*, and *Dorothy* his Wife, having been in the Country about their Lawful Occafions, (being Venders of *Oranges* and *Lemons*) and returning home again, were on *Tuefday* the 2*d*. Inftant between Seven and Eight at Night met by three Foot-Padders, near the crofs Road by St. *Pancrafs-Church*, in *Fig-Lane*: The Woman being foremoft they ftarted up out of a Ditch and Struck at her upon which fhe cried out, then they Shot at her as fhe fat upon her Horfe between her Dorfers, and the Bullet paffed in on the left fide of her Throat, then to make fure of her, knocked her off the Horfe with their Clubs, fo that fhe Died Imediately, and then Rifled her, throwing her Dorfers in two feveral Places, then left her, and prefently after meet her Husband, whom they Beat and Bruifed in a moft miferable manner, asking him for his

Money, and finding none, 'tis fuppofed he fared the worfe for it, as himfelf Relates; for his Wife had what Money they had taken, (which being about thirty Shillings) fhe hid in her Back, rapp'd in a Cloth: They cut the Girts from their Pack-Saddles, and turn'd their Horfes loofe, leaving them as is believed, both for Dead, and fo made their Efcape: The Woman was found by the Watch, and carried to the *Black-Horfe*, in St. *Pancrafs-Church-yard*, till the Coroners Inqueft have fat upon her: The Man was carried to the Golden *Sugar-Loaf*, near *Battle-Bridge*, where he lies, in hopes to be cured of his Wounds, and related the ftory of their Robbery; and that when the Thieves came to him all the Language he gave them was, if you have Killed my Wife you may do the like to me. He faith he can remember one of them who Struck him about his Head with his Piftol; and beat him on the Stomach with them and doth verily believe he could know him again, being a tall Man in Gray Cloths. Some hundreds of People went on *Wednefday* to vifit him, and knew him to be the same Perfon that ufed to crie Apples about the Street, and fay a *Lump, a Lump, a Lumping 'Penniworth*. So we leave him to be cured of his Wounds, and hope he may live to fee the Actors of this Bloody Tragedy and horrid Vilany, brought to condign Punnifhment.

FINIS.

This may be Printed, R.P.

LONDON,
Printed by *George Croom*, at the *Blue-Ball* in *Thames-freet*, near *Baynard's-Caftle*. 1685.

KENNETH ALLSOP: extract from *The Bootleggers*, London, 1961, by permission of the Hutchinson Publishing Group Ltd. RICHARD D. ALTICK: extract from *Victorian Studies in Scarlet*, London, 1970, by permission of the author and J.M. Dent & Sons Ltd. JACQUES BARZUN: introduction to *Burke and Hare: The Resurrection Men*, The Scarecrow Press, New Jersey, 1974, by permission of the author. DOROTHY DUNBAR: extract from *Blood in the Parlour*, London, 1964, by permission of Oak Tree Publications, Inc. JONATHAN GOODMAN: introduction to *The Trial of Ian Brady and Myra Hindley*, Newton Abbot, 1973, by permission of the author. RAYNER HEPPENSTALL's essay is published by permission of Margaret Heppenstall. LESLIE J. HOTSON's essay was first published in *The Atlantic Monthly*, June 1925; © The Atlantic Monthly, Boston, Massachusetts. EDGAR LUSTGARTEN: extract from *The Judges and the Judged*, London, 1961, by permission of the Curtis Brown Group Ltd. THOMAS M. McDADE: essay first published in *The New Colophon*, New York, 1950, under the title of 'Gallows Literature of the Streets', by permission of the author. EDMUND PEARSON: extract from *Masterpieces of Murder*, edited by Gerald Gross, London, 1964, by permission of the Hutchinson Publishing Group Ltd. WILLIAM ROUGHEAD: extract from *Classic Crimes*, London, 1951, by permission of Marjorie Roughead. DAMON RUNYON: extracts from reports that appeared in the New York *American*. F. TENNYSON JESSE's essay is published by permission of Joanna Colenbrander, for the Harwood Will Trust. HENRY DAVID THOREAU: extract from 'Thursday' of *A Week on the Concord and Merrimack Rivers*, August and September 1839 (published 1849). JAMES THURBER: the parodies from *The New Yorker*, 7 May 1927, © The New Yorker, New York; the essay, from *Vintage Thurber*, London, 1963, by permission of Hamish Hamilton Ltd.

A selection of bestsellers from SPHERE

FICTION

FAMILY ALBUM	Danielle Steel	£2.95 □
SEVEN STEPS TO TREASON	Michael Hartland	£2.50 □
DUNN'S CONUNDRUM	Stan Lee	£2.95 □
GOLDEN TALLY	Pamela Oldfield	£2.95 □

FILM AND TV TIE-IN

BOON	Anthony Masters	£2.50 □
AUF WIEDERSEHEN PET 2	Fred Taylor	£2.75 □
LADY JANE	Anthony Smith	£1.95 □

NON-FICTION

HENRY ROOT'S A-Z OF WOMEN	Willie Donaldson	£2.50 □
THE FALL OF SAIGON	David Butler	£3.95 □
LET'S FACE IT	Christine Piff	£2.50 □
A QUIET YEAR	Derek Tangye	£2.25 □

All Sphere books are available at your local bookshop or newsagent, or can be ordered direct from the publisher. Just tick the titles you want and fill in the form below.

Name _____

Address _____

_____

Write to Sphere Books, Cash Sales Department, P.O. Box 11, Falmouth, Cornwall TR10 9EN.

Please enclose a cheque or postal order to the value of the cover price plus:

UK: 55p for the first book, 22p for the second book and 14p for each additional book ordered to a maximum charge of £1.75.

OVERSEAS: £1.00 for the first book plus 25p per copy for each additional book.

BFPO & EIRE: 55p for the first book, 22p for the second book plus 14p per copy for the next 7 books, thereafter 8 p per book.

Sphere Books reserve the right to show new retail prices on covers which may differ from those previously advertised in the text or elsewhere, and to increase postal rates in accordance with the PO.